The Square Mile

THE SQUARE MILE

A Guide to the New City of London

John Plender
and
Paul Wallace

C

CENTURY PUBLISHING

LONDON

First published in Great Britain in 1985
by Century Hutchinson Ltd,
Brookmount House, 62–65 Chandos Place,
Covent Garden, London WC2N 4NW

British Library Cataloguing in Publication Data
Plender, John
    The square mile: a guide to the new City of London.
    1. London (England) – Description – 1981–
    – Guide-books
    I. Title   II. Wallace, Paul
    914.21′204858   DA679

ISBN 0 7126 1086 3

Photoset in Great Britain by
Rowland Phototypesetting Ltd, Bury St Edmunds, Suffolk
and printed by St Edmundsbury Press, Bury St Edmunds, Suffolk
Bound by Butler & Tanner Ltd, Frome, Somerset

Contents

market - the dealing system - a shortage of capital in the system - left behind by the international tide - extracting the last penny? - competition watchdogs dictate the pace of change.

or else - open season for conglomerates - winners and losers - the limits of popular capitalism - the economy's Achilles heel - sovereignty under pressure in the markets - a failure in banking supervision - what of the future?

The Square Mile is based on LWT's series of six programmes on the City of London. Indeed the main reason why we have written the book is the interest which the series aroused when it was first transmitted in the summer of 1984. We are both aware that we have built on work that was done while preparing the series. Our thanks go to all who helped to make the programmes. We would like in particular to acknowledge the parts played by Jane Hewland, executive producer, Julian Norridge, the editor, and Deborah Arnott, one of the two researchers on the series. In a tragic incident, the other researcher, John Warren drowned while the series was being transmitted. All of us who worked on *The Square Mile* know the contribution he made to the eventual success of the series and will sorely miss the fun he brought to the often fraught process of programme-making. We accordingly dedicate this book to his memory.

Preface

When Mrs Thatcher returned to power in June 1983 there was little in her manifesto to suggest that the City of London was to become the focus of sweeping reforms. Yet in the aftermath of the election, Tory radicalism found one of its most devastating outlets in the reform of Britain's financial markets. The upheaval began in the Stock Exchange and moved outwards to encompass other markets and institutions. Both the momentous scale of the changes and the sheer speed with which leading City firms regrouped to cope with a new, permissive climate were, by any standards, remarkable.

This near-instantaneous structural upheaval, which came to be known as 'The City Revolution', deserves a wide audience, not least because it provides a fascinating insight into the way in which institutional change takes place in Britain. The present book is, among other things, an attempt to unravel and explain the forces that combined to re-shape the landscape of the financial system in the two years that followed the general election of 1983. The changes come at a time of growing interest in the City, both from private investors who have been tempted into first-time ownership of shares by the governments privatisation programme and from those on the political left who are increasingly critical of regulatory failures in banking and at Lloyd's of London.

Inevitably the ground has moved under our feet. A definitive vade mecum to the new City of London is unlikely to be possible much before the end of the decade. Instead we have set out to provide an interim guide, in the form of a journalistic snapshot of the key strands in the revolution, which puts the changes into international and historical perspective. Perhaps it should also be said at the outset that 'revolution' is a very loose description, however evocative, for a complex pattern of changes that involve simultaneous moves to scrap restrictive practices and to tighten regulations designed to protect investors. If we have referred to revolution and counter-revolution in the course of the book, it is simply as a convenient shorthand. So, too, with the City itself, which is used both in its precise geographical sense and as a shorthand for the financial markets. The context will usually make the meaning clear.

Many people in and outside the City have given most generously of their time during the research that has gone into the book, most of which was written in Spring, 1985. Since many have preferred to shun the spotlight of attribution, it would be inappropriate to single out names. Our thanks therefore go to all who have helped us; the debt will be apparent to anyone who reads on. For editorial advice we are particularly grateful to Michael Brett and Garry Arnott. Our thanks, too, to Sarah Mahaffy and to Vivien James of Century Hutchinson, who helped steer the book through numerous obstacles to a difficult deadline.

The Road to Revolution

Nowhere is tradition treated with greater respect, or radicalism with more suspicion, than in the City of London, home of Britain's financial community. Yet in the space of eighteen months, between the summer of 1983 and the end of 1984, the City's markets were subjected to an upheaval so fundamental that it transformed the institutional landscape of the Square Mile.

During that brief period which followed the re-election of Mrs Thatcher's Conservative government in June 1983, a wave of takeovers and mergers engulfed hallowed names in broking, banking and insurance; the Stock Exchange itself laid plans to overhaul its system for dealing in stocks and shares – a system that had lasted more than three-quarters of a century; the laws and regulations governing investor protection in Britain were comprehensively reviewed; and the traditional barriers between different types of financial business such as banking, insurance, stockjobbing and stockbroking crumbled. In effect, decades' worth of custom and practice were unceremoniously thrown out by people who had always made a point of standing on ceremony. The nerve centre of British capitalism was being restructured to cope with a competitive threat to London's position as the world's main international financial centre.

The speed and enthusiasm with which normally staid City institutions went about the job of reforming the financial system have caused the upheaval to be dubbed 'The City

Revolution'. It is, however, a curious revolution that turns stockbrokers and jobbers into millionaires and offers them job security into the bargain. For these were among the more striking consequences of the game of musical chairs played out in 1983–4, in which banks, brokers, jobbers and discount houses swapped roles and forged new alliances. Something approaching £¾ billion had been committed by the end of 1984 for the purchase of Stock Exchange firms. A substantial part of it was to go into the pockets of individual partners and shareholders.

What is more, the government itself conspired to bring about the revolution, whose immediate cause was a deal struck in July 1983 between the chairman of the Stock Exchange, Sir Nicholas Goodison, and the then Secretary of State for Trade, Cecil Parkinson. Six weeks of secret negotiations between the Stock Exchange and the Department of Trade in mid-1983 resulted in a government decision to call a halt to a case where the Stock Exchange rule book was due to come under attack in the Restrictive Practices Court.

As part of the deal, the Stock Exchange was forced to make concessions in order to win exemption from the Restrictive Trade Practices Act 1976. Yet it looked suspiciously as though the government was dispensing favours to its friends in the City in the aftermath of its landslide victory at the polls that June. With hindsight the most remarkable feature of the government compact with the Stock Exchange was that few people, in or out of the City, had a clear idea of just how far-reaching and uncomfortable a reform it would unleash; or that the process of reform would stretch way beyond the Stock Exchange to encompass the whole financial structure of the City.

The need for change

The upheaval in the Square Mile was, in fact, long overdue – a necessary response to deeper forces affecting financial markets around the world. Three of the most important of these forces were the growing internationalization of the banking and securities businesses; the trend, especially in the United States, towards removing restrictions on competition in financial services through the process known as deregulation; and rapid technological change, notably in communications. If Britain was to retain its comparative advantage in providing financial services to the rest of the world, institutions in the Square Mile, together with the people who worked in them, had to adapt. That point was not lost on senior officials in the Bank of England, which played a crucial part both in the deliberations between Whitehall and the Stock Exchange, and in the subsequent rearranging of the City structure. Nor, indeed, was it lost on officials in the Treasury, whose respect for some City institutions was by no means unqualified.

These were the institutions – of which the Stock Exchange was the most notable – which had succeeded in protecting their members from the full blast of foreign competition since World War II. Their ability to do so resulted from the considerable freedom they enjoyed to run their own affairs. The Stock Exchange in particular had for centuries enjoyed the right to run the nation's main capital market in effect along the lines of a private club. Now, however, the government believed that the City's privileged position had caused its capital markets to become dangerously insular, which in turn was threatening to prevent the City from mounting an adequate response to challenges from other world financial centres such as New York and Tokyo.

The City's tradition of financial freedom had played a crucial, if paradoxical, role in its achievement in defying Britain's economic decline since World War II. On the one hand, the absence of heavy-handed government regulation had made the Square Mile a singularly attractive environment for footloose foreign financial firms whose enterprise accounted in large measure for the City's continuing success as the top international financial centre. On the other hand, the tradition of wide-ranging rights to run their own affairs had undoubtedly contributed to the lacklustre performance of many of the most illustrious clubs in the Square Mile. By the early 1980s, their failure was prompting increasing concern on the part of the government. So the key to understanding why a revolution was needed lies in the history of the Square Mile.

The special relationship with the state

The leitmotiv which runs through the City's evolution into a world financial centre is the unique relationship which it has for so long enjoyed with the state. From the Middle Ages and probably earlier, the merchants of the Square Mile were granted monopoly trading rights in return for the funds they raised for the Crown. The chief beneficiaries in the early days were the members of the City's craft guilds; today's livery companies – among them the Goldsmiths, the Merchant Taylors and the Skinners, to mention three of the oldest – are a tangible, if largely ceremonial, survival of the guilds, which history has endowed with some of the most valuable real estate in the Square Mile.

In due course similar privileges were granted to the guilds' successors, the chartered corporations. The Eastland Company began trading with Scandinavia and the Baltic in the fifteenth century; the second half of the sixteenth century saw the establishment of the Muscovy Company and the Levant Company; and the celebrated East India Company received a charter from Queen Elizabeth in 1600. As the names imply, these enterprises enjoyed exclusive rights vis-à-vis fellow British merchants to exploit the trade potential of specific parts of the globe.

Such privileges were largely responsible for London's increasing dominance in the economic life of the country. By the early seventeenth century, the economy of England was arguably more centralized than that of any other nation in Europe. However, while the City was already a great trading port, it was not yet itself a financial centre of note. It was Amsterdam which was developing new financial services to meet the requirements of a fast-growing commercial empire. The first stock exchange and the first national bank were both created in Amsterdam. Englishmen, jealous of Dutch prowess, described Holland as 'a counting house, protected by a navy'.

The City emerges as a world financial centre

The development of the City as a leading financial centre to rival and eventually eclipse Amsterdam rested on a new partnership between the City and the Crown which was established after the Glorious Revolution of 1688, when William of Orange displaced the last of the Stuart kings. This was a marriage of mutual interest. The City would provide funds for a series of trade wars through which Britain could win a great commercial empire centred on the Square Mile.

The nature of the new relationship between the City and the state is perhaps best exemplified in the founding of the Bank of England in 1694. In exchange for funds to prosecute the Nine Years' War with the French, which had started in 1689, the Bank was given a profitable near-monopoly of the issue of banknotes in England. Thereafter the Bank became responsible for assisting with the marketing of the national debt, which was issued to finance the many wars of the eighteenth century. Initially the government insisted on imposing the same conditions on the Bank as on other chartered corporations: charters were granted for specific periods, giving the government the opportunity to extract new conditions or a higher price from the merchants on renewal. Only when perpetual joint-stock companies were founded in the nineteenth century did such explicit quid pro quos start to fade away.

The acquisition of new colonial possessions as a result of the wars of the eighteenth century led to an enormous expansion in the amount of overseas trade handled by the port of London. This development, in which the chartered companies played a significant part, led in turn to the City's increasing importance in international finance. Foreign voyages locked up capital for long periods and entailed big risks, a situation which created a demand for both capital and insurance. By the early eighteenth century the need to finance trade and to hedge against the attendant risk had contributed to the emergence of many of the central institutions of today's financial system. There was an embryonic (and scandal-prone) stock market, where frenetic speculation and malpractice prompted a harsh verdict from Daniel Defoe. In a tract entitled 'The Anatomy of Change-Alley: A System of Stock-jobbing Proving that Scandalous Trade as it is now carried on to be Knavish in its Private Practice and Treason in its Publick', Defoe said: 'There is not a man but will own 'tis a compleat System of Knavery; that 'tis a

Trade founded in Fraud, born of Deceit, and nourished by Trick, Cheat, Wheedle, Forgeries, Falsehoods and all sorts of Delusions.' Edward Lloyd's coffee house was already set to become the centre of the insurance market. And there was a substantial banking community, with a complement of foreigners familiar with continental business.

The partnership between the City and the state bore fruit in the eighteenth and early nineteenth centuries. London overtook Amsterdam as the leading centre for trade around 1730; and its pre-eminence in finance dates from the time of the Napoleonic Wars, which brought about Amsterdam's demise as the most sophisticated provider of financial services to the rest of Europe. Yet paradoxically the City did little, after its emergence as the world's leading financial centre, to finance Britain's own industrial revolution.

Neglect of industry

Long-term capital for the early development of manufacturing industry in Britain was usually provided locally by entrepreneurs themselves, together with their families, friends and neighbours. Short-term finance for working capital was frequently provided by country banks in the form of loans – though London banks and discount houses did finance working capital by discounting domestic bills of exchange. Those entrepreneurs who sought access to substantial risk capital from the Square Mile were no less prone to frustration than their twentieth-century counterparts. When, for example, the growth of Boulton and Watt's steam engine business had eaten up all the savings of Boulton and his wife, it was not a London financial house but the great Dutch bank of Hope and Co. that came to the rescue.

The City's preoccupation with international finance was already attracting sharp-edged political comment in the nineteenth century – witness Disraeli's much-quoted verdict in *Endymion* on the railway boom before 1845:

> What is remarkable in this vast movement in which so many millions were produced, and so many more promised, was, that the great leaders of the financial world took no part in

6

it. The mighty loan-mongers on whose fiat the fate of kings and empires sometimes depended, seemed like men who, witnessing some eccentricity of nature watch it with mixed feelings of curiosity and alarm. Even Lombard Street, which was never more wanted, was inactive, and it was only by an irresistible pressure of circumstances that a banking firm which had an extensive country connection was ultimately forced to take the leading part that was required, and almost unconsciously lay the foundation of the vast fortune which it has realised and organise the varied connection which it now commands.[1] All seemed to come from the provinces and from unknown people in the provinces.

The golden era

The City did, however, play a crucial part in financing everyone else's railways. In the nineteenth and early twentieth centuries Britain had a huge surplus of domestic savings to export to the rest of the world. Markets in the Square Mile acted as a magnet for the capital accumulated by private individuals in the course of industrialization; that capital was recycled – in a twentieth-century phrase – not only to foreign enterprise but to foreign governments. The pattern was set by Baring Brothers, the merchant bank which, among other things, helped finance France's 700 million franc indemnity payment after the Napoleonic Wars. The Baring loan ensured that the indemnity could be discharged immediately, while the burden of repayment was deferred over the full term of the loan. It was this loan that led to the Duc de Richelieu's famous remark made in 1819: 'There are in Europe six great powers – England, France, Russia, Austria, Prussia and Baring Brothers.' The Baring indemnity formula was to be used again in 1871 after the Franco–Prussian War, and in 1924 to cope with the huge burden of reparations on Germany after World War I. Barings' other achievements included the financing in 1803 of the Louisiana Purchase, when Napoleon sold a large area of the South to the US government.

---

[1] The bank in question was Glyn's, which put up £100,000 for the London and Birmingham railway.

In the wake of the revolutions of 1848 the principal direction of British capital shifted away from Europe to the Americas and to the main outposts of British imperialism. India, Australia and, towards the end of the century, South Africa all absorbed substantial sums. The focus of much of this investment remained narrow; in 1883 no less than 93 per cent of the securities quoted on the stock market consisted of government and railway obligations. And much of the capital outflow was handled by merchant banks whose names remain familiar in the City – the Rothschilds, Barings and Morgans. Thanks to the Victorian middle class's propensity to make speculative investments overseas, Britain had, on the eve of World War I, become the *rentier* of the world – and on a scale that today seems scarcely credible. At the peak in 1913 (admittedly a somewhat freakish year) foreign investment took over half the total of British savings. Around one-tenth of Britain's national income came from interest on foreign investments, which were equivalent in total to around 180 per cent of gross domestic product.

London was similarly dominant in financing world trade. In the City's most self-confident period British bankers and merchants reaped huge profits as a direct result of empire and of sterling's central position in the world financial system. More than half the world's trade was financed in sterling, regardless of where the trade originated. It was normal, for example, for the movement of the American cotton crop from the Deep South to cotton mills around the globe to be financed by bills of exchange drawn on London's merchant banks. As holders of sterling were legally entitled to convert bank notes into gold, London's pre-eminence meant that much of the world economy was effectively on the gold standard. And because sterling was regarded as being 'as good as gold', foreign governments and enterprises held substantial balances in sterling in London. While France mounted a serious financial challenge to Britain in mid-century, Paris never became more than a European centre. The threat was more or less extinguished when the Bank of France was forced off the gold standard at the outbreak of the Franco–Prussian War of 1870–71.

Not surprisingly, all this activity in international trade and finance helped promote other related markets in London such as insurance and commodities, which had originally flourished in tandem with the growth of the port. Not only did Lloyd's of London become the biggest marine insurance market in the world, but British insurance companies spread their branches and subsidiaries through the main geographical areas of British influence to undertake all forms of insurance business. Similarly, all forms of merchanting, agency and advisory businesses grew up around, and fed on, London's central activity in international trade and finance. No other financial centre has ever enjoyed such a dominant worldwide position in such a comprehensive range of financial services.

Continuing privilege

The City's pre-eminence ensured its ability to retain a privileged position within the country. Explicit trading rights such as those granted to the chartered companies had been removed in the nineteenth-century Liberal assault on monopolies. However, City institutions were given the equally valuable privilege of running their own affairs; if necessary, Parliament intervened to give statutory backing to the organization of the financial system along the lines of a private club. The Lloyd's Act of 1871, for example, which remained in force until the beginning of 1983, gave the Society a constitution with the power to make bye-laws. The sonorous introductory clause gives a good indication of the self-confidence of City institutions such as Lloyd's:

> And whereas the affairs of the Society, and the business conducted by its members as such, are of large and increasing magnitude and importance . . . and the management of the affairs of the Society and the incorporation of its members with proper powers would be of great benefit to the shipping and mercantile interests of the United Kingdom. . . .

Presiding over the City was the Bank of England. It was to remain a private bank until its nationalization in 1946, but by the end of the nineteenth century it had assumed many of its present responsibilities. In addition to its developing role as a central bank, it had laid claim to the Square Mile as its bailiwick. Its influence was demonstrated in the 1890 Baring crisis. Baring Brothers, the most prestigious bank in London, faced collapse as a result of imprudent lending to Latin America. The enormous impact of such an event on confidence in the City and in Britain as a whole was greatly feared by both the government and the Bank of England. Over one weekend in November the Governor of the Bank of England, William Lidderdale, avoided Treasury involvement in the City by persuading a number of leading banks to provide a rescue fund for Barings.

Was decline inevitable?

The City's pre-eminence was, however, heavily dependent on continuing surpluses on the current account of Britain's balance of payments with the rest of the world. These were abruptly curtailed by World War I, when sterling went off the gold standard and returned to it only between 1925 and 1931, with disastrous consequences for the British economy. Thereafter sterling declined considerably in importance. By the time World War II had come to an end, and what was left of Britain's financial community contemplated the havoc wreaked on the Square Mile by German bombs, few felt sanguine about sterling's postwar prospects. It was widely assumed that Britain, as a debtor nation which had been forced to sell off foreign assets accumulated before the war, would play a dwindling part in international finance and that New York would take over London's international role.

History provided ample grounds for pessimism on this score. It was war that put an end to Antwerp's supremacy as a northern European financial centre in the late sixteenth century, and war again that completed the downfall of its successor, Amsterdam, in the early nineteenth century. But there were also practical economic reasons for expecting London's position to be eroded, which related to the capital structure of the financial businesses themselves and to the regulation of capital flows across the world.

An important characteristic of all financial firms, whether in banking, securities dealing or insurance, is that they need a cushion of capital to provide some protection against the risk of loss and of possible insolvency. Under the laws and regulations of a given country a bank might, for example, be required to keep at least £1 of capital for every £20 of deposits entrusted to it by its customers. Similarly, an insurance company might be required by law to have a minimum £1 of capital for every £5 of insurance that it persuaded its customers to take out. It follows that any bank or insurance company that is based in Britain, and whose capital is expressed in sterling, will be able to take fewer and fewer foreign currency deposits or foreign currency premiums if sterling is sinking against the world's leading currencies. Looked at from a wider perspective, the relative size of the capital base of Britain's financial system, and consequently Britain's ability to conduct international financial business, was bound to shrink if sterling went into decline.

A second, related, problem for the internationalists in the City lay in the maintenance of exchange controls after the war. To protect the pound, successive governments put obstacles in the path of both direct and portfolio investment overseas. Investors were forced to pay more than the going international market rate to acquire funds in a scarce pool of foreign currencies. As a result the ability of financial and other businesses to expand overseas was impeded. Professional fund managers and private investors held only small percentages of their assets overseas, and for some considerable time after the war London's commodity markets were prevented from opening for fear of exchange control abuses. Insurers faced unwelcome exchange risks where they were obliged to meet foreign claims from sterling reserves.

In the event the dismal performance of the British economy and the downward mobility of sterling in the postwar world gave the British government little incentive to lift exchange controls. The pound's role as a reserve currency in which foreign governments and corporations held their financial balances was gradually unwound. The dollar, with other currencies playing an increasingly significant part, became the main international unit of account as Britain struggled with balance of payments crises and successive devaluations in 1949 and 1967. In the meantime, a growing proportion of capital designated for economic development around the globe was channelled through international agencies such as the International Bank for Reconstruction and Development (the World Bank).

Against that background it was inevitable that the focus of the London financial community's attention should become more domestic, a post-imperial adjustment that was not unduly painful. After the immediate dislocation that followed the war, the City prospered as the British economy grew, albeit at a slower rate than Britain's main competitors. Yet surprisingly – and crucially – the diminished role of sterling did not put an end to the City's global role.

While exchange controls impeded capital flows, they did not kill off trade financing; and although the proportion of world trade financed in sterling had fallen from about 50 per cent before the war to nearer 25 per cent in the mid-1960s, that 25 per cent represented a share of a cake that had been greatly enlarged by economic growth in an increasingly liberal trade climate. Despite the restrictions on capital flows, for much of this period insurance continued to be Britain's biggest source of invisible earnings. Shipping, too, made a substantial contribution.

A new international role

More interestingly, the City that had lost its old sterling empire after two world wars found a new non-sterling international role in the late 1950s and early 1960s. That it did so was largely a matter of luck. For despite the enormous importance of the dollar in the postwar international system, the United States failed to grasp the financial opportunities that its status as political and economic top dog would clearly have justified. Instead, by imposing in the early 1960s tough fiscal and regulatory constraints on its own investors, banks and corporate borrowers, it drove them to conduct dollar business outside America.

The City's tradition of financial freedom made the Square Mile much the most attractive location for these victims of regulation. The Bank of England, the guardian of that tradition, played a crucial part in allowing London to play chief host in the 1960s and 1970s to the developing offshore markets in dollars, the so-called Euromarkets, which now constitute the biggest pool of expatriate capital in the world. It operated exchange controls in a way which allowed business in foreign currencies to be conducted virtually free of regulation while maintaining a tight grip on the use of sterling. And by adopting an open door policy to foreign financial institutions, it enabled the City to become a foreign banking centre on an unheralded scale. By the 1970s there were actually more American banks in the City than there were in New York.

The emphasis of the new non-sterling type of business which foreign banks were flocking into the City to conduct was 'wholesale'. It was concerned not with private individuals but with huge transactions between countries, companies and financial institutions. This policy was in marked contrast to, say, that of Switzerland, which established a comparative advantage in international finance by offering minimally regulated banking and investment services to the international 'retail' market – nervous private individuals for whom secrecy and security were more important than good investment performance. What Britain did was to offer services which complemented those of Switzerland. The City offered minimally regulated banking and investment facilities to multinational corporations and financial institutions that wanted to borrow, lend or invest in currencies other than sterling, at prices or in quantities that could not be obtained in their own domestic markets. Swiss and other banks could then find in London an investment outlet for the cash entrusted to them by their anonymous clientele.

The scope for putting this competitive advantage to good use magnified spectacularly in the 1970s as new sources of demand for financial services emerged in the global money system. The collapse in 1972–3 of the structure of fixed exchange rates established at Bretton Woods in the United States in 1944 proved a boon to London's foreign exchange market – if to no one much else. The resulting instability gave companies and banks a powerful incentive to move funds across the exchanges to anticipate changes in exchange rates and to hedge against volatility.

The volume of dealing was further increased by changes in US accounting requirements governing foreign currency trans-

13

lation and by the rapid development of communications technology. Foreign exchange dealers, in constant touch with each other in centres such as New York, Tokyo, Bahrein, Frankfurt and London, were among the first to discover what it meant to live in a global village. London vied with New York for supremacy, with a turnover by the mid-1980s of over $50 billion a day, in an extraordinarily volatile market in which 80–90 per cent of the transactions bore no relation at all to trade in physical goods.

This atmosphere of internationalism pervaded bank board rooms as well as the dealing rooms. While the Bank of England encouraged foreign banks into London, the United States maintained a similarly liberal attitude to foreign purchasers of American banks – indeed, it was a source of irritation to US commercial bankers that foreign banks enjoyed more freedom to operate branches across the country than they did. All the Big Four British clearing banks seized the opportunity to buy into American banks, although not with uniformly happy results.

Then the oil crisis in 1973 served to create a new demand for international finance. The richer members of the Organization of Petroleum Exporting Countries (OPEC) were unable to absorb in their own economies the huge volume of cash generated by the fourfold increase in the oil price. None of the OPEC countries had highly developed banking systems, so there was a need for someone to collect OPEC's surplus savings and to pass them on to oil consumers in the Third World whose balance of payments had been driven deeply into deficit by the spiralling price of oil. Britain was politically stable and had always shown an un-American readiness to divorce its role as a custodian of foreigners' money from wider political considerations; it also offered a high degree of banking confidentiality. It followed that London was ideally placed to do the job.

The task of intermediating the financial needs of these two groups of countries came to be known as 'petrodollar recycling'. But when the jargon is stripped away, the City can be seen to have gone halfway back to its nineteenth-century function. Once again it was managing the flows of capital from creditor to debtor countries. This time, however, the savings

14

were provided not by the British middle class, but by foreign governments and their state-owned agencies.

A tale of two Cities

The impact of all this on the Square Mile in the second half of the 1970s was remarkable. While the world economy sagged under the strain of two successive oil shocks, and Britain itself wilted under the additional blows of a banking crisis and a sterling crisis in the mid-1970s, the City of London, against all apparent odds, turned into a boom town. Most of the booming, predictably enough, was taking place in the foreign banking community. Indeed, a key point that will be reiterated through much of this book is that there were really two Cities in the 1960s and 1970s: one domestic and one international.

The international City, centred on the Euromarkets, was exclusive only in the sense that exchange controls prevented UK residents from doing business in it. The scale of its activities was growing at an exponential rate. By the end of the 1970s, about $60 billion of loans a year were being organized in Eurodollars within the Square Mile. For all that, this 'other' City remained shadowy, partly because a lack of regulation meant that little information was available about its activities – an information vacuum which the British financial press was initially slow to recognize or fill – but also because it was dominated by foreign financial institutions. Many of the top foreign bankers and dealers who worked in the Euromarkets lived a segregated existence. They tended, as did diplomats and multinational company executives, to gravitate to the upper-class residential ghettos of Knightsbridge, Belgravia and Regents Park, enjoying high salaries, special tax privileges and a way of life to which few Britons in managerial positions could aspire.

The domestic City centred on the trading floor of the Stock Exchange and the home operations of the banks and insurance companies. Its chief economic function was to channel the nation's savings into investment in industry and commerce. As in the Euromarkets, much of this business was 'wholesale'. It consisted of transactions between giant financial institutions in the interbank market, purchases of large blocks of shares by

15

insurance companies and pension funds, and the sharing out of huge risks between different insurance companies. While some of these institutions, notably the clearing banks and insurance companies, were quite heavily regulated, at least by British standards, others, such as the Stock Exchange, still believed in the gentlemen's club ethic; accordingly, they continued very largely to regulate themselves. Powerful though they were, institutional investors who constituted the main customers of the broking and jobbing fraternity were not invited to sit on the Stock Exchange's ruling body, the Council. Nor, in contrast with the arrangements on the New York Stock Exchange, were industrialists represented at this time. Even access to the payments system in Britain, including the all-important Bankers' Clearing House, was governed by a 'club', the Committee of London Clearing Bankers.

The formal dividing line between the two Cities was the system of exchange controls. However, this did not in itself mean that British banks could not participate in the Euromarkets and foreign financial institutions in the domestic City. Some British banks did build up a presence in Eurodollar lending, and certain foreign banks began to compete vigorously with the clearers in providing sterling loans to big British companies. However, the striking feature of the City in the 1960s and 1970s was the extent to which the offshore City was dominated by foreigners and the degree to which domestic financial concerns were able to shield themselves from competition from the foreign presence in their midst.

The City's success in achieving this measure of protection, at a time when it was loud in its criticism of British industry for failing to cope with foreign competition, was largely due to its continuing privileged, independent position. At the same time discount houses, a relic from the nineteenth century's system of financing trade through bills of exchange, were allowed to survive by grace and favour of the Bank of England, which allowed them to play a specialized role in the marketing of government debt. British banks could rely on the Bank to defend them from the threat of foreign takeovers. The City was thus left largely to its own devices through most of the postwar period.

A continuing special relationship

The City's continuing privileged status was still rooted in its relationship with government. Until Mrs Thatcher came to power, the main focus of dialogue between Whitehall and the Square Mile concerned the preoccupation of governments and financiers down the ages: the City's role in credit creation and in funding the government's debt.

Twentieth-century democracy had added a new dimension to the conduct of monetary policy and the marketing of national debt. Postwar governments strived ever more anxiously to protect voters from any upward movements in interest rates that threatened to make mortgage loans more expensive. Yet the implicit compact that had existed between City and state over the centuries was not fundamentally different in the postwar period, at least in the method of operation. While the nationalization of the Bank of England in 1946 gave the government considerable power over the banking system, that power was never exercised directly. Whitehall preferred to wield influence informally through a characteristically British activity that the distinguished Cambridge economist Dennis Robertson once described as 'ear-stroking' – that is, 'encouragements which are not quite promises, frowns which are not quite prohibitions, understandings which are not quite agreements'.

The system of nods and winks, as it is known in the City, survived largely intact even under the 1974–79 Labour administrations, whose Chief Secretary to the Treasury, Joel (now Lord) Barnett, cheerfully acknowledged its advantages. In a period of great pressure on public spending in the second half of the decade, investment institutions conveniently doubled their holdings of the government's gilt-edged stock, without statutory direction, despite a widespread distaste in the City for the Labour government's policies. Small wonder that it was 'hardly necessary to introduce direction of funds in order to induce a significant shift in the pattern of investment by long-term institutions'.

The responsiveness of the City to such 'ear-stroking' ensured that concern expressed by politicians over the financial community's relationship with industry remained only sporadic. In the mid-1970s Labour politicians argued vociferously, in the aftermath of the 1974 stock market crash, that the City was starving British industry of funds. Bank of England officials responded to this concern by paying increasing attention to problems of industrial finance. However, the City was able to ward off any real threat of statutory control over its freedom to invest. The Wilson Committee, which was set up by Prime Minister James Callaghan to investigate the issue of the relationship between the financial system and industry, came down largely in favour of the City, arguing that finance was generally available to meet genuine investment opportunities.

The one thing of which scarcely anyone in Westminster or Whitehall took any notice was the burgeoning activity in the Euromarkets. The existence of this huge unregulated pool of offshore money was a matter of interest and concern only to those Treasury officials responsible for international monetary relations and the Bank of England, which was anxious to preserve stability in the banking system. Almost by definition politicians in Westminster were unlikely to bother if Italian doctors and Belgian dentists, often bent on tax evasion, lost money in what amounted to the world's biggest black market in dollar funds. Few questioned the propriety of playing host to this vast pool of unregulated offshore money.

New concerns under Mrs Thatcher

Several things changed when Mrs Thatcher came to power. Not only did governmental interest in the City increase; it also broadened in focus. Where a Labour government in the 1970s had asked whether the City was failing British industry, a Conservative government in the 1980s asked whether the City was as competitive internationally as the national interest required. Whitehall looked to the City as a potential provider of service industry jobs as manufacturing industry came under severe pressure in the recession of 1980–81. And in doing so, it was obliged to consider how far the City's restrictive practices, which derived essentially from its considerable freedom to run its own affairs, detracted from its competitiveness as an international financial centre. It was also forced to ask whether a lack of formal regulation in the scandal-prone insurance market at Lloyd's was undermining international confidence not just in Lloyd's but in the City itself.

The government's interest in the City began to intensify in Mrs Thatcher's second term of office. Whitehall's customary concern for the City as a source of funds to cover public borrowing started to extend beyond events in the gilt-edged sector to the state of the equities market. The expansion of its interest partly reflected a change of emphasis in monetary policy. Like other Tory governments in the postwar period, Mrs Thatcher's administration – contrary to the general belief – failed to cut public expenditure. It was only able to meet its borrowing targets by selling off public sector assets such as the government's holdings in British Petroleum (BP) and great state enterprises such as British Telecom. The ability of the equity market to absorb the flood of shares spawned by the privatization programme thus became a matter of more than passing interest in both the Bank of England and Whitehall.

Equally important, Mrs Thatcher's government also started in its second term to address a wider range of economic issues. After devoting itself in its first term to measures designed to bring down inflation, it now turned to the 'supply side' of the economy – that is, to the examination of constraints and distortions that prevented particular markets in the micro-economy from working efficiently. The two most obvious distortions that touched on the City's concerns were the massive tax privileges given, first, to borrowers for home ownership and, second, to investors who put their money into institutional forms of saving.

While Mrs Thatcher remained blind to the absurdity of using taxpayers' money to subsidize the house price spiral, she and her ministers were ideologically predisposed to attack institutional forms of ownership – notwithstanding the readiness with which insurance companies and pension funds absorbed shares in privatized companies. Ministers became increasingly anxious to reintroduce the British people to direct share ownership, through both tax changes and specific inducements to take up shares in newly privatized state industries such as British Telecom.

Finally, Mrs Thatcher herself was temperamentally opposed to the club ethic in economic and business affairs, even if the club members carried the same ideological baggage as she did. Her instinctive lack of respect for established institutions and her desire to see more American-style capitalism in Britain had some impact on ministers and officials who were responsible for keeping an eye on the City.

A seminal decision

For the City, the most important new policy of the Thatcher government was a measure announced only a few months after the Tories first regained power in 1979. In the autumn of that year, without giving notice, the government sprang its decision on the House of Commons to lift exchange controls. It was a seminal event in the postwar history of the City, yet, ironically, the decision was taken with virtually no consideration about its potential effect on the structure of the City itself.

The new policy was adopted as part of a broader strategy designed to deal with the impact of North Sea oil on the economy. The sudden access of oil riches raised difficult questions about how far the structure of the economy should be allowed to change to reflect its new – but purely temporary – status as an oil producer. Because of the huge inflow of oil revenue Britain was likely to run a substantial surplus on the current account of its balance of payments for the rest of the new Tory government's term of office. The government had to decide how far, if at all, the non-oil-related sectors of British industry should be protected from the decline in competitiveness that seemed likely to result from a stronger pound while the current account surplus was building up.

One element in the strategy that finally emerged was a decision to offset the multibillion surplus by private capital outflows. Much of the outward investment was to be undertaken by the insurance companies and pension funds, which could be relied upon to exploit their new freedom from controls by investing part of their annual cash flow of £10–15 billion in the United States, Japan and other economies with open capital markets. By selling pounds in exchange for foreign currency in order to purchase overseas assets, the investment institutions – as the insurance companies and pension funds are known – were expected to restrain their appreciation of sterling, while accumulating a nest egg overseas for the day when oil ran down.

As it turned out, the effect of this policy was to expose mainstream industrial companies in Britain much more directly to the competitive pressures of the international economy. Part of its purpose was indeed to bring the return on investment in Britain into line with that of other countries and to ensure that the British economy ceased to be an isolated pocket of the world economy in which low returns were the norm. Yet the new freedom from capital controls meant that the City itself had come full circle. By dint of a fortunate discovery of a scarce natural resource on its own back doorstep the Square Mile was able to revert to something more like its nineteenth-century role. Having spent much of the 1970s managing other countries' financial capital, London-based financiers suddenly found themselves presented with an opportunity to handle Britain's own capital exports as well.

The lifting of exchange controls had further advantages for the City. Not only were private citizens now allowed to hold their money in whatever currency they chose; the financial community could now offer a wider and more flexible range of services to domestic and foreign clients. Lord Garmoyle, a vice-chairman of the merchant bankers S. G. Warburg, recalls advising the world's biggest insurance brokers, Marsh & McLennan of New York, on the takeover at that time of the London insurance broking firm of C. T. Bowring. Exchange controls were lifted in the middle of the transaction, immediately enabling Warburg's to advise the American concern to offer its own dollar-denominated stock to British shareholders as part of the consideration. British companies could likewise use international currency in making acquisitions overseas. The enormous flexibility that the new freedom gave to people in the financial advisory business amounted to a merchant banker's dream: all permutations of currency and commercial paper became possible in both domestic and international financing. For those more directly involved in broking and dealing, the scope for arbitrage – taking advantage of different rates of return on like products – between domestic and international markets increased enormously.

The decision to lift exchange controls was a characteristic

example of Thatcherite radicalism. It aptly symbolized the fundamentalist aspirations of a government that was anxious to hark back to the red-blooded economic liberalism of the nineteenth century. Properly speaking, the City Revolution starts here; not least because the government discovered that it could let loose instantaneous reform in the financial area without a serious political backlash in the House of Commons. The uncomfortable message for practitioners in the financial markets, though few recognized it at the time, was that the considerable freedoms enjoyed by the financial community in the profitable pursuit of its domestic business could no longer be taken for granted. The barrier between the two Cities had been removed; and this was to lay open the extent to which large parts of the Square Mile had become internationally uncompetitive. This unwelcome discovery explains to a large extent the intensification in the government's involvement in the City in Mrs Thatcher's second term of office, in the wake of the agreement reached between Cecil Parkinson and Sir Nicholas Goodison.

It would be wrong, however, to conclude that the government actually masterminded the City Revolution. The dramatic upheaval in the Square Mile in the mid-1980s was as much a matter of accident as of design. The point is, rather, that attitudes in government became more permissive, for all the reasons mentioned earlier. Even in the normally cautious Bank of England an uncharacteristically benign attitude to change began to emerge. It was summed up by a senior Bank official at the end of 1983, who told one of the authors of this book that, in looking at the structural upheaval in the City, the Bank no longer simply asked 'Why?'; it was inclined, for the moment, to ask 'Why not?'

Leading bankers and brokers may have had reservations about the pace of the change, but most recognized that it was necessary. For there was a growing consensus that without reform the City would not long survive as a leading international financial centre. Global economic changes were creating a competitive threat to the Square Mile that was simply too serious to ignore.

2

The Foreign Challenge

By 1984, none but the most complacent could overlook the foreign challenge which the City was facing. That was the year in which the influential American magazine *Business Week* ran a cover story on 'The New York Colossus'. The banner headline read: 'Its surge to world financial supremacy makes it the capital of capital.' The claim that New York had already outstripped London as the top international financial centre could certainly be contested; however, the article could not be dismissed as mere patriotic swagger. For 1984 was the year in which more shares in ICI, the barometer of the Stock Exchange, were traded in New York than in London.

The City Revolution is the response to the competitive threat facing London in the 1980s. Worldwide financial, economic and technological changes have been bringing to an end the tale of two Cities which characterized much of the postwar history of the Square Mile. They are making it increasingly clear that the City can no longer rely to the same extent on the foreign financial community in its midst to bolster up its international role. At the same time, together with the removal of exchange controls, they are undermining the barriers which used to protect much of the British financial system from foreign competition. Three developments in particular underpin the competitive threat that the City Revolution is intended to counter.

Three challenges

The first of these is that other major financial centres have started to emulate London in its role as an offshore island. The challenge which the Square Mile faces in the 1980s is that financial centres across the world are fighting for business on the same principle as free ports. They are stripping away the controls and regulations which once drove business to the City with its long tradition of financial freedom. Clearly it would now be unwise for the City to rely to the same extent on its attractions as an entrepot if it is to retain its international pre-eminence. The need for a stronger performance by British financial institutions has accordingly become apparent.

The second challenge which the Square Mile faces arises from the changed economic and financial conditions of the 1980s. The debt crisis has throttled the role of banks in borrowing and lending across frontiers, which has in turn threatened to undermine the part which the City played so successfully in the 1970s as a centre for international banking. The name of the game in the international financial system of the 1980s is for borrowers to raise money directly through the issue of securities which are purchased by investors instead of through banks. With it has come an increasing recognition that, if the City is to retain its pre-eminence, it will be as a centre for dealing in international securities. That realization has in turn highlighted the need for reform at the Stock Exchange, in order to galvanize British financial institutions into playing an effective part in this new growth sector.

The third and perhaps most pressing challenge has been the impact of new technology on the barriers which used to protect domestic financial institutions from foreign competition. Advances in telecommunications mean that dealing in stocks and shares can now take place virtually anywhere – subject to regulations. Shares in British companies can be traded in New York just as readily as in London. Equally they can be traded just as easily in the dealing room of an American securities house in the Square Mile as on the floor of the Stock Exchange. When banking can be done at home, the huge branch networks of the clearing banks no longer afford them the same degree of protection against competition from domestic and foreign rivals. New technology saps the fortifications which used to defend domestic financial institutions such as the Stock Exchange, the merchant banks and the clearers. In the eyes of many British financiers, it has certainly made the foreign presence in the City look more and more like a Trojan horse. More than the opportunities of the brave new world of international finance in the 1980s, it has been the dangers of losing domestic business to foreign competition which has prompted the City Revolution.

These developments have been affecting financial centres across the world; nowhere, however, has their impact been greater than in London. The major reason for the upheaval is the sheer size of the City's foreign financial community and the pivotal part it has played since the war in sustaining London in its international role. The problem the City now faces is that the international financial order no longer plays to its strengths to the same extent as before. The gravity of the foreign challenge now facing the Square Mile can therefore only be appreciated by understanding why conditions in the 1960s and 1970s served the City so well, as it became London's offshore island on the Thames.

The world's foreign banking centre

The role of host to foreign financiers is itself nothing new in the history of the City. In the early Middle Ages, London was first taught the principles of banking by the Lombards from northern Italy. In the age of sterling, the Square Mile proved to be a happy hunting ground for foreign-born entrepreneurs wishing to make their fortune by setting up a British bank in London. Many of the most illustrious merchant banks in the Accepting Houses Committee – one of the City's most select 'clubs' – were initially established by immigrants. The rollcall of names with such a connection includes Charterhouse Japhet, Hambros Bank, Kleinwort Benson, Lazard Brothers, Morgan Grenfell, N. M. Rothschild, J. Henry Schroder Wagg, and most recently, S. G. Warburg. At the same time, a small number of foreign banks had established a presence in the City during its Victorian and Edwardian heyday. Of the foreign banks in London today, about thirty had established themselves in the City before World War I. Half of the American and Canadian banks which have offices in London today had already established themselves by the early twentieth century.

These apparent elements of continuity only serve, however, to show how distinctive has been the City's more recent role as a foreign financial centre. Since the war, the Square Mile has not for the most part attracted foreign entrepreneurs wishing to establish British banks. Instead it has proved an attractive location for the branches of foreign financial enterprises. The scale on which this has occurred casts the City's previous role in this capacity in a shadow. At the end of 1984, there were 470 foreign banks with a presence in London; a further 97 foreign security houses were operating in London. The City is easily the most important foreign banking centre in the world. Finally, these foreign firms are in London in order to transact international business not in sterling but in Eurodollars.

Centre of the Euromarkets

The word Eurodollar is one of those terms which seem to have been designed to keep high finance arcane. So what exactly is this mysterious currency which proved to be the salvation of the City after 1945? The answer is perhaps disappointingly simple to those who prefer to keep their finance high. It is simply a dollar which is held in a bank outside the United States. If an American resident transfers a dollar from his bank in, say, New York to any bank outside the United States, the dollar has become a Eurodollar. It is an offshore currency which can be held both by American residents and by institutions and individuals who do not live in the USA. Similarly, any other currency which is held outside its country of origin is termed a Eurocurrency. However, the Eurodollar is the principal offshore currency. In the 1980s, approximately four-fifths of all money held in the form of Eurocurrencies has consisted of Eurodollars.

The Euromarkets comprise the array of financial activities based upon the offshore use of currencies. These are broadly similar to some of the principal features of any developed financial system. Just as there is a money market in London in which banks borrow funds from each other and from other holders of surplus cash, so there is a Euromarket in bank deposits, which forms the basis of the Euromarket in loans. And just as funds can be raised in the capital markets of Britain and America through the issue of bonds, so there is a Eurobond market.

The Eurodeposit and loan markets are dominated by the big commercial banks such as Britain's high street banks and their foreign equivalents. These compete with each other both in bidding for funds and in making loans. With a Euroloan, the banks therefore stand between the borrower and the ultimate source of finance, the holder of the deposit. By contrast, a borrower who issues a Eurobond raises money directly from the investors who purchase the securities. This business is largely dominated by the investment (or merchant) banks and security houses which organize new issues, sell them to investors on behalf of their clients, and make a market in Eurobonds.

The growth of the Euromarkets has been quite spectacular. In the last quarter of a century they have outstripped any domestic market as a source of international funds. Two statistics give some indication of their sheer size. Since 1982, the gross volume of bank deposits held in the form of Eurocurrencies has exceeded $2 trillion, according to the calculations of the American bank Morgan Guaranty, which monitors the markets. In 1984, $80 billion was raised in capital through the issue of Eurobonds.

The City's attractions

The burgeoning of the Euromarkets goes a long way towards explaining London's dynamic performance since the late 1950s as an international financial centre. The Square Mile became the principal centre of the Euromarkets because of the many attractions it offered to foreign enterprises wishing to conduct offshore business.

One obvious advantage which the City possessed over possible rivals on the continent, such as Paris, is that English is the lingua franca of modern finance. At the same time, English law is considered to provide a superior framework to continental law for international financial transactions. As the senior partner of a leading City firm of solicitors, explained, 'English has a head start over continental law because it is explicit and positive. Continental law is much more conceptual and general.' Legal expertise was just one of a repository of financial skills built up over centuries which the City could offer. A further attraction was that the Square Mile lay at the hub of an infrastructure of world communications, which had been established during the days of Empire.

However, the City's trump card in becoming the main centre of the Euromarkets was the particular appropriateness of its long tradition of financial freedom to the emerging international financial order of the 1960s and 1970s. The hallmark of the offshore markets is that they thrive on lack of regulation. Those centres which offer a liberal financial regime free of political interference act like magnets to funds charged by the twin forces of fear and greed. The City's history made it uniquely endowed to provide just such an environment.

Fear and greed stimulate London's offshore banking market

The origins of the very term 'Eurodollar' bear witness to the role of fear in creating the offshore markets. The story of the Eurodollar is generally considered to have begun not in London but in Paris, at the height of the Cold War. The Soviet Union was concerned that Washington might block its holdings of dollars if it kept them with banks in the United States. So the USSR deposited dollars outside America, initially at the Banque Commerciale pour l'Europe du Nord. Because the telex address of this bank was EUROBANK, dollars held outside the USA came to be called Eurodollars.

There can be little doubt that fears of this nature contributed not just to the origins but to the continuing growth of the Eurodollar markets. Such worries were particularly important in the 1970s when members of OPEC were wary of placing their petrodollars in New York where they might be vulnerable to pressure from Washington. Whatever part Paris may have played in the inception of the market, the City was undoubtedly the chief beneficiary of such fears. The Square Mile's long tradition of political independence served to re-assure nervous holders of funds that they could deposit them safely in London. However, when Iranian dollar assets were frozen by President Carter during the Iranian hostage crisis, it emerged that this security did not extend to funds deposited with US bank branches in the Square Mile.

Although fear has therefore been an important force in the growth of the Euromarkets, their real dynamo has been greed. The lack of regulation which characterizes the Euromarkets has allowed financial institutions operating in them to offer better overall terms to their clients and to make more money themselves than they can on the same business in regulated domestic markets. At the same time it encourages greater innovation than in more heavily regulated domestic markets. The Euromarkets are usually in a ferment of new financial products, packages and wheezes.

Thus, although the Soviet Union may have played midwife to the birth of the Eurodollar, its initial prodigious growth in the 1960s and early 1970s was fostered by the United States. In a spectacular own goal scored against New York, a battery of draconian controls was imposed on American financial in-stitutions in the early 1960s to restrict them from providing funds to overseas clients. These special measures were intro-duced by the American government with the aim of reining in the balance of payments deficit, by curbing international lending out of the USA. The result was that a large part of the American capital and credit system simply migrated over-seas.

The Square Mile was the first port of call for the American banks in this mass exodus. Between 1964 and 1973, the number of American banks with a presence in London jumped from fourteen to fifty-one. They found in the City the relaxed regulatory climate they were seeking. London thus became the chief centre from which American banks serviced the needs of their corporate clients as they expanded into Europe in the 1960s and 1970s, in what the French journalist and politician Jean-Jacques Servan-Schreiber dubbed 'le défi américain'.

In 1974, most of the regulations which had originally driven American banks out of the USA were lifted. In the wake of the collapse of the Bretton Woods system, the American government no longer needed to bolster the balance of payments through such controls in order to defend the value of the dollar. Despite this development, London's relaxed regulatory climate meant that it remained an attractive location for international banks.

The continuing existence of the Eurodollar deposit market is founded above all on the fact that international banks can offer holders of dollars higher returns if they deposit them offshore, in a centre like London, than if they deposit them in the domestic financial system, which is subject to monetary regulation. This margin is created mainly as a result of the absence of reserve requirements on banks accepting deposits in the form of Eurodollars. In contrast, monetary regulations in the USA mean that banks there have to hold as reserves, which yield no interest, a small proportion of any deposits which they accept. If, for example, an American bank is paying 10 per cent on domestic deposits but has to hold as reserves five out of every hundred dollars' worth of deposits, this raises the effective cost of these funds to a little over 10.5 per cent. In addition, American banks have to protect depositors by subscribing to a federal insurance scheme, which increases the effective cost of their funds by a further small margin.

The effect, then, of even minimal domestic monetary regulation is to spur the development of offshore deposit markets. During the 1960s and 1970s, this was particularly advantageous to London, largely because no other major financial centre sought to emulate its laissez-faire approach. Any number of 'brass-plate' centres in offshore tax havens like the Cayman Islands were established; they enjoyed an advantage that the City could not offer in that banks escaped tax on profits derived from business conducted there, and were therefore able to win a substantial amount of business. However, London remained the major centre, with a third of all deposits in the 1970s – two to three times the share of its nearest rival. No other financial centre could match its unique blend of advantages: the financial freedom of an offshore island, combined with all the skills and facilities of a great city, and the traditions of hundreds of years as the world's leading international financial centre.

The Eurobond market is founded in London

The development of the Eurobond market, like the Euro-deposit banking market, has similarly been spurred on by the opportunities which lack of regulation offers to satisfy fear and greed. The mainstay of the Eurobond market is the facility that it affords investors to minimize and often evade tax. Unlike the registered bonds issued, for example, in the United States, Eurobonds are 'bearer-only' certificates which do not identify their holders, thus ensuring their owners' complete anonymity. Produced by specialist security printers, the certificates have attached to them the interest coupons which are physically clipped from the bond when interest falls due, generally on an annual basis. No tax is deducted from these interest payments. The onus is on the investor to declare the income. By contrast in America, until 1984 foreign investors purchasing US bonds were subject to withholding of tax on interest income. The opportunity which Eurobonds offer for tax evasion is evident. The archetypal investor is the Belgian dentist who holds his Eurobonds in Luxembourg out of reach of his tax inspector.

The Eurobond market was first established in London in 1962. The City did not provide an environment where such tax fiddling could occur – that was left to financial centres such as Switzerland and Luxembourg. Much of the buying power in the Eurobond market comes from the Swiss banks which manage the accounts of the anonymous rich to whom Eurobonds are so attractive. What the City provided from the outset was a very free environment for the actual issue and trading of Eurobonds. Investment banks may issue Eurobonds as and when they please without any timetable established by the Bank of England.

The founding father of the market was S. G. Warburg, the last of the long line of foreign entrepreneurs to establish a British merchant bank. Warburg, a member of one of the oldest banking families in Germany, first came to Britain in the 1930s after Hitler had come to power in his homeland. However, his background in the business did not prevent the City establishment from looking down on this Jewish immigrant 'with the utmost snobbism', as he later recalled. Perhaps he reminded too many top merchant bankers of their own foreign pedigree; or perhaps they simply had short memories. Whatever the reason, their attitude simply spurred Warburg on to make financial innovations in an area outside the influence of the charmed circle from which he was excluded.

The Bank of England's role

In establishing the market, the Bank of England's attitude was crucial because of the potential difficulties presented by exchange controls. Sir George Bolton, former chief exchange dealer and executive director of the Bank, is thought to have played an important part in persuading the Bank that it was in the City's interest to promote this international capital market in dollars in the Square Mile, and in soothing the Bank's concern about the implications for the regime of exchange controls. Bolton is himself often given the credit for originally spotting the opportunity which Eurodollars presented for regenerating London's international role as sterling came under more and more pressure in the post-war period. This flamboyant Bank of England director turned buccaneer in 1957, and used a relic of Empire, BOLSA, the Bank of London and South America, to take advantage of the chance to conduct borrowing and lending in offshore dollars.

Many foreign bankers have told the authors that the Bank played a vital part in fostering the new offshore markets in London. The Bank combined a light regulatory touch with an open door policy to foreign banks. Its approach of 'nods and winks' was greatly preferred by American bankers to the more legalistic framework of American regulation. The advantages of the Bank's methods were summed up in a few pithy words by Otto Schoeppler, former chairman of Chase Manhattan Ltd. It made the City, he said, 'a very warm place for doing business'.

Boom town

The Bank's approach meant that by 1970 the City was the focal point of both the Eurodeposit banking market and the Eurobond market. In the 1970s, the City's position as the centre of the Eurodeposit banking market was to prove the more important role of the two. London's position as the key foreign banking centre in the world meant that the City stood poised to take advantage of the frenetic expansion which occurred in the Eurodollar market, increasing its gross size twentyfold by 1982. This extraordinary growth was fuelled primarily by the unprecedented imbalances of payments which followed the Yom Kippur War and the subsequent fourfold increase in the price of oil. Whatever problems this created for the world economy – and they were many – this development presented a golden opportunity for the City. The job of recycling the petrodollar surpluses fell, largely by default, to the private commercial banks operating in the Euromarkets. (After the onset of the debt crisis in 1982, the question was whether the result of their efforts would be their own default.) Because the Square Mile played host to much the biggest concentration of international banks in the world, the City could not fail to benefit from the prominent role which they assumed in the petrodollar merry-go-round.

International banks recycle the petrodollars

The dominance of international banks in the massive recycling of the 1970s stands out as an exceptional episode in the history of funding of payments imbalances between countries. Until World War II, these were generally met by private investors in surplus countries who bought securities issued by governments and companies in deficit nations. After the war, governments assumed a greater significance in the financing of payments shortfalls, both through direct country-to-country loans, organized by their central banks, and through international organizations such as the International Monetary Fund, the IMF.

The leading role played by international banks in petrodollar recycling was rooted first in the international relations of the 1970s. Oil-rich states were perhaps understandably unwilling to put their oil ransom into international funding agencies over which they could exercise no real control. Western governments for their part were reluctant to become involved in recycling for fear that it would draw them into a financial commitment to the main group of deficit countries, the oil-importing developing nations. It was much easier to flunk the whole issue and shuffle off responsibility onto the commercial banks. Developing countries for their part were given a means of avoiding the need to reduce their balance of payments deficits through deflation, with unpleasant political consequences. In contrast with help from the IMF, there were no strings attached to loans from private banks.

A further reason for the international banks' involvement in recycling was the abnormal economic environment of the 1970s. Indeed, in retrospect the whole exercise may be seen as the grand finale to the world inflation which had begun in the mid-1960s. The behaviour of both surplus and deficit countries was based upon the prospect of continuing and possibly accelerating inflation. Holders of funds sought to keep their assets as liquid as possible so that they would not incur losses in the event of a surge in interest rates caused by a rise in the rate of inflation. Short-term deposits in the Euromarkets satisfied this requirement. For developing countries, inflation appeared to make borrowing relatively painless, even if debt was incurred at floating rates of interest. The calculation seemed deceptively simple. On past experience, any rise in interest rates would occur as a result of higher inflation. Although they would have to pay more in interest, the higher rate of inflation would reduce the real burden of the principal they had borrowed. And to the extent that their export prices rose in line with any increase in world inflation, higher export earnings would enable them to service the debt, even at higher rates of interest.

Such explanations only go so far, however, in accounting for the key part played by international banks in recycling. For if anything, the whole episode was a monument to mass irrationality – on the part of bankers. They chose to ignore the countless examples in financial history of sovereign states defaulting on their debts. They made no attempt to monitor the use to which the money was put. Much of it simply financed consumption and the purchase of military hardware, instead of enhancing the countries' productive potential, and thus their ability to service the debt. Yet in a sustained bout of self-fulfilling optimism the bankers succeeded in convincing

34

themselves of the creditworthiness of Third World countries, even when new borrowings began to be used by increasingly indebted countries to pay interest on their old debt.

The City takes a turn on the petrodollar merry-go-round

More than any other financial centre, the City benefited in the 1970s from the delusions of bankers and the disorder of the world economy. As the principal emporium of international banks, the Square Mile became the principal place where the highly lucrative business of international syndicated loans was managed. Such loans provided a means for banks to use the short-term funds they had accepted from surplus countries to provide massive medium- to long-term finance for the deficit nations. A key feature was that the borrower would agree to pay a fixed margin, or spread, over the floating rate of interest which banks would themselves have to pay for their short-term deposits over the length of the loan. The City's leading role in this lending was indicated by the fact that the bench-mark interest rate was generally defined as LIBOR, the London Interbank Offered Rate, at which banks in the Square Mile would themselves borrow funds from other banks. The other main feature of the loans was the process of syndication in which banks clubbed together to pool their resources and thus assemble huge loans to meet the borrowing requirements of nations.

The sheer concentration of banks in the Square Mile gave London a major advantage in this activity. In a typical loan, as many as a hundred major banks are united into a lending group. The lead bank, with the responsibility for working out the terms and conditions of the transaction and organizing the group, clearly found the process much easier to manage in a centre like London where more foreign banks were repre-sented than anywhere else in the world.

The collective involvement of banks in a syndicated loan is recorded in advertisements called 'tombstones' which are placed in the financial press to mark each loan. The origin of this curiously appropriate term, in view of the trouble which such loans were to stoke up for the world economy, goes back to the mid-nineteenth century, when British merchant banks found that the only place where they could advertise their accomplishments for their clients was next to the obituaries. The position of the bank's name in the order of wording in these tombstones, which make so many financial publications a weighty, if not meaty, read, is all-important, since it indicates the bank's prominence in the loan. An elaborate protocol has been established to designate precedence: the lead bank takes pride of place at the top, followed by members of the management group, and then all the other banks which have participated in the loan, in alphabetical order. Some banks are reputed to have changed their names just to advance further up the tombstone. According to Rudiger Eisenhart-Rothe, managing director of Chase Manhattan Ltd, the subsidiary which The Chase Manhattan Bank set up as its investment banking arm in Europe, this change of title 'gave rise at that time to some rather unfriendly discussions with some of our friendly competitors'. No doubt that was a banker's way of referring to the Chase's arch rival, Citicorp, which from that time came after Chase in the alphabetical pecking order.

The City's advantages as a centre for syndicated lending were so great that, according to one estimate, some 63 per cent of all syndicated loans made in 1979 were organized in London. Indeed, earlier in the decade the City's share of this activity was probably even higher. The importance of this leading role is indicated by the fact that the volume of loans had grown from about $5 billion in 1970 to over $80 billion in 1979. At its peak, in 1981, the total amount of international syndicated lending reached $133 billion.[1]

The international banks' role in recycling thus gave London a tremendous if largely unearned fillip as an international financial centre. Furthermore, although the business of international syndicated lending was dominated by foreign banks, the big British banks such as NatWest and Barclays had the resources to join in the activity and win a respectable share of this booming sector of international finance. One estimate is that British banks accounted for some 10 per cent of total

[1] Robert McDonald International Syndicated Loans Euromoney Publications.

syndicated lending in the late 1970s. However, this achievement (as it seemed at the time) must be put in perspective: in 1982 the share of the Big Four clearing banks was roughly the same as that of just one American bank, the market leader, Citicorp. British banks were slow to get in on the act, and when they did eventually enter the market in a big way they generally tended only to participate in the loans rather than 'lead manage' them.

During the 1970s, then, the City went from strength to strength as an international financial centre. Business in the Square Mile boomed as the volume of financial transactions in the Euromarkets exploded. More and more banks flooded in, many simply seeking representative status in order to get a listening post in the world's leading international financial community. Between 1970 and 1980 the number of foreign banks with offices in London more than doubled, from 163 to 353; this influx further reinforced the City's position. The Square Mile appeared to have found an elixir that protected it from the ills afflicting the rest of the British economy.

The music stops

The charge of the Panglossian bank brigade continued until August 1982, when the great syndicated loan bubble finally burst. A tremor ran through the Euromarkets as Mexico teetered on the brink of default, soon to be joined in the debtors' dock by Brazil. It rapidly became apparent that many of the world's most indebted countries were in no position to pay the interest on their debts, let alone repay the principal.

The debt crisis emerged as the inevitable consequence of the transformation in the world economy during the 1980s. The prolonged postwar inflation has been stopped in its tracks as a result of the adoption of tight monetary policies and a rebellion of savers worldwide. The new regime of high real interest rates which has thus come into being, while inflation has been tamed, has been sustained and made yet harsher as a result of the American budget deficit. The massive flows of capital which have been attracted into the USA by the magnet of high interest rates, together with the reduction in dollar lending by international banks, have in turn made the dollar soar. This combination of disinflation, high real interest rates and a strong dollar proved a lethal brew for the developing countries. Because they had agreed to pay interest on their Euroloans at floating rather than fixed rates of interest, the cost of servicing the debt jumped to unprecedented levels. Since at the same time the vast bulk of borrowing had been denominated in dollars, the appreciation of the dollar added still further to the difficulty they faced in generating sufficient foreign earnings to pay their interest bills. Not surprisingly, one country after another was forced to go cap in hand to the IMF. By the end of 1984 some thirty-five countries were unable to service their debt.

Since late 1982, the heady days of go-go international syndicated lending have given way to the more melancholy pursuit of rescheduling agreements. The commercial banks have been dragooned by the IMF into lending new money to the debtor countries simply in order to allow them to pay the interest on existing borrowings. Debtor countries for their part have been forced to squeeze their economies remorselessly in order to generate the trade surpluses necessary to service the debt. By early 1985 this improbable solution seemed to be working beyond the wildest dreams of the international bankers who had convened, shellshocked, at the IMF meeting which took place in Toronto late in 1982 in the wake of Mexico's moratorium. All the big four Latin American borrowers – Brazil, Mexico, Argentina and Venezuela – had succeeded in producing sufficient export surpluses in order to pay the interest on their borrowings without recourse to fresh credit. Whether this happy state of affairs could be maintained remained, however, open to doubt. For the solution to work, for years to come Brazil and Mexico would have to continue to generate relatively larger trade surpluses as a proportion of total output than Japan did in 1984.

A more challenging environment

Whatever the eventual outcome of the debt crisis, it has marked a watershed in the development of the Euromarkets – one which has presented an altogether more challenging environment for London in its role as an international centre. As the principal foreign banking centre, the City was bound to be most affected by the contraction in international banking which has followed the debt crisis. As if this were not enough, the 1980s have brought growing competition from other financial centres for this diminished business.

Since the onset of the debt crisis, international bankers have been gripped by fear and caution. In the halcyon days of the 1970s, the order of the day was expansion of the balance sheet through more and more loans. Now the day of reckoning had come, and banks found themselves with hopelessly inadequate amounts of capital to back their commitments of credit. The priority for international banks in the 1980s has therefore been to rebuild capital ratios. With access to new share capital largely blocked as a result of the fall in bank ratings which has occurred since the onset of the debt crisis, banks have been trying to avoid any new business which would expand their balance sheets. Asset management rather than asset growth has become the battlecry.

In this new environment, the Eurodeposit market has ceased to be the dynamo driving the international banking system. The gross size of the market had increased by no less than 24 per cent in 1981. In 1982, this rate of growth fell back to 11 per cent; in 1983 to 5 per cent; and in 1984 to 4 per cent. The outstanding reason for this development has been concern about the creditworthiness of many commercial banks. Nervous depositors, whether individuals or corporations, have wherever possible shifted funds out of the banking system in order to lend directly to borrowers. Instead of placing spare cash with commercial banks as Eurodeposits, they have preferred to buy short-term securities issued by the American government or by corporations. To a considerable extent they have been joined in this 'flight to quality' by many banks, which no longer lend automatically in the market. The memory of 1982, when they discovered that certain banks of debtor countries had been called upon by their governments to finance the payment of interest through short-term borrowings in the interbank market, remains far too vivid.

The impact of the debt crisis on international syndicated lending has been even more dramatic. According to Morgan Guaranty, Eurocurrency bank credits amounted to $74 billion in 1983 – half their 1981 level; in 1984 they recovered to $113 billion. In fact the real picture has been even gloomier than these bare statistics paint, since the totals include considerable amounts of credit arranged, in conjunction with the IMF, in the various debt rescheduling exercises. For example, in 1983 less than 10 per cent of the $15 billion of funds raised by Latin American borrowers comprised loans made outside the debt rescheduling process. Such 'involuntary' lending continued on a similar scale in 1984. The apparent recovery in 1984 was also something of an illusion since it included about $30 billion of exceptional credits arranged to finance takeovers in Wall Street, many of which were never even drawn.

The threats from New York and Tokyo

The problem facing London is not just that the cake is smaller than it used to be. The City now confronts much greater competition from other financial centres for a slice of that cake. The introduction of International Banking Facilities, known as IBFs, in the USA in 1981 has already demonstrated the fragility of the City's position as an international banking centre. IBFs create the conditions of an offshore dollar market within New York, much as if Manhattan had been towed out into the Atlantic beyond the reach of the American financial authorities. The offices of banks are physically in New York; the pretence is that they are not. Banks can therefore transact international banking business in exactly the same way as if they were operating in London, the Cayman Islands or wherever. The Facilities mean that they are not required to back transactions with the reserves that are necessary for ordinary domestic banking in the USA. By the end of 1984, IBFs had captured nearly 10 per cent of the total Eurocurrency banking market – adopting Morgan Guaranty's convention of including IBF dollars as Eurodollars. Much of this activity consisted of business which had been diverted from Caribbean offshore centres. The City remained the principal centre of the Eurocurrency banking market. However, London's share of the total Eurodeposit market had fallen to under a third by the end of 1984.

Perhaps equally worrying for the City is the fact that a

similar scheme is likely to be introduced in Tokyo in 1986. The potential impact of such a move arises out of the key role which Japanese banks now play in the Eurodollar market in the City. Since the early 1980s they have commanded a bigger share of total Eurodeposits than the American banks which formerly dominated business in the Square Mile. At the end of 1984 Japanese banks held 160 billion pounds worth of Eurodeposits, over half as much again as American banks and 25 per cent of the total pool of Eurodeposits in London. The proposal to establish IBFs in Tokyo forms part of a much broader wave of deregulation transforming a financial centre which used to be one of the most restricted in the world. The catalyst to these changes has been pressure from an American administration which believes that Japanese regulations have kept the yen artificially low, thus contributing to the huge imbalance of trade between the two countries. However, there is reason to believe that the Japanese are acquiescing in these demands because they believe that liberalization may well serve the interests of Japanese financial firms. It would appear that the authorities in Tokyo, like the British government, increasingly consider their banks and security houses an industry as much as a source of finance for industry. As a result, the agreement which was reached between US Treasury and Japanese Ministry of Finance officials in May 1984 is leading to the dismantling of many of the restrictions which formerly shackled the use of the yen as an international currency. These changes are bound to heighten the attractions of Tokyo as a rival to London.

The party ends . . .

The combination of the debt crisis and increased competition from other financial centres has cast a shadow over the City's role as a foreign banking centre. The flood of foreign banks seeking a corner in the Square Mile has dwindled to a trickle. The harsh reality for many foreign banks is that their London operation has ceased to be the moneyspinner that it was in the 1970s. Kent Price, head of Citicorp's London office, accepts that the Square Mile's position as the focal point of international syndicated lending once made it a highly profitable

41

location for a foreign bank. The banks were making 'a lot of money', he told the authors, through the recycling process. However, now that the boom had collapsed, he continued, 'There's a lot of folk who are feeling a lot of pain.'

The prestige of a London operation, together with the perks it presents for globetrotting international bankers – the so-called 'Ascot factor' – have so far prevented major departures. However, a number of important American banks are known to have conducted reviews of the future of their London operations. One factor that has tilted the balance in the City's favour has been the strength of the dollar, which has greatly reduced the cost of a presence in the Square Mile for American banks. Rudiger Eisenhart-Rothe warned the authors that 'in the event of the dollar weakening, I wouldn't be surprised if you see quite a number of banks moving their operations out of London. In recent years, the profit and loss calculation has become much more finely balanced.' Two American banks, the Indiana National Bank and Wells Fargo, closed down their London offices in the first half of 1985. It is likely that many more will eventually be forced to leave. This is certainly a view taken by Kent Price, who said: 'I expect that people's pocketbooks will get the better of their pride, and I think that a lot of them will just disappear.'

. . . and another begins?

At the root of the challenge which the City faces in the 1980s is the transformation occurring in the form and pattern of international lending. Banks are no longer required to mediate to the same extent between holders of funds and borrowers. They are being bypassed more and more as investors increasingly purchase securities issued by borrowers. The phenomenon has been dubbed, in the ugly jargon of finance-speak, the 'securitization' of international lending. This key development for the future of the Square Mile as a world financial centre is underpinned by certain fundamental changes in the world economy.

The first of these changes is the shift which has taken place in the global balance of payments. In the 1970s the major disequilibrium lay between the developing countries and members of OPEC. Since neither group had well-developed securities markets, it was natural for them to turn to international banks. In the 1980s the major imbalance lies between the United States and Japan. America's cumulative current account deficits have been on such a scale that in 1985 the United States, the world's chief international creditor since World War I, joined the ranks of debtor nations. This development has happened as overseas savings flood in to finance the huge budget deficits which the American government has been running under the regime of Reaganomics. Since the United States has highly developed security markets, overseas investors are plugging the shortfall by purchasing securities. The main source of these funds is Japan, which suffers from exactly the reverse problem to America's. Japan is running current account surpluses on a scale comparable to those achieved by members of OPEC in the 1970s. These in turn reflect the chronic surplus of consumer savings, a consequence of a uniquely high propensity to save and the shortage of domestic investment outlets that has emerged as Japan has ceased to be a super-growth economy. As a result, Japanese investors have a rapacious appetite for overseas assets.

The long-term decline in world inflation has also made it much more attractive for both borrowers and lenders to dispense with international banks as intermediaries. At high rates of inflation, the risk in locking into a fixed-rate commitment is high for both borrower and lender. If inflation falls faster than anticipated, the issuer of a fixed-rate security may find that he is paying well in excess of market rates. If inflation rises more than expected, the lender will lose. Such risks are geared to the overall level of inflation; as inflation comes down, they are greatly reduced. The decline in world inflation has thus given another push in the direction of 'securitization'.

The City's strengths as an international securities centre . . .

As a result of these developments, the issue and trading of securities have been and are likely to continue to be the most buoyant sector of international finance in the 1980s. This has made it clear that the Square Mile's future as a world financial

43

centre depends upon its attractions for those dealing in international securities. However, there is considerable doubt
whether the City can ever attain the same pre-eminence in this
role that it achieved as a centre for international bank lending
in the late 1970s.

London's chief asset is that it remains the centre of the
Eurobond market. During the 1970s this market became
something of a poor relation to the burgeoning business of
international syndicated lending. By 1973 such loans were
providing five times as much credit as the issue of Eurobonds.
By contrast, the 1980s has seen the Eurobond market
flourishing as never before. Demand has soared as investors
have sought to take advantage of the highest real interest rates
of the century. Meanwhile, the reduction in inflation has
encouraged issuers to commit themselves to long-term borrowing through bonds. The total volume of new issues in all
currencies doubled between 1980 and 1982, and then doubled
again in 1984, to reach the staggering total of $80 billion.
Turnover in the market increased to $1550 billion, ten times
the level of 1979, and according to some estimates greater than
the combined turnover of the New York and London Stock
Exchanges.

One telling indication of the rude health of the market is the
inflated remuneration on offer in the Square Mile to key
individuals. Stanley Ross, an extrovert veteran of the market,
who likes to recount how he makes million-dollar deals using
the carphone in his Porsche as he speeds along the M4, told us
that at least ten individuals were tempted to move from one
firm to another in 1984 by payments in excess of a quarter of a
million dollars. For the top players in the first division of the
Eurobond market, such transfer fees have become the norm. In
today's booming market, each player who succeeds in putting
together a major new issue is feted as if he has scored a winning
goal; all that is lacking in the ensuing congratulation is the
physical contact of the football pitch. This cult of personality,
which has become one of the less attractive features of the
market, is assiduously fostered by its own trade press.

London's position as the centre of the Eurobond market
means that the major investment banks and security houses
which operate in this market have all established a presence in

London. This has concentrated in the City skills, expertise and ancillary services which no other financial centre can match. The City's dominant position was confirmed towards the end of 1984 by the decision of Deutsche Bank to move its Eurobond operation from Frankfurt to London.

A further advantage which London enjoys in the new international securities market stems – at first sight, paradoxically – from its position as the leading foreign banking centre. As traditional international bank lending has gone into decline, many commercial banks have sought to move into the field of securities, once the preserve of investment banks and security houses. The most notable of these commercial banks is Citicorp, which in 1984 announced that it was winding up its London-based syndicated loan department to replace it with a capital markets division which would operate in the field of Eurosecurities. Citicorp's strategy indicates the way that the barriers which used to separate one financial institution from another are being eroded.

Mirroring this development is the proliferation in the Euromarkets of financial instruments which bridge the former gulf between the Euroloan and Eurobond markets. This innovatory ferment, centred in London, is considered by many bankers to be one of the City's principal strengths. Chief among these hybrid instruments is the Floating Rate Note, a bond in which the issuer agrees to pay the investor a floating rather than a fixed rate of interest. Borrowing in this form was relatively unusual until the 1980s, during which it has greatly increased in importance: in 1984 it accounted for over a third of all issues of Eurobonds. The latest innovation is the Euronote Facility, which boasts any number of outlandish acronyms ranging from RUF (Revolving Underwriting Facility) to NIF (Note Issuance Facility). Banks arranging such a facility do not themselves make a loan to the borrower; instead they act as guarantors of a long-term credit facility under which funds are raised through periodic sales to investors of short-term securities issued by the borrower. One corporation which has raised money in this way is ICI, which secured $400 million in a deal arranged by Citicorp. The dangers for banks involved in such facilities is that their extended underwriting commitment might lead to unforeseen calls on banks' capital in the event of investors refusing to buy a borrower's Euronotes. Such worries have not hindered the spectacular growth of the new market. By early 1985 over $30 billion worth of such facilities had been arranged, most since the beginning of 1984. The Euromarkets had demonstrated once again their capacity to invent new, if potentially destabilizing, financial products.

The other main asset which London enjoys as an international securities centre is its position in the world's time zones, which enables it to deal with both the Far East and New York during a single working day, albeit extended. This is impossible for London's two main rivals, New York and Tokyo. Some financiers regard it as a major advantage, as the accent of international finance falls more and more heavily on trading. It is a major reason why a great deal of international fund management is done out of London, including a sizeable portion of America's huge ERISA (Employment and Retirement Income Security Act) pension funds.

... and its weaknesses

For all these strengths, the transition from bank lending to dealing in international securities was beginning to cause alarm bells to ring within the City by the early 1980s. The essential cause for concern was that the development highlighted the weakness of British financial firms in this new growth sector of international finance. Neither British merchant banks nor Stock Exchange firms were participating significantly in the boom in international securities dealing.

The failure of British merchant banks to win any real share of the Eurobond market was all the more galling in view of Warburg's pioneering role in establishing the market. In the 1960s and early 1970s Warburg had continued to play a significant part in the market, and other British merchant banks like Rothschild had also participated to some extent. However, by the early 1980s Warburg remained the only British bank with any real presence at all; and its share of the market was only 3 per cent. *Euromoney*'s league table was headed by Credit Suisse First Boston, the London-based investment bank, whose major shareholders are the Swiss bank

Crédit Suisse and the American investment bank First Boston. CSFB had 12 per cent of the market in 1984, more than the combined share of all British banks. All the other major players were foreign. Five of the top ten were American: Morgan Guaranty, Merrill Lynch, Morgan Stanley, Salomon Brothers and Goldman Sachs.

Eurobond business has also bypassed all but a handful of Stock Exchange firms, such as Strauss Turnbull. However, the weakness of British stockbrokers has been highlighted by their poor performance in the international market in equities which has begun to emerge on a large scale in the 1980s. In particular, they failed to seize the opportunity presented to them by the great outflow of portfolio funds from Britain which built up after 1979 as the counterpart to the build-up in North Sea oil revenues.

Between 1979 and 1984 Britain's stock of overseas assets rose, on Treasury estimates, from £12.5 billion to £70 billion, equivalent to a rise from 6.5 per cent to 22 per cent of gross domestic product. The increase was a sizeable jump, even if it fell well short of the level of 180 per cent of gross domestic product reached before World War I. The greater part of the increase simply reflected changes in the value of the investments or in the parity of sterling over the period. But some £18 billion of the total represented net new investment; and more than two-thirds of that outlay consisted of portfolio investment undertaken by insurance companies and pension funds. This outflow was expected to be a windfall for British stockbrokers; instead it simply demonstrated their weakness. While there are no official estimates of how much of these capital exports was handled by foreign and British brokers, it is generally reckoned that British firms missed out on all but a small fraction of the business. According to one calculation, 95 per cent of the investments made by the top twenty British pension funds were handled by foreign firms.

The evident weakness of both British merchant banks and Stock Exchange firms was undoubtedly an important reason why the Bank of England, and later the government, was so keen to promote change in the City. The dominant foreign houses in both the Eurobond and the international equity markets are investment banks, which combine the functions of underwriting new issues, research and market-making which had always been split in the London capital market among merchant banks, stockbrokers and stockjobbers. Charles McVeigh, head of the London office of Salomon Brothers, the leading American securities firm, explained to the authors why outside pressure was necessary:

> The City would not have changed of its own accord. It would have remained compartmentalized because this divided structure meant that it was possible to get a very high return on a limited base of capital. Without pressure from outside, the indigenous City wouldn't have participated in the boom in international securities dealing. The changes have come at the eleventh hour.

The poor performance of British merchant banks and brokers was worrying because of London's inherent weakness as an international securities centre. As a result of Britain's economic decline, the capital market of the UK is only a fraction of the size of America's and Japan's. The value of shares quoted in the United States accounts for more than half the total of the world's shares. Tokyo accounts for nearly a quarter. The Stock Exchange comes a poor third with less than a tenth. The growing challenge presented by Tokyo is particularly serious. In the words of Citicorp banker Kent Price, 'They've got such a massive capital market, people are literally tearing the doors down to get in.'

It is precisely because of this inherent weakness that London's position as the centre of the Eurobond market has been so important. However, this role is coming under increasing challenge in the 1980s. In July 1984 the American government abolished the withholding tax which had acted as a disincentive to foreign investors to purchase bonds issued in New York. One of the most vociferous lobbyists for this change was Morgan Stanley, the Wall Street investment bank, which argued that the measure would 'transfer the centre of the worldwide dollar bond market back to the US where it properly belongs and used to be'. Such appeals had a ready hearing with the American administration which was anxious to tap the Euromarkets in order to help finance its burgeoning budget deficit. Although the change has so far had little impact on the City's position, it forms part of the broader deregulatory challenge to London. The proposal to set up IBFs in Tokyo itself forms part of a broader package of liberalization in Japan. The finance of trade in yen is being facilitated by the creation of a market in yen-denominated bankers' acceptances. At the same time, the doors have been opened to the issue of Eurobonds in yen for both foreign and Japanese companies. Furthermore, withholding tax has been removed on Eurobonds issued by Japanese companies and purchased by foreign investors.

Moment of truth

Worrying though all these developments have been for British firms, what transformed concern into action was the gathering challenge mounted by foreign firms on the home ground of the Square Mile. By 1984, new technology was showing just how vulnerable the Stock Exchange had become to foreign competition. The trading of ICI shares in New York was not an isolated example. Soon after the privatization of British Telecom, it emerged that Morgan Stanley, which had acted as lead underwriter for the Wall Street end of this monumental £4 billion issue, was making an active market in the shares for British clients, as were other American houses. Although the government's sale of Telecom shares constituted the largest issue of equity the world had ever seen, British institutional investors were allocated far fewer shares than they had wanted. Morgan Stanley was quick to seize the opportunity to make good the shortage through its international dealing operations, as Americans sold out at a quick profit back to British institutions. US firms were also dealing actively in other leading British shares such as British Petroleum (known to the Americans as 'British Pete') and Glaxo. Most of this dealing took place in the form of American Depository Receipts, a kind of proxy security which carried the rights to a bundle of underlying British shares that remained lodged with leading American banks in London. Many big British institutional investors were happy to play the American game because by dealing in American Depository Receipts they could escape stamp duty, and they could deal in larger quantities than was possible on the London Stock Exchange itself.

By the early 1980s, then, it was apparent that the international financial order that had so favoured the City since the war had altered to the detriment of London. The future prospects of the Square Mile depended now to a far greater extent on the performance of British financial institutions. And there was an uncomfortable recognition that many of these were second division players, unused and ill-equipped to play in the top international financial league. The question that was being increasingly asked was why British firms had fallen behind since the war despite the City's continuing pre-eminence as a world financial centre. This in turn led to the question of what, if anything, could be done about it.

3

The Domestic Dilemma

If anyone can claim responsibility for coining the phrase 'The City Revolution' it is Jacob Rothschild of the well-known banking family. The occasion he chose to put his stamp on the proceedings was a conference organized by the *Financial Times* in autumn 1983. In a trenchant speech to a largely City audience he delivered what amounted to a damning critique of the Square Mile's *ancien régime*.

Members of the financial community are rarely outspoken in public; in the clublike atmosphere of the City, straight talking tends to be equated with rocking the boat. Yet Rothschild's speech attracted universal attention. Since his thinking – and dealing – proved influential in the development of the City Revolution, it is worth exploring briefly how he came to be regarded as a maverick in the financial community, yet one whom no one could afford to ignore.

One of Jacob Rothschild's more endearing characteristics is that he is not as easily categorized as the name might imply. The only son of the scientist and former head of the government's 'Think Tank', Lord Rothschild, he managed to combine a conventional education at Eton and Christchurch, Oxford, from which he emerged with a first class degree in history, with a less orthodox background in the army, where he had to enlist as a private for his national service before becoming an officer in the Life Guards. On joining the family bank he rapidly proved to be a throwback to the more opportunistic, nonconformist strain in the Rothschild family which had not been much in evidence at N. M. Rothschild & Sons since World War II.

Though he owned only a small shareholding and never became chairman, in the 1960s he was the driving force in establishing the bank in the Eurobond markets and turning it into one of the most active merchant banks in takeovers and mergers. To overcome the problem of running a family bank with only modest capital – the English Rothschilds are not rich by the standards of their cousins in Europe – he set up a quoted investment trust in tandem with the bank. In itself there was nothing original about the move; but other family banks had gone about the job in more genteel fashion. Rothschild Investment Trust was an acquisitive, buccaneering and highly personal outfit which made large profits in the bull market of the early 1970s on stock market deals that were often controversial. It also took stakes in private companies such as London's leading jobbing firm, Wedd Durlacher Mordaunt, and Sotheby's, the auctioneers, both of which it subsequently sold.

Rival bankers acknowledged that Jacob Rothschild was the cleverest male Rothschild of his generation. Some, however, questioned whether his frenetic dealing was enhancing the solidity of N. M. Rothschild's reputation. So, too, did members of his own family. In the mid-1970s, when the financial climate had become less favourable for buccaneers, Jacob's cousin Evelyn de Rothschild, a much richer and less flamboyant member of the family, took a more active role as chairman of the bank. From that time Jacob was obliged to devote more of his time to Rothschild Investment Trust, where his activities ultimately became the source of an acrimonious family row that burst into the press headlines of 1980. He was forced to resign from the board of his family's bank and took Rothschild Investment Trust away with him into the outside world. The directors of the bank then sought, with partial success, to impose legal restrictions on his ability to use the world's most famous banking name in any of his business ventures. Whatever their differences, the maverick and establishment sides of the Rothschild family were at one in their dynastic aspirations: both valued their own name immensely.

The case for revolution

Jacob Rothschild was thus something of an outsider in the City despite his family background. And his criticism of the London financial community in 1983 carried an echo of the criticism he had made of the family bank under Evelyn de Rothschild's more conventional style of management. Quoting with approval Disraeli's remark: 'I have ever been of the opinion that revolutions are not to be avoided' (and name-dropping rather grandly across the centuries by referring to Disraeli as 'a nineteenth-century English Prime Minister who was a friend of my family'), Jacob pointed out to his audience at the *Financial Times* conference that the rules by which London had so successfully played the financial game in the past were being rewritten by its international competitors. He went on to sketch what he called 'a nightmarishly complicated scenario' in which the financial world would come to be dominated by financial conglomerates which would provide a complete range of services to citizens, companies and governments around the globe. The menu, he argued, would cover insurance, credit, options, futures, stocks, bonds, cash management, money transfer, exchange and mortgages, together with financial, legal and travel advice. He went on:

> But the giant institutions of the future will not be satisfied with providing comprehensive financial services. Those with a banking capacity will seek to find an alternative to the 1970s' balance of payment lending so that their crucial role in financing international trade and projects can go on. To correct the failures of past lending policies, there may well be a reorientation to the tried techniques of linking credit to goods. The financial sector will try to re-establish its close relationship with the commodities and products which countries and corporations must produce and move around the world to sustain economic recovery. Trading companies may develop their financial arms and the banking system will become more deeply involved in trading, commodities, barter and counter-trade. As the process of deregulation continues, the two broad types of giant institutions, the worldwide financial service company, and the international commercial bank with a global trading competence, may

53

Market capitalization of British, American and Japanese financial institutions as at July 1983, as quoted by Jacob Rothschild

United Kingdom

	£ million
Clearing Banks	
Barclays Bank	1,603
National Westminster Bank	1,528
Lloyds Bank	1,045
Midland Bank	753
Royal Bank of Scotland	276
	5,205
Merchant Banks	
Kleinwort Benson	235
Hill Samuel & Co	184
Charterhouse Group	171
Mercury Securities	165
Hambros	122
Schroders	95
	972
Money Brokers	
Exco International	296
Mercantile House Holdings	272
	568
Discount Houses	
Gerrard & National	56
Union Discount	55
	111

United States

	£ million
Commercial Banks	
Citicorp	3,170
BankAmerica	2,285
Chase Manhattan	1,154
	6,609
Financial Services and Brokers	
American Express	4,800
Merrill Lynch	2,648
Phibro-Salomon	1,392
E. F. Hutton Group	779
Paine Webber	430
	10,049

Japan

	£ million
Banks	
Dai-Ichi Kangyo Bank	3,250
Sumitomo Bank	3,120
Fuji Bank	3,110
Mitsubishi Bank	3,110
	12,590
Securities Firms	
Nomura Securities	3,278
Nikko Securities	1,356
Daiwa Securities	1,219
Yamaichi Securities	1,046
	6,899
Trading Firms	
Mitsubishi Corporation	1,756
Mitsui	973
Sumitomo Corporation	737
C. Itoh	669
Marubeni Corporation	647
	4,782

Insurance Companies with Life Interest

Prudential Assurance	1,223
Guardian Royal Exchange Assurance	720
Legal & General Group	661
Eagle Star Insurance Co.	580
Hambro Life Assurance	470
	3,654

Insurance Brokers

Sedgwick Group	460
Willis Faber	220
C. E. Heath	94
Minet Holdings	90
Stewart Wrightson Holdings	44
	908

Insurance Companies with Life Interest

Cigna Corporation	2,143
Travelers Corporation	1,778
Transamerica Corporation	1,141
	5,062

Insurance Brokers

Marsh & McLennan*	1,092
Alexander & Alexander Services	307
Frank B. Hall	225
F. S. James	195
Corroon & Black	114
	1,933

* including other financial services

55

themselves converge to form the ultimate, all-powerful, many-headed financial conglomerate.

How well was the City of London equipped to cope with a brave, if unbeautiful, world peopled with these hydralike creations? The verdict was unflattering. Jacob Rothschild detected a tendency for the domestic City to be averse to risk, and conservative; its success stories did not emanate from the established firms. Above all, British financial houses lacked the capital that their foreign competitors brought to the securities trading and underwriting businesses. The point was vividly demonstrated by a comparison of the size of British financial institutions and service companies compared with their US and Japanese counterparts (see table). N. M. Rothschild was excluded from the exercise (as, coincidentally, is any reference to the bank in Jacob Rothschild's recent entries in *Who's Who*) because it was not a quoted company. But the omission merely served to underline the implicit criticism: British merchant banks had long since dropped out of the big league.

The comparison was equally damaging for leading members of the Stock Exchange. Rothschild argued that by maintaining a closed shop, minimum brokerage commissions on share transactions and unlimited liability for its members, the Stock Exchange had inhibited the accumulation of capital that was needed to ensure liquid markets in which it was possible to deal in large sums. He pointed out that the combined capital of London's jobbers, the market makers in the Stock Exchange system, amounted to less than £100 million, while the combined profits of the whole Exchange came to less than the $500 million earned by a single New York firm, Salomon Brothers, in a single year. Taken together with the 2 per cent stamp duty imposed on broking transactions, which raised the cost of dealing in London compared with other financial centres, these factors had set in motion 'a vicious circle of low levels of liquidity, leading to low levels of activity' – liquidity here being the ability to deal in large sums without causing large price changes. Equally important, the traditional distinction between brokers, acting as agents for outside investors, and jobbers, acting as principals on their own behalf as they dealt exclusively within the confines of the Stock Exchange, left

London out of step with dealing arrangements in the much larger markets in New York and Tokyo. Finally, Rothschild pointed to the City's lack of retail competence, its lack of skill in dealing directly with the consumer.

Some people were prepared to argue with Jacob Rothschild's futurology in the light of the troubles encountered by some of the biggest American financial conglomerates such as American Express, Sears Roebuck and Merrill Lynch. But few found it easy to toss aside the basic diagnosis on which he based the case for revolution. This critique of the City coincided with the private view of many other merchant bankers, as well as officials in the Bank of England. But how was it that London had slipped behind? Why were so many firms under-capitalized? And what was the reason for the survival of uncompetitive practices on the Stock Exchange?

The answers to these questions clearly hold the key to how far British banks, brokers and other financial institutions can hope to rise to the competitive challenge of the City Revolution. And some of them are obvious: Britain's relative economic decline was bound to have some influence on the fortunes of the financial sector. But there are other, equally fundamental, explanations which relate to the balance of forces at work between competition, restrictive practice and regulation in the banking and securities areas. Since they help explain why Britain was a slow starter in the international race for financial supremacy in the mid-1980s it is worth looking in some detail at how the British clearing banks, merchant banks and securities houses performed in the period before Cecil Parkinson made his compact with the Stock Exchange in 1983.

The clearing banks' place in the big league

At the heart of the financial system the clearing banks did, as was explained in Chapter 2, achieve a respectable share of Euromarket business. But it was not conspicuously greater than their size in the world's financial markets would naturally have justified, and in their wider international aspirations they fell a long way short of runaway success. The main area of the Big Four clearers' geographical expansion in the 1970s was the United States, where their investment was slow to yield returns even remotely comparable with those in their domestic business. In the case of the Midland Bank, the acquisition of a majority stake in Crocker National Corporation in California led to devastating losses; so when the City Revolution came along its response was somewhat muted.

The transatlantic traffic in the other direction was heavy, and it raised a serious challenge to the clearing banks in their own corporate back yard. In the period between the Radcliffe Report in the late 1950s and the Wilson Committee report (the two major post-war reports on the financial system) at the turn of the 1970s American banks took their share of bank lending to British manufacturing industry from virtually nothing to more than 30 per cent. While some loss of market share was only to be expected when the big US banks invaded Europe, this rate of attrition was rather too high. American bankers told the authors that they were greatly helped by the clearing banks' heavy reliance on all-purpose branches and their slowness to offer a more specialist service to corporate (and other) customers.

It is, however, the business carried out through the clearing banks' merchant bank offshoots that is perhaps of most importance in relation to the City Revolution. For securitization – the process by which banks are turning from direct lending to the issue of tradable debt securities and other commercial paper – calls for the skills traditionally deployed by merchant bankers in raising capital for their clients. Here the big British banks have a notable advantage in international capital markets vis-à-vis their American and Japanese competitors, who are largely prohibited by regulation from carrying on both commercial and investment banking simultaneously in their domestic markets. Yet the clearing banks appear, once again, not to have risen much beyond the position that their size in the world would naturally indicate. This is partly because the main investors in the Eurobond market are non-British. But that handicap has not inhibited the independent British merchant bank, S. G. Warburg, from establishing a much bigger market share than the clearing banks' offshoots, despite its smaller capital resources.

It may be that the clearers' unspectacular performance in this respect reflects a fundamental managerial problem: the endemic tension between two very different types of banking animal. A persistent refusal to grant more autonomy to the merchant banks – or, from the opposite perspective, a persistent tendency of merchant bankers to over-reach or to divide and rule in dealing with the clearing bank parent – has in recent years been a contributory factor in the departure of Sir Charles Ball, a brilliant exponent of the takeover defence, from Barclays Merchant Bank; of John Padovan, who built up National Westminster's County Bank subsidiary, to Hambros; and of the ambitious Swede, Staffan Gadd, from Midland's accepting house subsidiary Samuel Montagu. In the case of Montagu, problems of integration were exacerbated in the 1970s by the Bank of England's insistence that the accepting houses should enjoy a high degree of autonomy, and in the 1980s by joint ownership with America's Aetna Life group. If Lloyds Bank does not feature in the list, it is only because it chose not to devote time, effort and money to building up an autonomous merchant banking operation until 1985. As will be shown in Chapter 6, the ability to integrate the operations of very different firms will be of supreme importance in the new types of corporate finance that are opening up as a result of the City Revolution. So the clearers' past experience is not an altogether happy pointer.

The retail gap in the clearers' defences

Of all the big players in the revolution the clearing banks are the best equipped to exploit the new opportunities in retail finance. Yet here the Big Four have suffered a significant loss of market share on the deposit side of their balance sheet to a major competitor group outside the City, the building societies. In round numbers the banks saw personal deposits increase from £43 million to just under £59 million in the five years to the end of 1984, while the building societies' soared from under £50 million to more than £90 million over the same period. These mutually owned organizations, whose lending was restricted to housing finance, offered more convenient opening hours, better marketing and efficient administration of their admittedly simple range of deposit services.

On the other side of the balance sheet the clearers' critics claim that they have been slow to exploit the potential of their branches for cross-selling a wide range of financial products – which is the key to success in a revolution where the regulatory barriers between different types of financial institutions are breaking down. According to Mark Weinberg, the South African-born entrepreneur who built up two successive insurance groups on the back of clever salesmanship, the Big Four have within their groups virtually every financial service known to man. They have loyal customers, many of whom have unfulfilled financial needs. Yet each of the companies responsible for handling different products within the clearing bank groups is separately administered, as if it were an independent company. Staff in bank branches are not encouraged to sell insurance and investment products as actively as they might, argues Weinberg, even though the banks now have substantial subsidiaries in insurance broking, life assurance and unit trusts; and the cost of the banks' huge investment in branches is not spread efficiently across a wide enough range of actively marketed products. A fundamental problem in cross-selling concerns the inability of the banks' computers to give a full picture of the relationship with the customer. The records do not show, for example, whether a current account holder has made use of the bank's insurance or investment services.

The British clearing banks are now addressing all these problems and some – most notably Barclays – confronted them earlier than others. But the fact remains that much of the innovation in the British commercial banking system seems to be going on outside the Big Four (or the Big Three and a Half, as the wags have dubbed them after Midland's problems in California). It was the Nottingham Building Society and the Bank of Scotland that pioneered home banking via the television set and the telephone in Britain – whereas in the United States it was the establishment banks such as Chemical Bank and Bank of America that led the market. The British bank that most successfully cross-sells financial services, including own-brand insurance and unit trusts, in its branches is, rather surprisingly, that Johnny-come-lately, the Trustee Savings Bank. Mark Weinberg's Hambro Life, the highly successful direct selling insurance and financial group, was a prime mover in Britain in developing all-in-one packages of banking, insurance and investment products catering for a comprehensive range of private individuals' financial requirements. With its scheme for on-line payments at filling stations in Scotland the Midland's Clydesdale Bank subsidiary can admittedly claim to be in the vanguard in electronic funds transfer; but in corporate cash management the British clearers are not as advanced as the Americans. Nor have they been consistently at the forefront of innovation in the Euromarkets.

Regulation and the shape of British banking

Why the mixed record? Once again history holds a number of clues. In the 1950s and 1960s the clearing banks used to see their main function as tapping the public's savings cheaply via their countrywide branches and channelling that money into industry and commerce. In so far as there was glamour in the clearing banks' business it was on the corporate side; servicing the personal customer came second. They also had to run a public utility, the payments system, the burden of whose heavy expense was not shared by their main competitors, the building societies. But if there is a single key to the performance of the British clearing banks, it is their position at the centre of the monetary system. It has condemned them to an existence in which they are perpetually torn between the conflicting obligations of national (and sometimes party political) interest on the one hand, and private profit for their shareholders on the other.

Until 1985 the tax system discriminated heavily in favour of the building societies in allowing them to deduct at source a composite rate of tax on the interest they paid out. Since this was based on the average tax rate of their depositors, who included many pensioners and others who were not subject to income tax at all, the building societies were deducting less than the standard rate of income tax from their depositors' interest. So their rates were more attractive than those of the banks. The societies were also outside the restrictive system of monetary control operated by the Bank of England, being responsible to the Chief Registrar of Friendly Societies. And on occasion the clearing banks were victims of more blatant attempts by politicians to win votes from would-be home owners. In a cynical move in the mid-1970s the Heath government imposed a crude ceiling on clearing bank interest rates on small deposits of up to £10,000, thereby diverting small investors' funds to the building societies, which could pay higher rates.

The banks have also been subjected to heavy regulation – and granted the benefit of exemption from competitive pressure – in the interests of financial stability. For much of the postwar period officials at the Bank of England and the Treasury believed that some limitation on competition was necessary to underpin the financial structure and to facilitate monetary control; hence the restrictions, for example, on the ability in the 1970s of the National Girobank, the Trustee Savings Bank and the building societies to compete over a wider range of products with the clearing banks. There was more to this view than idle bureaucratic prejudice, for abrupt moves towards liberalization in the banking system have, in the past, led to disaster; and since one such move, initiated under the Heath administration in the early 1970s, was really a predecessor of the present City Revolution it is well worth looking at in some detail. The episode affords valuable insights into the effects of deregulation in the financial sector and the risks inherent in encouraging the creation of financial conglomerates.

An earlier revolution

This previous revolution was prompted by the belief that the regulatory climate in banking had become so restrictive that it was stifling efficiency and innovation and creating economic distortions in the system. It began with the abolition of the clearing banks' interest rate cartel and the introduction by the Bank of England of a new policy called Competition and Credit Control. At around the same time the clearing banks themselves decided voluntarily to disclose their true profits, even though they enjoyed the legal right to conceal profitability and to maintain hidden reserves. These moves coincided with a steady relaxation of the regulatory boundaries between different financial intermediaries. In the 1960s and early 1970s the clearing banks moved first into instalment credit, leasing and factoring, then into merchant banking.

This experiment in deregulation was to have a profound influence on the behaviour of both clearing banks and merchant banks in a cautionary direction. For instead of leading to dramatic innovation in the banking establishment, it led to explosive credit growth and to an upsurge of activity in new, under-regulated money markets. 'Fringe' banks, which were not subject to adequate regulation from either the Department of Trade or the Bank of England, competed ferociously to lend large sums to property entrepreneurs; and via the impersonal mechanism of the money markets the clearing banks scrambled to lend to the fast-growing 'fringe' property banks.

Financial entrepreneurs also started to experiment with conglomeration, bringing together very different types of financial activity in a single group in the hope of achieving what they called 'synergy'; that is, economies of scale and opportunity that came to more than the sum of the parts. The fringe financier Jim Slater, who was lionized by some sections of the press as the chief revolutionary of his day, declared that banking, insurance and property offered the perfect business combination to beat the wave of inflation that was engulfing the British economy and undermining the value of orthodox investment and savings media. Slater was widely imitated.

The bubble burst at the end of 1973 when London and County Securities, an outfit whose board included the then Liberal leader Jeremy Thorpe, suffered an outflow of deposits. The loss of confidence was contagious: it swept through the secondary banking sector and on to the big finance houses such as Mercantile Credit and United Dominions Trust. In a rescue bid that was carefully orchestrated by the Bank of England, the clearing banks were forced to set up a 'lifeboat' to prevent the collapse of the whole banking system. The government itself had to rescue the semi-official Crown Agents, which had plunged into speculative property dealing.

The financial crisis of the mid-1970s thus holds a dire warning for participants in the City Revolution of the 1980s, for it clearly demonstrated the problems inherent in trying to reintroduce competition into the financial sector while maintaining prudential control over a system that was undergoing rapid structural change. New institutions doing new types of business were found to have a way of falling through the regulatory net. Old institutions doing new types of business, such as the Crown Agents, were unable to make the transition from acting in an agency capacity to dealing in markets on their own account – which is precisely what many stockbroking firms were to start doing in the mid-1980s. And the moves towards financial hybrids, in which banks, insurers and investment companies joined forces, turned out to carry severe risks of cross-infection.

Jim Slater, for example, found that property and banking made dismal bedfellows in foul weather because nervous depositors pulled their cash out faster than the property market could absorb sales of speculative property. The Bank of England had to mastermind an expensive rescue for Slater's bank, and, for fear that the exposure of freewheeling practices in this freebooting period would further erode the City's freedom to regulate its own affairs, argued fiercely and successfully in Whitehall against a Department of Trade investigation. Another fringe financier, Oliver Jessel, discovered that his whole industrial and financial empire was unable to withstand demands for fresh capital from its troubled insurance subsidiary, London Indemnity. When the empire crashed, the insurance company itself turned out to hold stock in the parent, which underlined the fragility of the structure and the dangers of cross-infection.

From the point of view of the long-term health of the financial sector the policy of competition and credit produced the worst of both worlds. It generated instability on a scale that ultimately threatened the whole system; and the survivors, including the clearing banks, who had to pick up much of the bill, were after that experience scarcely in the mood for imaginative risk-taking, even though the clearers' own viability was, in effect, underwritten by the Bank of England. Monetary control became more restrictive; and industry was saddled with sky-high interest rates and a soaring cost of long-term capital as the stock market plunged.

Comfortable ownership

Against this background of a return to tighter monetary control in the second half of the 1970s, what pressure did ownership bring to bear on clearing bank management as a spur to innovation and efficiency? In practice, very little. Following the Radcliffe Report on the monetary system, the number of London clearing banks shrank from eleven to just six: Barclays, National Westminster, Midland, Lloyds, Coutts (a National Westminster subsidiary) and Williams & Glyn's, which was owned by the Royal Bank of Scotland. This heavy concentration of financial power was cocooned from outside takeover threat by a protective central bank. The Bank of England was happy to operate an open door policy for foreigners who wished to do business in the Euro-markets; but it was reluctant in the extreme to tolerate foreign takeovers of British clearing banks. Indeed, when the Hongkong and Shanghai Banking Corporation broke all the rules by making a contested bid for the Royal Bank of Scotland Group in 1981, so disrupting a cosily arranged marriage with the Standard Chartered group to which the Bank of England had given its fiat, officials at the Bank could not conceal their intense annoyance. A fierce argument in Whitehall and the City only reached stalemate when the Monopolies Commission ruled against a bid by either party.

Nor could the clearing banks' institutional shareholders be accused of extracting a high degree of accountability, despite the growing readiness of pension funds and insurance companies to intervene in corporate management in the 1970s. This apparent immunity from institutional prodding led to some perverse happenings in the financial sector. When Mercantile House, one of the most innovative of the new money broking groups in the Square Mile, sought to buy into a New York brokerage firm, Oppenheimer & Co., a group of pension funds led by Hugh Jenkins, the powerful manager at that time of the National Coal Board fund's investments, questioned the move. Mercantile's founder and chairman, John Barkshire, persisted with his deal in the face of their opposition. It proved to be one of the few British moves into the US financial sector that came to be regarded in the City as both timely and inexpensive.

In contrast Midland Bank's appallingly costly foray in the early 1980s into Crocker National Bank, which badly scarred its balance sheet when Crocker's loans later turned sour and the rise in the dollar magnified the resulting losses, prompted no ballyhoo from the pension funds at all, any more than earlier questionable strategic moves by the Midland had done; and the Bank of England, without whose approval such moves cannot generally be made, did not stand in the way. All this was despite the fact that a key condition of the deal allowed local management of this huge subsidiary-to-be of the Midland to continue to enjoy autonomy. At the meeting called to approve the takeover, the shareholders appeared more concerned about Crocker's head office being on top of California's San Andreas fault than with issues of control. The press, it has to be said, was no more far-sighted.

Some experts argue that the Big Four are not notably worse than the general run of commercial banks around the world, and much better than some. They certainly suffer from being an easy and heavily regulated target. Their peculiar misfortune is that, come inflation or disinflation, they make too much profit for their own good. Under Mrs Thatcher they were subjected first to a windfall tax on their politically unpopular profits, then to corporation tax changes that plugged the tax avoidance loophole that they had enjoyed by virtue of running leasing subsidiaries. It was a poor return, one might think, for sparing the government political embarrassment by discreetly rescuing many labour-intensive firms in the heartland of British manufacturing in the early 1980s in another lifeboat operation orchestrated by the Bank of England. It was also a considerable disadvantage when a strong capital base held the key to a major role in international corporate finance in the new deregulated markets of the 1980s.

Merchant banking in a competitive world

The starting point of the merchant banks in the City Revolution ought, in many respects, to have been more advantageous than that of the clearing banks. They were not at the centre of the monetary system, and so had less opportunity to raise the hackles of politicians; and their lives were more competitive for the simple reason that there were more of them. They had little in the way of a profitable retail cushion because they were instinctively (though not exclusively) wholesale animals. The nature and attraction of wholesale business is that there is an obvious economy of effort in taking tiny percentages on multi-million pound deals with giant companies and institutions that want the best service at almost any price, as against a rather larger percentage on hundreds and thousands of small, labour-intensive, retail deals with cost-conscious private individuals. A merchant bank frequently has to devote as much work to raising £10 million for a client as it does to raise £100 million. But since the bank's fees are related to the size of the deal, big capital issues for corporate clients are potentially very profitable indeed.

There is, however, genuine competition for those profits. The accepting houses (so-called because they 'accept' or guarantee commercial bills) still dominate a business in which acceptances play only a marginal part. But the clearing banks' merchant bank subsidiaries are, after a difficult start, beginning to disprove the adage that the art of merchant banking is so alien to the commercial banker that it defies any useful participation in the game. The merchant banks do not enjoy a monopoly. Stockbrokers, and latterly even some of the big accountancy firms, have tried to muscle in on their corporate finance business. As yet, however, they have made little impression except at the small company end of the spectrum where larger merchant banks are happy to let them do less profitable work.

Corporate wizardry, pension profits

Perhaps the merchant banks' biggest problem in confronting the City Revolution is that the focus of their activities in the postwar period has been increasingly domestic and relatively low-risk. In fact it was in the 1950s that they discovered the activity that was to provide them both with profitable growth and a glamorous image. They became the new wizards of corporate manipulation, advising clients on how to gobble up or fend off other companies in a world where takeovers became an ever-present threat to the management of quoted companies. Coming out on the winning side became an important way of marketing the merchant banks' wider range of services. So while most of them continued to make profits from low-risk lending and the provision of trade finance to corporate and other clients, they complemented this activity by moving further into fee-earning advisory business that did not need the support of a big capital base.

As providers of advice to corporate clients the merchant banks were also well placed to exploit a second profitable game: the trend towards saving via company pension schemes. In the postwar period tax reliefs on saving via life assurance and pensions gave a powerful incentive for people to abandon direct investment in the stock market. At the same time employees were dragooned into company pension schemes, more often than not as a condition of employment. This combination of carrot and stick dramatically – and unintentionally – changed the pattern of ownership in Britain.

Recognizing that they were unlikely to match the government-subsidized returns on life assurance policies and pensions through their own efforts on the stock market, each year between 1945 and 1980 private individuals sold to investment institutions an average 1–1½ per cent of the share capital of British quoted companies. Having owned more than 80 per cent of the ordinary share capital of British companies listed on the Stock Exchange at the start of World War II, four decades later the private investor owned less than 30 per cent. The reverse side of this coin was that management of long-term savings became heavily centralized in the City. Stockbrokers Phillips & Drew estimate that between 1963 and 1984 the market value of all pension fund assets rose from £4.5 billion to £126.5 billion.

While some of this money was managed in-house or by insurance companies, stockbrokers and other independent investment groups, merchant banks controlled the biggest share of the investment advisory business, which grew dramatically in the early 1970s when the Heath government introduced a pay policy that provided employers and unions with an inducement to agree to improve occupational pension benefits in lieu of direct pay increases. In addition to fund management most of the accepting houses occupied other profitable niches in the City's traditional markets, ranging from gold dealing to shipping finance.

International oversight

The merchant banks' domestic existence was, then, far from uncomfortable. But what of their international activities? In the context of the City Revolution the failure of most merchant banks in the 1960s and early 1970s to take the upstart Eurobond market very seriously was a crucial oversight. And the example set later on by the fast-growing futures and options markets in the United States failed to fire the imagination of the people who ran established merchant banks. It took an outsider, John Barkshire of Mercantile House, to dream up, promote and propel through a cautious Bank of England the idea of the London International Financial Future Exchange (LIFFE).

In the early 1980s the people with an appetite for risk in investment banking tended not to be members of the accepting houses committee. Leaving aside the acquisition by Kleinwort Benson of a small primary bond dealer in the United States, the two biggest US broking acquisitions were undertaken by Jacob Rothschild, whose company acquired a 50 per cent stake in L. F. Rothschild, Unterberg, Towbin (where the Rothschild in question was no relation), and by John Barkshire with his purchase of Oppenheimer. The prize for the outstandingly successful venture into the United States goes to Exco, run by John Gunn, which was quick to perceive that the scope for financial innovation lay as much in the related technological services as in banking and securities dealing itself. Exco's investment in Telerate, a hugely successful computer-based market information system used by the US financial community, generated profits on a scale that was the envy of the British financial community (and no doubt a cause of chagrin to the Guinness Peat group, parent of one of the smaller accepting houses, Guinness Mahon, which sold a large stake in Telerate before the shares climbed to dizzy heights). With its computer-based systems Reuters, the famous press agency, has, incidentally, performed in the rest of the world a feat comparable to Telerate.

By the mid-1980s the accepting houses had their regrets. In their basic banking business they were up against tough competition from both commercial banks and investment banks. Long-standing relationships with company clients ceased to guarantee preferential treatment from the corporate treasurer, who was influenced increasingly by US-style treasury management methods. In mergers and acquisitions life had become more competitive: two banks, S. G. Warburg and Morgan Grenfell, had achieved a dominant position at the others' expense. In fund management, pension fund trustees were becoming more demanding and prone to change investment advisers more often.

That is not to say that merchant banking was unprofitable. At that stage most of the threats were still in the future, and the accepting houses could congratulate themselves that the American banks had failed to make serious inroads into the domestic corporate finance market. And for good measure the Tory government's privatization programme helped keep the financial community in fees. On the British Telecom issue alone these amounted to more than £200 million for the British and foreign banks, brokers and other commission takers who helped the government find a home for the shares; though there is a rider in that the merchant bank handling the issue, Kleinwort Benson, claims to have made little direct profit on the deal. This is less implausible than it sounds, since merchant banks make more money out of rights issues by companies that are already quoted on the stock market than they do on new issues. But the publicity and promotion can hardly have been other than invaluable for Kleinwort's wider business.

Capital raising in international markets

No merchant bank could afford to plan for survival in the mid-1980s, however, on the basis of carrying on much as before. In the context of the City Revolution the fundamental problem for the accepting houses was that, despite having prided themselves on their flexibility and international outlook, they were late in seeing that the big growth area of merchant banking in the 1980s would relate to the international securities markets and that their basic business of raising money for corporate, institutional and government clients could not be carried out in the face of serious international competition unless it was combined with a readiness to take positions in and distribute the clients' stocks, shares or bonds.

Lack of regulation meant that the Euromarkets had done away with formality in raising capital for multinational companies and governments, while the abolition of exchange controls in Britain opened up new international capital-raising opportunities for the merchant banks' British clients. Those clients were becoming much more sophisticated. In the highly volatile markets of the late 1970s and early 1980s, borrower power prevailed: the borrowers wanted a rapid, cheap money-raising service from the bankers. Increasingly they got it from the larger American investment and commercial banks, which were prepared to bid for the multinational companies' bonds *en bloc*, taking the bonds onto their own books in the hope of reselling rapidly at a profit to investment institutions. This Euromarket approach to capital raising was adopted in US markets in 1982. But, at least in the UK domestic market, British merchant banks continued to lay off their risks by bringing investment institutions into the underwriting of their clients' issues at an early stage. They were not able to sell or deal in stocks and shares because they were not able to become members of the Stock Exchange. And in many cases they felt more comfortable acting as agent than as principal, since they lacked the capital to take hundreds of millions of dollars' worth of bonds onto their books even if they wanted to.

As Win Bischoff, group chief executive of Schroder's, pointed out to the authors, back in 1973 there was no great difference between the capital resources of leading merchant banks in the City and some of the top names on Wall Street. Yet by 1983 the British had been outdistanced because they had failed to see how quickly the market would become global and that the American way of designing capital issues, making the capital available to the borrower and distributing the resulting bonds or securities to investors, would become the international norm.

So what should the merchant banks have done to prepare

themselves for a world in which trading in commercial paper and securities was to become a more important part of the merchant banking business? Bischoff points out that the Euro-markets are driven by the dollar. It follows that merchant banks need to have a strong position in the United States, as well as Europe, in order to exploit the opportunities for trading and arbitrage between the US and European markets. Even in the early 1970s it is doubtful whether any of the British merchant banks had the muscle to take over one of the top US investment houses. So the perfect strategy, says Bischoff, would have been to forge links with the United States through cross-shareholdings, much as the big Zurich-based bank Crédit Suisse did, first with White Weld, then with First Boston.

The opportunities were undoubtedly there. In the years that followed the abolition of fixed commissions on the New York Stock Exchange in 1975 there was a huge reshuffle in the investment community. Some of Wall Street's oldest invest-ment houses, such as White Weld, Dillon, Read, Shearson and Lehman Brothers were open to offers, and some British bankers did, in fact, read the future. While Sir Siegmund Warburg was still alive S. G. Warburg made a bid for inter-national power by linking up with the powerful French com-mercial and investment bank, Paribas. In 1973 the British bank's parent, Mercury Securities, exchanged shareholdings with the French, a deal which immediately provided Warburg with a network of European contacts and the combined strength to buy into an American investment house, A. G. Becker. Even earlier, at a time when most British banks' view of Japan was still coloured by World War II, Warburg handled bond issues for Japanese companies in the international mar-kets. It was thus able to establish earlier than most a branch office in Tokyo, with the right to transact securities business, a status that is taking years of negotiation for other banks to establish. Warburg was equally quick to see the potential of a new international advisory market. In the wake of the first oil crisis, Third World countries and central banks urgently needed help in managing their reserves and servicing their debts. The bank had built up a strong position by the end of the 1970s.

In none of these cases, however, was the going easy. Advising governments makes huge demands on top management's time and talent. It is also risky in the sense that the bank is a natural scapegoat when politicians are fighting for survival in financially stretched circumstances. In the United States A. G. Becker, which was one of the top three banks in the new market in commercial paper, failed to break into the wider corporate finance area. Warburg's competitors argue that joint ownership did not help in sorting out management problems at Becker. So in 1983 Warburg sold its interest in the American firm to Paribas, and it unscrambled its cross-shareholding with the French group following the nationalization of Paribas by the Mitterrand government in France. Despite the acuteness of its strategic vision Warburg was left to rebuild its US operation at just the moment when a well-established business would have given it a huge competitive edge as a global investment bank.

A surfeit of good housekeeping

Why did other merchant banks let slip opportunities that were later to prove important for the City's international competitiveness? Perhaps the domestic markets were simply too profitable to have made it necessary for them to look for big opportunities on the international stage. But the economic climate in Britain in the mid-1970s almost certainly had a great deal to do with it. Most merchant bankers felt that in the banking crisis of 1974 they had stared into the abyss. Jewish banks faced problems in handling the business of the world's new *rentiers*, the Arab oil producers. Attention turned to good housekeeping rather than bold risk taking; and any banker who looked like a whizz-kid was more likely to be seen as a liability than as an asset. Those who did have anything of the whizz-kid in their make-up had as like as not done deals in the early 1970s that rebounded on them. Jacob Rothschild was a case in point: his Rothschild Investment Trust found the going much tougher in the stock market crash of the middle of the decade, when the scope for entrepreneurial dealing was reduced.

As with the clearing banks, the structure of ownership

among the merchant banks was highly relevant to their managerial performance, though in a rather different way. Unlike their clients, those who belonged to the top merchant bankers' club, the accepting houses committee, did not have to exercise the corporate martial arts on their own behalf. The Bank of England carefully vetted would-be acquirers or applicants for admission to accepting house status. It also guaranteed survival for all who stuck to the rules: in the curiously literal *argot* of Threadneedle Street (which usually incorporates an implicit moral imperative) accepting houses were 'undoubted'. And unlike the clearing banks, most leading merchant banks even today draw a discreet veil over their true profitability by hanging tenaciously onto their statutory right to maintain hidden reserves.

The accepting houses, then, were highly protected. But it should not necessarily be assumed that they are all down and out, or that all of them have been asleep. Soon after the crisis of 1974 Morgan Grenfell substantially increased the size of its balance sheet, played to its strength in trade and project finance, and built up a country advisory business. Several others did perceive the importance of acquiring skills in broking and distributing stocks and shares; they used Far Eastern markets as a learning ground. N. M. Rothschild already had a profitable outpost on Wall Street, which it secured with the French Rothschilds. And a handful recognized early that fund management could be handled on an international scale. Baring's, though a shadow of its nineteenth-century self, still holds a much envied contract, alongside Merrill Lynch, to advise the Saudi Arabian Monetary Authority on the management of its short-term funds; it is one of a clutch of British merchant banks to have established itself in broking and investment management in Japan. The consensus in the City is that London has a competitive edge in analysing and judging the relative attractions of international currencies and stocks that could give it a lead of three to five years over the international opposition. But it is not easy, especially in Japan, to make a mark in non-sterling investment.

A shift in the balance of power within merchant bank management is also taking place, with the internationalists, whose experience is rooted in markets, catching up with or replacing domestic acquisition and merger experts at the top. It is no coincidence that Schroder's Bischoff, for example, happens to be a West German who was educated in Johannes-burg, New York and London; he worked on Wall Street before joining the bank, and made his name building up Schroder's Hong Kong operation. But it will still take a huge managerial effort to wrench the British merchant banks away from the comfortable, risk-averse world that they used to inhabit, into the aggressive, American-style corporate finance that charac-terizes the international merchant banking business in the second half of the 1980s. They will need more capital, as well as fast footwork, if they are to offer their corporate clients the kind of service in raising money that competitors like Salomon Brothers or Goldman Sachs are now offering. That is some-thing which will not make life easy for family-controlled or -dominated banks such as Baring Brothers, N. M. Rothschild, Schroders and Hambros, for whom raising new capital means a potential loss of control.

It is a fair bet that some of the less powerful members of the accepting houses committee will see a change of ownership before the decade is out. Perhaps membership of the commit-tee will become much less highly prized. There is, after all, something rather anachronistic in the importance attached to membership of this once exclusive – but now very disparate – club when the big players are outside it. In today's inter-national capital markets the real competition is American and Japanese. There is a risk that the accepting houses will (or indeed have) become as quaint and irrelevant as their name suggests.

The freedoms of the Stock Exchange

The City Revolution is, in the final analysis, about the reform of one of the central institutions of the Square Mile: the Stock Exchange. And the case for reform, as outlined by Jacob Rothschild and others, rested on the assertion that parochial-ism had prevented the Exchange's members from coming to terms with the new international securities business of the 1980s. The trouble was partly that the Exchange's members could all too easily afford to be insular, at least in the short term, because they enjoyed privileges and freedoms unparalleled elsewhere in the Square Mile, with the single exception of Lloyd's.

At the start of the decade the Stock Exchange was the only exchange of any significance in Britain, with floors in a number of provincial cities as well as London and, oddly enough, Dublin. Its members enjoyed the privilege of being able to deal in securities without taking out a licence from the Department of Trade. Among the world's larger stock exchanges it was unique in having been totally free from any form of governmental or statutory control except in the purely theoretical sense that the Department of Trade could revoke a statutory order whereby it was the only recognized stock exchange. Since revocation was such an extreme option, it was not really an option for the Department of Trade at all.

Within this framework there had existed since 1912 a key constraint on free competition. For acting as agent for their clients all brokers had, from that time, enjoyed the benefit of a scale of minimum commissions on most transactions. For their part the jobbers took a turn, or margin, on dealing in the shares – that is, they reckoned to sell for slightly more than the price at which they bought. In the postwar period those fixed commissions served the brokerage community well in the same benign climate that had favoured the merchant banks – though whether they had served the interests of investors well was another matter. The question was taken up, in the second half of the 1970s, by the Office of Fair Trading, which was under a legal obligation to look into such restrictive practices.

Takeovers, with attendant flurries of share dealing, 'dawn raids' and the rest also served brokers well because they generated turnover in the market and that was good for business. The Stock Exchange's members lived handsomely off the huge transfer of share ownership from individuals to institutions as the size of the transactions increased and the number of clients who had to be serviced decreased. The larger brokers, meantime, expanded into a range of other services of which institutional fund management was probably the biggest. While they made no direct charge for this service, they enjoyed commission on all the transactions, so putting themselves into a curious position where they were both user and provider of their own broking service. The resulting potential conflict of interest gave an incentive to 'churn' clients' portfolios – that is, to deal actively in the shares to generate a higher commission income. Fund management was a lucrative business to be in, though the merchant banks sometimes resented the brokers' intrusion into what they regarded as their territory and penalized the firms in question by passing less of their own stock market dealings through them.

Throughout the postwar period the profits derived from fixed broking commissions were protected by restrictions on the Exchange's membership. Individual membership with unlimited liability was the norm for Stock Exchange firms; this gave members considerable tax benefits and freedom from disclosure, but it did indeed make it hard for them to accumulate capital, as Jacob Rothschild suggested, since partnerships distributed their profits each year. Stockjobbers enjoyed an additional protection from competition outside the Exchange through a statutory exemption from full stamp duty which only applied to jobbers who were Stock Exchange members. They were also protected by the Bank of England. The nearest thing to competition experienced by the Exchange in the 1970s was a challenge from a computer-based share trading system called Ariel (Automated Real Time Investment Ltd), which was set up by the accepting houses in the belief that the Stock Exchange's scale of minimum commissions was far too high. But while Ariel succeeded in prompting a reduction in the Stock Exchange's commissions, it failed to win more than 1 per cent of the available business. The explanation, according to some of Ariel's merchant bank shareholders, was that the Bank of England excluded Ariel from dealing in gilt-edged securities, the area in which fixed commissions most irritated the accepting houses. The Bank has always kept a firm hand on the gilt-edged market because that market plays a vital part in the implementation of the government's monetary policy; and it has chosen to reinforce the dominance of the Stock Exchange in order to preserve maximum liquidity in a single marketplace. Since the jobbers' gilt-edged business was generally reckoned to subsidize their equity trading, the constraint on Ariel appeared a tough one. However, some fund managers question the validity of this excuse: they doubt whether Ariel would have attracted much gilt-edged business even if the Bank had given it a fair wind and argue that brokers in the gilt-edged market were offering a whole range of services that a computerized system could not hope to match.

Friendly customers

In equities, Ariel's failure to win a bigger share of the business undoubtedly owed something to the cumbersome nature of the system itself. But it is worth noting, too, that the merchant banks' own incentive to reduce the level of fixed commissions in equities was far less than in gilts. For, in addition to charging fees based on the value of the funds under management, the merchant banks derived indirect income whose level was determined both by the Stock Exchange's monopolistic pricing practices and their own level of share dealing. This was because Stock Exchange commissions varied according to the size of the transaction. It was common for banks to deal in large amounts at low commission on the Exchange, and then charge their clients larger commissions as they parcelled out smaller chunks of the transaction between different clients. This turn, sometimes called the retail–wholesale split, gave the merchant banks a powerful incentive to deal actively, or to 'churn' portfolios. And sure enough, one of the more telling findings of the Wilson Committee was that the average period for which insurance companies and pension funds held their shares had fallen from around twenty-four years in 1963–67 to eight years for insurance companies and six years for pension funds in 1973–77. The shortening of time horizons brought about by inflation no doubt influenced the trend, but merchant bankers and stockbrokers can usually be persuaded to make a jocular admission that their competitors churned pension fund portfolios vigorously until investment performance surveys became commonplace in the second half of the 1970s. This imposed some check on the practice because high costs, including commission, incurred through wildly excessive dealing acted as a brake on good investment performance.

It should also be said in passing that the clearing banks' arrangements to share commission with stockbrokers on transactions carried out through branches gave them little incentive to press the Stock Exchange for reduced commissions in equity dealing. All of this helps explain why it was left to the Office of Fair Trading to bring pressure to bear on the fixed commission system. The main users of the Exchange had other interests to weigh against the case for deregulation. To return to Ariel, the merchant banks would probably have been disturbed if this computerized competitor of the Stock Exchange had succeeded in bringing about more draconian cuts in the Exchange's dealing costs. From the point of view of their own profitability, the ideal combination of circumstances for the merchant banks was the ability to deal cheaply outside the exchange while charging clients expensively at the Stock Exchange's fixed rates.

In this confined world of the domestic securities markets the growing power of the investment institutions ensured that the brokers did have to compete actively with each other. But because of the scale of minimum commissions the pressure was reflected increasingly in non-price competition such as the offer of extras and ancillary services, which could cover anything from large lunches and days at the races to brokers' research on government economic policy or the prospects for pump and valve manufacturers. In terms of the City's competitiveness as an international financial centre the research was an important plus.

Meritocracy comes to market

Such analytical work by stockbrokers emerged partly in response to a marked change of climate in the postwar City. Many of the people who managed investments for the insurance companies and pension funds had not gone to Eton and were more interested in whether a broker gave professional service than in where he went to school. In dispensing fees, commissions and other forms of patronage to bankers and brokers they placed diminishing emphasis on a shared educational background or club. Leading stockbrokers responded by opening up their ranks to bright young analysts and dealers, many of them admittedly from Oxbridge, but who lacked City connections and expensive public school educations.

Actuaries and chartered accountants found their way into broking partnerships. Some firms went largely meritocratic. Phillips & Drew, which is famous for its extensive research, has more in common with an aggressive American-style brokerage house than with a traditional firm such as Cazenove, which continues to cultivate a clublike – though still very profitable – style of doing business and scarcely bothers with research. Grieveson, Grant sports a chairman and chief executive like any industrial company and prides itself on the fact that the firm's capital is more evenly spread between the senior and junior partners than in some of the more old-fashioned broking houses.

Rigid City Toryism is also on the wane. Labour peer Lord Donoughue, who was an economic adviser to Sir Harold Wilson and James Callaghan, is a partner in Grieveson, Grant, while his former colleague Gavin Davies, also a political adviser in the 1974–79 Labour government, heads the research effort at Simon & Coates, a firm which has long been regarded as faintly left-wing, at least by City standards. In the late 1970s Phillips & Drew even took the bold step of advising the unions at the Ford Motor Co. on the presentation of a pay claim – without apparent damage to the partnership's own business or reputation.

The dealing system

The only problem with the growth of non-price competition in the shape of research was that the investment institutions found themselves confronting an ever-increasing mountain of paper, much of it of poor quality. And by the 1970s the institutions themselves were outgrowing the structure on which the whole market operated. Since early in the twentieth century trading on the Stock Exchange had been rooted in two fundamental principles: the first, known as 'single capacity', was a way of describing the unique distinction in London between broker and jobber; the second required jobbers to act as competing market makers – that is to say, jobbing firms competed with each other in offering prices to tempt the broker to give them business.

In the textbooks the system was usually said to work along

the following lines. The client would contact a stockbroker to give an order to buy, say, a thousand shares in Courtaulds. In handling the client's order the broker would act purely in one capacity, that of agent; the rules made it unattractive for him – there are still very few female members of the Exchange – to sell to the client shares that he (or his firm) owned personally. The broking firm's order department would then instruct a dealer to enter the market to execute the order with a jobber at his 'pitch' on the Stock Exchange floor.

The jobbers were accurately described as sharp-witted middlemen, or wholesalers, who stood or sat around hexagonal booths on the Stock Exchange floor; these booths were the equivalent of market stalls. The stallholders in question acted only in one capacity – in this case that of principal – dealing on their own account in the shares displayed on a board above the jobber's pitch. The broker, knowing that the jobber had a position in the shares, would protect his client's interests by sounding out the other competing jobbers, without revealing whether he was a buyer or seller. For their part, the jobbers would quote two prices: a lower one at which they were prepared to buy and a higher one at which they would sell. Competition between the jobbers was meant to ensure that the 'turn', or margin, did not become exorbitantly wide. Like a bookmaker, the jobber would aim to minimize risks by seeking to balance his book as far as possible at the end of the day. Once a bargain was struck between jobber and broker, they noted the transaction in their respective dealing books without signing any formal contract. Hence the Stock Exchange's motto, '*Dictum Meum Pactum*' – 'My word is my bond'.

This system of single capacity had, in fact, been outlined in the Stock Exchange's deed of settlement of 1802. But while the Exchange's rule book of 1847 banned partnerships of brokers and jobbers as 'highly inexpedient and improper', this did not stop individual members acting in both capacities. As E. V. Morgan and W. A. Thomas show in their history of the Stock Exchange, what finally caused a firm line to be drawn was not so much scandals arising from conflicts of interest towards investors as tensions between brokers and jobbers who trespassed on each others' territory. In 1908 the London Stock

Exchange agreed to a new rule (which was opposed by many of the larger firms but not by the small ones) by which members had to declare whether they were acting as broker or jobber. From that time brokers were required not to make prices or to deal with non-members unless they could obtain better prices for the client; and jobbers were not allowed to deal with non-members unless it was in arbitrage outside Britain. Fixed minimum commissions were introduced soon afterwards, in 1912, on the ground that they strengthened single capacity by preventing jobbers dealing with non-members outside the Exchange while negotiating a purely nominal commission with a broker to pass business through the Exchange. The whole system derived subsequent support from the introduction of stamp duty, which was followed by a special exemption from duty for Stock Exchange jobbers. The underlying compact between the two classes of Stock Exchange animal was that the brokers agreed to bring all their business to the central marketplace – in other words to provide the jobbers with an assured flow of orders – on condition that the jobbers did not approach the investing public direct with a view to cutting out the agent's commission. One important merit claimed for the system, though not the main purpose behind its introduction, was that the whole thing was potentially self-policing. Continuous dealing offered investors fair prices in a central marketplace. There was genuine protection, in that jobbers competed only with each other for the brokers' business while brokers had no direct incentive to overcharge the client.

A shortage of capital in the system

That is how the theory went, anyway. The subsequent practice was that in the two decades to the end of the 1970s the number of jobbers in the market declined from 104 firms to thirteen; and of those thirteen, five accounted for 90 per cent of the market's turnover. Noting the trend, the Stock Exchange Council became worried in the late 1960s. For while the amalgamations did not necessarily mean that the number of individual jobbers was going down, there were growing signs that the whole jobbing system lacked the capital to ensure liquid markets when insurance companies and pension funds were dealing in larger and larger lines of stocks and shares. So the Council changed the rules to permit 100 per cent outside ownership provided that no single owner held more than 10 per cent of a single broker or jobber. The new ruling broadened the ownership of jobbing firms, some of which turned themselves into companies, and ultimately led to two of them, Akroyd & Smithers and Smith Brothers, becoming quoted on the Exchange.

Nonetheless the move failed to solve the problem, because as the institutions grew incessantly the firms were having to cope with continuing increases in the average size of stock market bargains, while simultaneously struggling with the impact of inflation on the cost of financing their inventory of stocks and shares, and on the costs of running their own business. In 1976 a review of the degree of competition in the jobbing system carried out by the Exchange's chief executive, Robert Fell, concluded that the loss of one more big jobber would threaten the whole system of single capacity. A proposed merger in 1977 between the fourth and fifth largest jobbing firms, respectively Smith Brothers and Bisgood, Bishop, was not surprisingly referred to the Monopolies and Mergers Commission. The verdict was that competition between jobbers in equities had indeed become somewhat limited, but that the proposed merger was unlikely to have a significant adverse effect on the public interest. In the event the firms decided not to merge. But by the time the Wilson Committee came to report on the City, at the turn of the decade, it was unable to say for sure whether competition had been seriously undermined.

What the committee did find was that there had been considerable erosion in the system of single capacity. It pointed out that jobbers did not appear to be behaving as competitively as they might. They were, for example, prone to agree on a minimum spread between the prices at which they were prepared to buy and sell equity shares and to run joint books in the shares of individual companies. There was sometimes only one jobber in the smaller stocks and even in some of the bigger ones there were only two or three. The market had thus become very much less liquid and yet faced huge, volatile swings in sentiment as institutions tended to move in the same direction all at once. A growing proportion of big transactions was being arranged by brokers who matched the requirements of their institutional clients outside the Stock Exchange and then put the business through the jobber as a cut-price formality. These 'put-throughs', as they were known, constituted an interesting reversal of the situation at the start of the century where the jobbers passed their business with non-members cheaply through brokers on the Exchange.

Left behind by the international tide

A further problem of the unique distinction between broker and jobber was that the system was out of tune, as Jacob Rothschild and others argued, with the rest of the world. In the 1970s jobbers in London lost much of their international business, especially in South African mining shares – or 'Kaffirs' as they were called. This was because they were not only hampered by exchange controls but also forced to deal expensively through brokers instead of going direct to other dealers to exploit arbitrage opportunities in the international market. By the time pressure had built up to change the rules, much of the business had gone; and in the end it was not until 1984, when the City Revolution was well under way and business in domestic equities was being lost to the Exchange, that the Stock Exchange permitted firms to set up international dealerships that were allowed to trade under dual capacity. Yet most brokers found it easy to overlook such problems in the 1970s because – with the exception of the savage collapse in prices in 1973–4 – domestic business was booming. Fixed commissions on gilt-edged dealing, in particular, provided an alternative goldmine in the second half of the 1970s when high public spending and a shift in the emphasis of monetary policy required the market to absorb huge volumes of government stock.

While this was going on, Wall Street was in turmoil following the introduction in 1975 of negotiated commissions at the behest of the Securities and Exchange Commission. One result was that securities trading came to be dominated even further by big 'block trading' houses that dealt in huge blocks of stock amounting to 10,000 or more units at a time. And those same capital-intensive block traders applied their techniques and skills in dual capacity dealing not just on Wall Street but in London in the Euromarkets. Most members of the Stock Exchange were unbothered by this development, since few of them were active in the Eurobond market and Britain's domestic market was in any case impenetrable to foreign firms. So by the time exchange controls were lifted by the Chancellor of the Exchequer in 1979 British broking firms were, by international standards, short of capital and very small.

The effect of this parochialism can be seen by comparing the performance of British stockbrokers with their counterparts in insurance broking. Rowe & Pitman is generally considered to be a top-flight stockbroker (among other things, it looks after the Queen's investments). Its pretax profits in 1980, shortly after exchange controls were scrapped, amounted to £2.86 million, of which less than 16 per cent came from operations overseas. Willis Faber, a firm of more or less equivalent reputation and status in insurance broking, with a leading position in the Lloyd's insurance market, in the same year made profits of £19.4 million and ran a totally international business. And whereas Rowe & Pitman had a capital at that time of just under £1 million, Willis Faber had accumulated capital of more than £50 million. The insurance broker's huge reserves reflected the profitability that came from doing international business in a period of sustained sterling weakness; much of its commission income was in dollars. Part of the cost of making these large profits was, admittedly, that the original owners of Willis Faber, when it was unquoted, had to dilute their interest in the business. But at the end of the day it had the capital and the market share to be a significant player on the international stage, with options that extended beyond the pure insurance field.

It would be wrong to tar all broking firms with the brush of insularity. Some, like Vickers da Costa, established a bigger presence overseas, in North America and the Far East, than in the British market. And Rowe & Pitman itself went on to build up business in the United States and Japanese markets in the first half of the 1980s. But the fact remains that, when the British institutions poured more than £18 billion into foreign securities between 1979 and the end of 1984, most of the business bypassed the Exchange. The general run of larger brokers were simply doing too well before then to have felt the need to worry about the trends in international securities trading, so they contributed little to Britain's invisible earnings on the balance of payments. And they were open to the accusation of being poor salesmen and sluggish innovators.

Some outsiders argue that the Exchange was slow to exploit the full potential of options, futures and other new instruments pioneered in North America in response to increasing volatility in financial markets; or, indeed, to see that futures were an important part of the armoury of an international financial centre since the hedging facility they offered added liquidity to volatile markets. It also took some prodding and pushing, as well as a hint of competition from new over-the-counter markets outside the Stock Exchange, before the Stock Exchange Council decided to promote a full unlisted securities market to offer a cut-price service to smaller companies so that they could have access to risk capital with less heavy regulation than on the Stock Exchange itself.

Counter-arguments from brokers are that innovation is of little use unless it is profitable – a dig at LIFFE, which has some way to go before it can claim to be a convincing winner. London's strength, they add, has been in developing markets rather than setting them up from scratch, and the quality of its research is second to none. The Stock Exchange itself has good information systems, together with effective regulation and a compensation scheme. It is much respected on these counts by the foreign investment community in London. The real problem, however, was that the Stock Exchange's rules militated against participation in the international markets that were developing at the turn of the 1980s, leaving British firms vulnerable as foreigners started to deal in British stocks and shares. Because of the system of single capacity, British member firms could not deal effectively in North America, as will be shown in Chapter 5. And because they acted only as agents and enjoyed the benefits of fixed commissions, they felt no need to accumulate capital until late in the day when they saw that business in big British shares such as ICI, British Telecom and Glaxo was emigrating from the Exchange.

Extracting the last penny?

A more fundamental criticism of the Stock Exchange, however, might be that it actively encouraged business to emigrate
through changes in its own fixed-commission structure. In
1982 the Stock Exchange Council proposed the first major
adjustment in its commission rates since 1976. And much to
the surprise of many of its customers, it made only modest
concessions to their lobbying. While gilt commissions were
reduced (though by far less than the big institutions thought
reasonable) commissions on equity transactions were actually
increased. The net result was to promote the survival of the less
efficient brokers and to make private share ownership less
attractive, at least in the short term, at a time when a Tory
government was hoping to revive popular capitalism. It also
seemed a cavalier gesture, given that the watchdogs of the
Office of Fair Trading were examining the dealing system at
the time. The impression given was that the Stock Exchange
was willing to take risks, as dealing costs in London rose
relative to those in New York, in the hope of extracting the last
ounce of benefit from a waning monopoly in the United
Kingdom. And if the attentions of the Office of Fair Trading
led to the abolition of fixed commissions, commissions would
at least start to be negotiated downwards from a high base.

Objectively it could still be argued that the Stock Exchange's
time-honoured system of single capacity had much to com-
mend it, especially in terms of investor protection. But the
degree of protection had eroded markedly in the 1970s and the
customers' hostile response to the 1982 commission increase
suggested that the Exchange was asking too high a price for its
services. Moreover, there was a serious risk that as more
business in British shares disappeared overseas the point might
be reached where the Stock Exchange became a residual
backwater of the international financial system, one in which
the main trading was undertaken by the locals in second- and
third-line companies.

It was small wonder that by the early 1980s members of the
bigger British firms had begun to perceive that they were
playing the part of the Greeks in a Roman world and that the
Romans – under the guise of Merrill Lynch, Goldman Sachs,

Drexel Burnham Lambert, Pru-Bache and the rest – were camping on the doorstep. Or perhaps a more exact analogy could be drawn with the Square Mile in the eighteenth century, when the burghers of the City of London still confined admission to the brokerage fraternity to freemen of the City, who were then required to comply with the City's own regulatory fiat in relation to their conduct. The growing size and financial power of the Jewish community at that time posed a serious threat to this closed community. In the end a dozen Jewish brokers were admitted – though not without being expected to bribe the Lord Mayor for the privilege.

Competition watchdogs dictate the pace of change

Either way, twentieth-century members of the Stock Exchange recognized that there was no future in unprofitable isolation. The only question was how to make a break so late in the day, because the Exchange had become embroiled in a court case under the Restrictive Practices Act of 1976. This legislation posed a major problem for the City because it took for granted that agreements between competitors were likely to operate against the public interest; yet such agreements were the very basis of the self-regulation on which the City set so much store. The Secretary of State for Trade did, as it happened, have the power to exempt organizations from the Act's provisions. But under a Labour government in the second half of the 1970s this was a forlorn hope. The Stock Exchange was obliged to deliver its rule book to the Office of Fair Trading to be included on a public register of restrictive trading agreements; and the Director General of Fair Trading then had a legal duty to refer those agreements, including the ones on single capacity trading and the exclusion of outside corporate control of Stock Exchange firms, to the Restrictive Practices Court for a ruling as to whether they operated against the public interest. This was done in 1979.

Any open discussion of the Stock Exchange's invidious position in relation to the international capital markets then became virtually impossible, for the Restrictive Practices Court's *modus operandi* was a rare one in English law: the Stock Exchange was guilty until proved innocent. Against that background everyone concerned, in both government and the Exchange, faced an intractable dilemma. In some parts of the financial sector, such as the clearing bank system, there were natural as well as artificial barriers to foreign entry. As long as the Americans were prevented from making an outright takeover of a British clearing bank, the Big Four could console themselves with the thought that no foreigner would build up a prohibitively expensive full branch network in Britain, and that home banking would be sufficiently long in catching on to give them all a breathing space against the invader. Their own customers were also notoriously loyal (or, as their critics would have it, notoriously inert).

Members of the Stock Exchange were in a wholly different position. The predominantly wholesale nature of most big brokers' business meant that they were very vulnerable both to the foreign competition on the doorstep and to competition from each other if the regime on the Exchange was liberalized. There was no need for American and Japanese investment houses to invest in new infrastructure or in expensive retail distribution networks to poach the British broking firms' business; they were already at work in the Eurobond market, and more familiar with the dealing methods that prevailed there than were their British competitors. If the Stock Exchange was to play a significant part in the new game of twenty-four-hour dealing in international securities, its membership had to be opened up. But once the foreign wolf was actually allowed through the door, what hope was there that hitherto protected British firms would be able to cope with the onslaught?

4

All Change at the Stock Exchange

For the first three and a half years of the 1980s the Restrictive Practices Court proceedings against the Stock Exchange created a logjam in the institutional structure of the City of London. The impasse was finally broken when Cecil Parkinson and Sir Nicholas Goodison agreed to a deadline lasting a further three and a half years for what was later dubbed 'The Big Bang' – a blunt but evocative epithet for the proposed abolition of the Exchange's fixed minimum commissions. It was this controversial agreement between one of the more durable postwar holders of the office of Stock Exchange chairman and one of the most ephemeral postwar Secretaries of State for Trade that finally unleashed the City Revolution. But by far the most important role in the affair was played behind the scenes by another discreet but powerful actor: the Bank of England. The Old Lady of Threadneedle Street played a pivotal part not only in the Parkinson deal itself, but in the subsequent unfolding of this increasingly turbulent drama.

To understand the Bank's manoeuvrings in relation to the Stock Exchange it is necessary to appreciate the rather curious position that it occupies within the British public sector. Although it was nationalized in 1946, and was once jocularly described by the Labour Chancellor Sir Stafford Cripps as 'my creature', the Bank retains a far greater degree of autonomy than any of the big state industries. Under the 1946 Act the Chancellor of the Exchequer is empowered to issue directives to the Governor, but the right is never exercised. Instead there is a fluctuating balance of power between Bank and Treasury (with the Treasury having the best of it of late) in which the Bank's clout derives from the authority of the Governor, who is appointed by the Prime Minister for a five-year term. The Bank's independence is further underwritten by the profitability of its operations, which ensures that the Governor never has to go cap in hand to the Treasury, and permits pay scales and perks more in line with those prevailing in the better-heeled merchant banks than in the Civil Service.

The Bank of England is thus able to combine apparently conflicting roles. On the one hand it is owned by government and acts as the government's banker in the City; on the other, it chooses to act as a spokesman for City interests in Whitehall. Over the past thirty years successive Governors have been staunch advocates of self-regulation in the Square Mile and determined guardians of City freedoms in the face of government encroachment. And Whitehall mandarins have cast envious eyes at the Old Lady's pay scales.

It was entirely in character, then, that the Bank of England should have argued from the outset against any referral of the Stock Exchange's rule book to the Restrictive Practices Court, and from 1978 the Bank fought a sustained battle to persuade Whitehall that the court proceedings should be curtailed. The thrust of its argument was not so much that the Stock Exchange's rule book was beyond reproach; it simply claimed that the court was a wholly unsuitable place in which to settle the future structure of the Exchange.

The campaign failed, predictably, with Labour's Secretary for Prices and Consumer Protection, Roy Hattersley. It failed less predictably with Mrs Thatcher's first Trade Secretary, John (now Sir John) Nott – a former merchant banker with S. G. Warburg who has since returned to the City as a chairman of Lazard Brothers – and with Nott's successor, John Biffen. Both Tory ministers were conscious that the 1980 Competition Act had included specific provisions designed to give the Restrictive Practices Court flexibility in handling the Stock Exchange's legitimate complaint that there would be turmoil if its rules were simply declared illegal. The Act allowed a six-month period of grace, in which the Stock Exchange would be able to submit revised rules, together with a right of appeal against the court's findings. The Stock Exchange nonetheless argued that this was far too short a time in which to overhaul a sophisticated market structure, especially since it was unable to consult its membership while the legal proceedings ran on; but its pleas for a Royal Commission or a Monopolies Commission inquiry in lieu of the court case met with no more success than the lobbying efforts of the Bank.

By 1982 what had started as an instinctive concern in the Bank of England at outside interference in the City's self-regulatory arrangements turned into a far wider worry about the competitiveness of the City of London as an international financial centre. Part of the focus of this new anxiety was an internal study that had been set in train by an executive director of the Bank, David Walker, a former Treasury official who had taken the unusual step of emigrating to the Square Mile at the suggestion of Gordon (now Lord) Richardson, Governor of the Bank between 1974 and 1983. Walker, who brought a sharp mind, driving energy and a persuasive charm to the job, was regarded in and out of Whitehall as an instinctive interventionist. As well as overseeing the clearing banks' industrial lifeboat in the early 1980s, he was anxious to promote a sponsorship role for the Bank towards the financial services sector, much as government departments sponsored individual industries that came within their area of policy-making. The purpose of Walker's study was to quantify British firms' penetration of international financial markets.

The results of the study pointed to a lopsided performance. In international banking, British institutions had established themselves as a force in the important syndicated credit market. In insurance the British had more or less held their own despite growing protectionism and increasing competition around the world; and in insurance broking British firms had won an impressive place towards the top of the international league. Even in commodities the City had performed creditably in terms of market share. In stark contrast Britain's stockbrokers stood out for their failure to make a mark on the international stage. Their share of international business had declined steadily over the years.

The Bank of England looks to the national interest

With the growth in international financial services shifting away from the banking sector towards securities markets, this failure on the part of British securities houses was regarded by the Bank as running counter to the national interest. Official concern extended beyond the implications for the invisible side of the balance of payments current account. With much of the British manufacturing sector laid waste by a combination of tight monetary policy and overvalued sterling as North Sea oil revenues built up in the early 1980s, the government was looking to the service sector, in which the City loomed large, to provide new jobs.

Seen from the Bank of England's perspective, the most worrying thing was not just that the Restrictive Practices Court case against the Stock Exchange was preventing change. Either outcome of the case was potentially disastrous: if the Stock Exchange won, its constitution risked being set in concrete for another decade in which business would ebb away from the central market; if it lost, there was a powerful and more immediate threat from outside. Though in their speeches to foreign audiences Bank governors traditionally upheld the virtues of free trade and liberal investment policies, this liberalism had never extended to a desire to see domestic banking and securities markets opened up to the full force of foreign competition. The Bank had little doubt that the immediate removal of the ban on 100 per cent corporate ownership of Stock Exchange firms would open the way to American domination of the more profitable end of the Stock Exchange's business, notwithstanding public protestations to the contrary by Sir Nicholas Goodison, the Stock Exchange chairman.

There were, however, formidable difficulties in breaking the logjam. For a start there is no harder task in Whitehall than to reopen an old argument that someone else has won. The Department of Trade was convinced that the Bank was simply talking its own book and that it had no interest in fostering competition. Any politician who contemplated the course of action advocated by the Bank risked being accused of constitutional impropriety, given that it involved disrupting a judicial process. Against that the Bank could argue that things had

93

changed dramatically in the international financial system since 1978; and it was able to offer the politicians an argument about jobs.

In late 1982 high-level discussions on the question began between David Walker at the Bank and permanent secretaries in the Department of Trade and the Treasury. But there was little movement until the talks shifted to ministerial level, at which stage the recently appointed Trade Secretary, Lord Cockfield, took an interest. Cockfield had never fought shy of controversy, and with him the Bank had got its breakthrough: he found the case put by the Governor persuasive. Action was finally on the cards. Even so, the Bank was forced to work hard, as the deadline for an out-of-court settlement loomed, to steer the campaign to its desired conclusion. Among other things the argument was overtaken by a change of Governors, from Richardson to Robin Leigh-Pemberton, and by the ministerial reshuffle that followed the general election in mid-1983. But happily for the Bank the new Trade Secretary, Cecil Parkinson, was readily persuaded, and the radically inclined Chancellor of the Exchequer, Nigel Lawson, took the view that making a constitutional concession to the Stock Exchange was a price worth paying if the government extracted a commitment to change. The only question that then remained was the precise form that a deal between the government and the Stock Exchange should take.

No one involved was prepared to argue for outright liberalization. If the Bank's outlook was tinged with chauvinism, there was a far more powerful streak of economic nationalism in Mrs Thatcher's cabinet. And without some degree of protection it was certainly questionable whether even the biggest British houses would stand up to American competition. So the Bank's preferred outcome was for the Stock Exchange to soften the blow by phasing out minimum commissions over a period, while creating pressure to bring fresh capital into member firms; it was keen to see some restrictions on foreign entry retained, provided that it was made clear that barriers would not remain indefinitely. And it wanted dealing costs brought down in relation to those of other financial centres by persuading the Chancellor of the Exchequer to cut the 2 per cent stamp duty on share transactions. Key objectives were the

94

need to maintain liquidity – the ability to deal consistently at reasonable prices in large sums in a unified market – in both the gilt-edged and equity markets; and also to ensure reasonable standards of investor protection. The more specific details of the future structure of the market could then be left to the Stock Exchange's own members to decide, within a framework of continuing consultations among the Stock Exchange, Bank and government.

When the government finally approached the Stock Exchange in June 1983 the Bank's view had more or less prevailed. There was little in the way of hard negotiation because there was little in the government's position for the Stock Exchange chairman, Sir Nicholas Goodison, to object to. He was delighted at the prospect of escaping from the clutches of the court because he knew that if legal proceedings continued the Exchange was sure to lose its case on fixed commissions and was at risk on both the membership rules and the market structure. The only real dispute was over the speed with which liberalization should proceed. Goodison wanted the changes to be phased in over five years in order to secure what the Stock Exchange called an orderly transition; he was supported in this attitude by the Bank of England.

A controversial package

In the event the Stock Exchange got just under three and a half years, which was considerably more than the six months that the Restrictive Practices Court would have been able to offer. When the deal was finally struck between Sir Nicholas Goodison and Cecil Parkinson, it called for fixed commissions to be abolished by the end of 1986; outsiders were to be brought onto the Stock Exchange Council; and the Bank of England was to have a monitoring role in the interim, alongside the Department of Trade.

It is not hard to see why this deal, struck behind firmly closed doors, was regarded in both the Commons and the press as a post-electoral sell-out to the City. Even on the Tory benches there were some, like Enoch Powell, who questioned whether there was any precedent for introducing new legislation to put a stop to litigation that was being brought under existing legislation. While the government made it clear that the circumstances surrounding the deal were exceptional, the affair was still very damaging to the authority of the Office of Fair Trading, whose Director General, Sir Gordon Borrie, seriously considered resigning. In the end Borrie confined himself to pointing out that if the government tried to proceed simply by placing a statutory order before Parliament, as some ministers wished to do, the order might not affect his existing legal obligation to pursue the case; primary legislation was necessary. In the meantime an enormous quantity of research and evidence was consigned to oblivion without any discussion of the public interest issues involved.

An equally surprising feature of this compact between the government and the City's most important club was the remarkable degree of freedom it left to those whose commercial interests were at stake. Sir Gordon Borrie was concerned, for example, that there was no formal agreement in relation to granting full access to corporate members. In 1982 the limit on individual shareholding by outside companies in Stock Exchange firms was raised from 10 per cent to 29.9 per cent at the request of a leading broker, Hoare, Govett, which wanted to bring in the Californian banking group Security Pacific as a shareholder. But there was no public commitment to raise this to 100 per cent or even 51 per cent. Nor was there any formal agreement on the future of the market structure. Ministers were conscious at the time that legislation had just been enacted to prohibit members of Lloyd's of London acting in dual capacity, albeit in very different circumstances. And in the course of the secret discussions in July the Stock Exchange had told the Department of Trade that it would be feasible to continue for the moment with the old system of single capacity. So Cecil Parkinson told the Commons that the old system, with the protection for investors that was claimed to come from the sharp distinction between broking and jobbing, was to be maintained for the time being. Parkinson told us that there was genuine uncertainty, both in the Department of Trade and the Stock Exchange, on the question of whether single capacity could survive; but the Stock Exchange was, he added, reluctant to commit itself to giving up single capacity when it did not know what to put in its place.

The 'link' argument

Yet this raised all manner of doubts. For in presenting its case to the Restrictive Practices Court the Stock Exchange had argued that the abandonment of fixed commissions would put the system of single capacity at risk because the two were inextricably linked. Once brokers' profits came under pressure as a result of much lower negotiated commissions, so the argument ran, they would increasingly be tempted to cut out the jobber by matching the purchases and sales that their clients wished to transact. To the extent that they failed to match up exactly, brokers would be forced to take positions in the shares in much the same way as a jobber. The jobbers would then demand to approach the brokers' clients direct because they were being cut out of the business. In the circumstances it would not be easy for the Stock Exchange Council to turn down the request.

Many (though by no means all) in the Bank of England believed by this time that a move to the American-style system of dual capacity trading was inevitable. Months before Cecil Parkinson made his announcement, papers had, in fact, circulated in the Bank discussing the potential problems associated with any move towards a system modelled on the American over-the-counter market NASDAQ (short for National Association of Securities Dealers Automated Quotations). Why, then, were the details of the Parkinson deal so sketchy?

One reason was simply that the Department of Trade's main concern lay with the narrow aspect of competition policy. It was, the authors were told, the Stock Exchange's monopoly power to fix commissions that the government found most offensive. Trade ministers took the view that it was for the Stock Exchange to see to the issues of membership and market structure. All concerned also recognized that Sir Nicholas Goodison had to sell the package first to the Stock Exchange Council, then to the membership. There was a feeling that Goodison should be given the maximum flexibility – a word much favoured by officials in Threadneedle Street – because his proposals on the market's structure and membership

97

would have to be put to the vote. Nor should it be overlooked that the looseness of the arrangement suited the purposes of the Bank.

The Old Lady widens her horizons

In the past the Bank had had little formal power over the Stock Exchange. Its supervisory role extended primarily to the banking system. But from the mid-1970s, at a time when the Bank's influence over the government's economic and monetary policies was waning, officials had shown a renewed interest in industrial finance, much as they had done in the 1930s when Montagu Norman's Bank was heavily involved in restructuring declining sectors of British industry. The capital-raising ability of the equity market was thus of increasing interest to the Bank, and in the early 1980s the erosion of the traditional boundaries between the banking and securities markets gave an added incentive for central bankers to keep a closer watch on securities markets.

Against that background the government–Stock Exchange deal gave the Bank of England a unique opportunity to extend its influence. As the government's arm in the City it was the Stock Exchange's most important customer: the turnover in gilt-edged stock was substantially greater than in equities. By raising funds for the government exclusively through the Stock Exchange it helped preserve the attractions of the Exchange as Britain's central market in stocks and shares. But the protection that this arrangement afforded had always been conditional on the Stock Exchange's providing a satisfactory degree of liquidity and regulation to facilitate the raising of government funds. The Bank's implicit leverage over the Exchange was thus enormous when it came to any change in the market structure, even though it was devoid of statutory power, and the Bank also increased its formal powers through the monitoring role granted under the Parkinson deal. In addition it obtained a veto, now incorporated in the Stock Exchange's revised deed of settlement, over the lay members of the Stock Exchange Council; or, as officials prefer to put it, the Governor has the right to 'bless the names of outsiders'.

In practice day-to-day relations between the two institutions were close and amicable. So from the Governor down, every-one at the Bank of England was confident that the Stock Exchange Council would come up with mutually satisfactory reforms. The real questions, seen from their point of view, were whether the smaller firms would accept those reforms and whether the bigger ones that saw reform as inevitable would be able to cope with the consequences.

The uncertainties and the risks were, in fact, far greater than generally appreciated at the time. Sir Nicholas Goodison might have won a victory over the Office of Fair Trading; but the victory posed a serious threat to the smaller firms on the Exchange whose voting power was disproportionately large in relation to their financial muscle. The shares in the Exchange were owned by 4500 or so individual members. If the terms on which outsiders were allowed to buy into the Exchange were not satisfactory to the smaller firms, or if they were too expensive to tempt in the big outsiders, there was a risk that the market would fragment as big banks and broking firms started to deal outside the Exchange over the telephone in leading stocks and shares. The Bank of England might then be obliged to take the gilt-edged market away from the Stock Exchange.

It was also unclear how outsiders would respond to the lifting of restrictions on ownership of Stock Exchange firms. Would they really be keen to put money into businesses whose return on capital might shortly be cut down to size by the arrival of the international brigade, with Merrill Lynch, Salomon Brothers and the rest among the assembled cohorts? Or would there be a stampede to establish a foothold in the newly liberalized market? There was a further question mark over how far the market structure would have to be changed to cope with the new arrangements.

In the event the two main planks of the strategy jointly agreed among the government, the Bank and the Stock Ex-change Council – a phased move to negotiated commissions and the perpetuation of the distinction between brokers and jobbers – collapsed within months, if not weeks. Because of the Restrictive Practices Court proceedings it had been impossible for any of those involved in negotiating the July deal to consult practitioners in the markets. When the practitioners came to look at the options for dismantling fixed commissions bit by bit they concluded that they were unworkable.

If, for example, negotiated commissions were introduced in one part of the market, but not another, big investors would simply demand terms in the negotiated sector that reflected the fact that they were required to pay fixed commissions to the same broker in other parts of the market. All the other suggestions for moving to negotiated commissions by stages were open to the same criticism – that big investors would simply rearrange their business in such a way as to overcome the distortions that had temporarily been introduced into the market. The City consensus was that no alternative existed to the abolition of minimum commissions for all securities at one fixed date; this was the option that came to be known as the Big Bang. So the government, the Bank and the Stock Exchange were forced to concede the point. An informal deadline was then fixed for the Big Bang: October 1986.

Goodbye to single capacity

Any fears that might have been entertained about the readiness of outsiders to pump capital into a market that was soon to be exposed to competitive reality turned out to be wholly unfounded. Many of the interested parties concluded at the outset that the old distinction between jobber and broker was doomed; and the power of their chequebook was ultimately to ensure that their view prevailed. This was certainly the case with the two most powerful domestic financial groupings that were to emerge in the wake of the reforms, Barclays de Zoete Wedd and Mercury Securities, the parent company of S. G. Warburg.

Lord Camoys, vice-chairman of Barclays Merchant Bank, heard about the Parkinson deal while on holiday in Ibiza. He immediately telephoned his office in the City to initiate papers on future strategy, in which it was taken as read that the Stock Exchange would move to American-style dealing where members enjoyed the freedom both to make markets in shares on their own account and to distribute the shares to their clients. Camoys' assumption was that from the moment negotiated commissions came in, securities trading would become central to the business of merchant banking in Britain just as it was in the international markets. If Barclays was to retain its big corporate clients, its merchant banking and securities trading arm would have a key role to play, not least in handling 'bought deals'; the art of corporate finance in the new era was expected to lie very largely in the ability to take a complete block of a company client's securities onto the bank's book and then to lay off the risk as rapidly as possible by distributing the securities to investors. For distribution Barclays clearly needed a broker. The only question in anyone's mind at that early stage was whether the bank would also need a jobber to make a market in the securities. But the hunt for acquisitions was on.

The thinking was not dissimilar at S. G. Warburg. The bank's chairman, David Scholey, and his vice chairman Lord Garmoyle had long been conscious of the disadvantages of the British way of handling capital issues. These feelings were confirmed in 1977, when both had been closely involved in a £565 million issue in London and New York of British government shares in British Petroleum. The government had committed itself to the sale as part of a package of commitments made to the International Monetary Fund in December 1976, one of whose objects was to bring down the public sector borrowing requirement. As the government's banker, the Bank of England had been charged by the Treasury with putting in train the arrangements for the sale. The Bank turned to David Scholey to organize the underwriting – a commitment, in effect, to take up any shares that remained unsold – who in turn asked Lord Garmoyle, then at BP's brokers J. & A. Scrimgeour, to devise a way of handling a simultaneous issue of the shares on London and Wall Street. Mullens, the government broker, provided an operations room for the huge team that worked on the transaction.

This immensely complex issue was the biggest that Britain had ever seen. In London, no fewer than ten top merchant banks, five leading stockbrokers and more than 400 sub-underwriters were involved. On Wall Street, by contrast, Morgan Stanley did the job of all ten merchant banks in handling the sale of a fifth of the total issue, and brought in five brokerage houses to distribute the shares. Scholey, Garmoyle and the Bank of England were impressed by the relative neatness and efficiency of the US proceedings; and with the fact that Morgan Stanley was providing advice, performing the equivalent of the underwriter's job and preparing to stabilize prices in the market after the issue all at the same time, yet involving itself in much less risk than the British underwriters.

In Britain the price at which the shares were offered to investors was fixed at a discount to the market price when the offer was announced. The underwriters then had to wait on tenterhooks for two weeks to see whether the price of BP shares held up; any fall would narrow the discount and thus reduce the incentive for investors to take up the shares, leaving the underwriters to take up the unwanted shares. In exchange for taking on this risk, they received a fee from the seller (usually 1½ to 2¼ per cent of the offer price), the greater part of which was passed on to the sub-underwriters and brokers.

In the United States Morgan Stanley and its five brokerage houses sold the issue to investors on the basis of a so-called 'red herring' prospectus which contained all the information on the BP issue except the price. At the end of this marketing period, Morgan Stanley negotiated a price and an underwriting discount with the seller, the British government; together with its team of five brokers it then bought all the shares and sold them to investors within a week of distributing a final prospectus containing the price. Instead of receiving a percentage fee, the American underwriters simply took a turn between the price at which they bought the shares from the British government and the price at which they sold to the public. In other words American salesmanship was used to reduce the risk inherent in taking on, as principal, much larger amounts of stock than the big British merchant banks could afford to do.

Scholey's and Garmoyle's feelings about the cumbersome nature of raising capital in Britain were reinforced by recent trends in the Euromarkets. There, banks had discovered that it was essential to offer an integrated service. Little money was to be made in issuing bonds unless the issuer also distributed the bonds to investors; and investors were reluctant to buy bonds from a house that was not prepared to make a subsequent market in those bonds. In other words there were not three rewards to be had in the business, but only one. Failure to offer an integrated service was likely to put the issuing house at a huge competitive disadvantage. So when the Parkinson deal was announced, Warburg concluded that the international way of handling issues would ultimately drift over to the British market; it started to plan its strategy accordingly.

What the revolutionary game was about

This desire to provide an integrated financial service was, in effect, a return to the capital-raising methods employed by merchant banks such as Rothschild and Baring in the nineteenth century. It was also the fundamental justification for the biggest purchases agreed in the City Revolution. Yet it involved the purchasers in huge new risks. Why were Barclays, Warburg's and others prepared to contemplate such risky acquisition and merger commitments when the Stock Exchange had given no undertaking to permit outside corporations to take control of member firms? And why were they so convinced that the market structure would evolve in the way that most suited their interests, notwithstanding the sketchiness of the Parkinson deal?

The first point to note is that few of the new alliances forged in 1983 and 1984 amounted to absolute commitments: they were conditional on a change in the Stock Exchange rules to allow them to go ahead. And in the immediate aftermath of the July announcement there was some hesitation, which partly reflected the fear that a broker–merchant bank merger would immediately alienate the broker's other merchant bank clients. This phenomenon was known as 'taint', and it gave brokers good reason to think hard about selling to foreign purchasers since this would involve fewer conflicts of interest and less risk of loss of commission income from valued clients.

But the hesitation did not last long. In the close-knit City community news soon leaked out that the Stock Exchange Council seemed likely to accept the principle of outside control of member firms. Then in late 1983 government ministers started to send clear signals about what they expected from all concerned. Alex Fletcher, Minister for Corporate and Consumer Affairs, who also regarded himself as having a sponsorship role in relation to the City, told the *Financial Times* in an interview that it was 'time for pretty fast change' and declared that there was a need for more financial conglomerates.

More important, the word soon spread that the Bank of England wanted to see the big foreign securities houses come into the gilt-edged market. This was a crucial pointer; so was the Bank's refusal to lend its support to those who wanted to preserve the jobbing system. Quite apart from the manifest difficulty of replacing the judgement of the Restrictive Practices Court with an edict from the central bank, the Old Lady was not convinced of the preservationist case. Bodies such as the National Association of Pension Funds, which represented the Stock Exchange's biggest investment customers, along with several senior figures in the market, argued the case for single capacity – the preservation of the distinction between broker and jobber – in vain. While the Bank's public position, like that of the government, was that these were matters for the Stock Exchange to decide, everyone knew that its position in the gilt-edged market gave it a crucial say in the reform of the Exchange. As Robin Leigh-Pemberton, the Governor, was later to confirm in a speech well stocked with sporting metaphors, the Bank's rather lofty view was that the time had come for the customers to broaden their vision:

It is not open to us simply to choose the best market system for our domestic purposes, without regard to the realities of the outside world. These realities are – and have been for some time – intruding most insistently. The inescapable fact is that securities trading is now an international activity and if we in this country wish to play any significant role in the world securities market, we must be equipped to compete. There must, however, be doubts over our ability fully to meet international competition, if our central market for securities conducts its trading in a way which is unique to this country and which thereby may handicap its members in regard to its non-member competitors at home and overseas. It is rather like sending the principal players in the UK team onto the international playing field bound by the rules of rugby league when the rest of the team and all the opposition are in fact playing association football. And we must not be led into thinking it is possible to play rugby at home and soccer away, since important parts of what we might regard as the home pitch are, in fact, now part of the international playing field and, indeed, it is in our interest that it should be so. In my estimation, the mounting competition would by itself eventually have brought about the demise of the jobbing system as the exclusive or principal trading system on the Stock Exchange, even if there had been no Restrictive Practices Court case and hence no agreement with government to abolish minimum commissions.

Despite the inherently implausible notion that a soccer team would triumph over a rugby league team that was permitted to pick up the ball and run, the message was one that the City had understood. A combination of hints, winks and nods, together with the scent of profit in the air, was enough to ensure that active overtures were soon being made by potential buyers and sellers. By the end of 1983 Cecil Parkinson had been swept out of office by a noisy (but by past Tory standards uncolourful) sex scandal. Yet in his short tenure as Trade Secretary he had unleashed a reform that was developing a swirling momentum of its own. By then people in City markets were beginning to sense that the structure of both the equity and gilt-edged markets were about to be subjected to a radical overhaul in order to cope with 'dual capacity' dealing in which anybody could act in the capacity of both agent and principal if he so wished. Brokers and jobbers were constantly in and out of banking parlours in search of congenial partners offering lucrative dowries; and rumours were mounting that a stampede was about to develop.

The temptation to join the stampede was rendered all the more compelling by the figures involved in some of the earliest deals. The most eye-catching concerned Citicorp, the American giant, which was revealed in November 1983 to have bought a 29.9 per cent stake in the medium-sized firm of Vickers da Costa, on terms that valued the whole firm at around £22 million. Ironically Citicorp's chief interest was in Vickers da Costa's overseas interests and had nothing to do with the revolution. Yet the deal gave the revolutionary band-wagon a powerful impetus because Citicorp was not only buying full control of Vickers' overseas operations but taking an option on the outstanding shares in the British part of the business. The all-embracing nature of the arrangement convinced everyone that there would be no going back. It was only a matter of time before outsiders moved to full control of Stock Exchange firms. And the Stock Exchange itself started to close the gap between British and international practice by allowing members to set up international dealerships which could operate in dual capacity.

Confronting the foreign challenge

Neither the Bank nor the government publicly admits to having encouraged individual firms towards particular partners. The official line was merely that the government wished to see the establishment of a number of strong British investment houses capable of taking on the international competition. In a speech in March 1984 that succeeded in combining protestations of liberalism with a hard core of protectionist sentiment, Robin Leigh-Pemberton declared:

> I believe that greater foreign involvement in our securities industry could bring substantial benefit, in particular through enhancing market liquidity and trading volume. But such participation needs to be properly accommodated in a way that has regard to the stake of existing British firms in the Stock Exchange structure and does not permit any firm to establish, by virtue of its size elsewhere, a dominant position that could then be exploited in an anti-competitive way. . . . Recognition of the benefits that foreign participation can bring does not of course imply indifference to where control of major participants in our markets lies, and we would not contemplate with equanimity a Stock Exchange in which British-owned member firms played a clearly subordinate role, any more than we would like to see Lloyd's or any other City market dominated by overseas interests.

The explanation for the change of gear from first person singular to a magisterial 'we' is perhaps no more than a reflection of the fact that the Governor was speaking for the government as well as for the Bank. But the clear implication was that if foreigners had a comparative advantage in financial services, they would not necessarily be allowed to exploit it to the full in Britain. In the same speech the Governor enunciated a principle of reciprocity, which carried an implicit warning that the big Japanese securities houses would not be allowed to play in all the markets to which they sought access unless the Japanese authorities offered comparable access to British firms.

In an otherwise permissive climate virtually everyone else clambered enthusiastically onto a revolutionary bandwagon that careered off in several directions at once. Stockbrokers and stockjobbers fell into the arms of every conceivable kind of financial institution, British and foreign, ranging from clearing banks and merchant banks to insurance companies and independent fund management groups. Then the discount houses were caught up in the process as the Bank of England relaxed its restrictions on ownership even to the point of allowing a foreigner to buy into one of the smaller houses.

Some of the participants were seeking stakes in brokers for reasons quite unconnected with the City Revolution. America's seventh largest bank holding company, Security Pacific, was attracted by Hoare Govett's research and its presence in Far Eastern markets long before it was aware of the opportunities that were opening up for 100 per cent ownership in Britain. As described above, similar factors were at work in Citicorp's purchase of its stake in Vickers. Hoare was just one of a number of firms that had seen the way the wind was blowing and had started to sound out the banks with a view to bringing in outside capital.

The high cost of independence

There came a point in 1984 when announcements about pending alliances were being put out almost by the week. Events started to impose a logic of their own. Simon & Coates, a medium-sized firm well-known for its equity research and its business in the Unlisted Securities Market, originally had no wish to tie up with anyone. At the start it considered staying away from the action and even contemplated going public on the stock market to bring in new capital. But as the number of merger announcements multiplied and the revolution became all-embracing the independent option simply became untenable. The thinking was explained to the authors by the senior partner of Simon & Coates, Michael Prag, one of the City's most thoughtful analysts, who argued that there was no satisfactory answer to the question of how the firm would perform if its peers were all part of some megacorporation backed by billions. The last independent stockbroker might stand to make a lot of money, he said, but that was not a strategy on which he and his partners could afford to gamble.

Even some of the biggest firms which had hoped to remain independent, such as Phillips & Drew, came reluctantly to the same conclusion and joined the Gadarene rush. The rush was at times exceptionally haphazard, with some firms approaching the business of their own sale with more professionalism than others. Since all the barriers between different types of financial institutions were crumbling, would-be sellers could not always turn with confidence to the traditional sources of advice on mergers and acquisitions for fear of giving away trade secrets: all the merchant banks and brokers were potential players in the new game, and so many sellers felt obliged to take their own counsel. Others, including leading jobber Wedd Durlacher Mordaunt, turned to specialist firms such as Phoenix Securities, run by a well-known international banker, John Craven, who rapidly established a reputation as an efficient marriage broker in the wake of Wedd's link with Barclays.

In some cases negotiations bordered on the chaotic. In 1983, before the Parkinson deal, Midland Bank embarked on lengthy discussions with W. Greenwell, one of the biggest brokers and one who had a well-merited reputation in the gilt-edged market. The talks, according to one participant, failed to achieve any real momentum, partly because Midland was distracted with the problems of its troubled US subsidiary, Crocker. Following Cecil Parkinson's announcement an impatient Greenwell told Midland that the situation had changed so dramatically that it wished to terminate the talks. Midland subsequently came within an ace of signing up the less expensive firm of Simon & Coates, only to see negotiations stall at the last fence. Senior executives at the big clearing bank were then taken aback to discover that their 60 per cent-owned merchant bank subsidiary Samuel Montagu, which had been only marginally involved in the earlier dalliance with Greenwell, had subsequently carried on independent discussions with the big broker. Midland found itself presented with a last-minute choice on whether to block or sanction a Montagu–Greenwell marriage. In the end the clearing bank gave its fiat. But Montagu's energetic Swedish boss, Staffan Gadd, who was the driving force behind the marriage, was obliged to part company with the bank shortly after; though the Greenwell saga was not the chief reason for his departure, it was a contributory factor.

The failure rate in all these talks was relatively high. Some mishaps, like Midland's, never surfaced publicly. Others were common knowledge. Everyone had several balls in the air at any given moment because they felt they had no option but to involve themselves in simultaneous talks and negotiations. After the event the financial press was full of articles in which top bankers explained how they had implemented carefully laid plans. In some cases the plans were real; others were simply post-hoc rationalizations of how they came to wind up with a second-rate broker or jobber.

Crucial in this hectic lottery was the ability of individuals to hit it off. These were businesses in which the chief assets were people and, in the case of brokers, those people's relationships with customers. The purchasers were buying market-making skills, in the case of jobbing firms, and 'placing power' – the ability to distribute large lines of shares to customers – in the case of the brokers. Since most of the firms were partnerships, where many individuals had to be involved in the ultimate decision, agreement was not always easy to come by. The criteria which dictated the outcome were often very different from those that would have applied to quoted companies; and chauvinism was by no means confined to the government and the Bank. James Titcomb, senior partner of de Zoete & Bevan, whose founder was an eighteenth-century Dutch immigrant,

Who Owns Who in the New London Securities Business
– the line-up at June 30th, 1985

Ultimate owner	Stockbrokers	Jobbers	Banks, discount houses, other	Comment
British clearing banks				
Barclays	de Zoete & Bevan, 5% (March 84)	Wedd Durlacher Mordaunt, 29.9% (March 84)	—	Barclays Merchant Bank is the vehicle for the big clearer's ambitious 3-way merger with one of the two top jobbers and a leading broker. The bank proposes to take its stake in both firms to 75 per cent after the merger. Its new investment banking subsidiary has been christened Barclays de Zoete Wedd. The most ambitious of the clearing banks' moves in the revolution.
National Westminster	Fielding Newson-Smith, 5% (July 84)	Bisgood Bishop, 29.9% (Feb 84)	—	NatWest's County Bank subsidiary is to combine with these two second league firms to pursue first league investment banking ambitions. The clearer plans to take 100 per cent of each when Stock Exchange rules permit.
Midland	W. Greenwell, 29.9% (March 84)	—	—	The stake in Greenwell was acquired by Midland's 60 per cent-owned merchant bank subsidiary Samuel Montagu, which expects to move to 50 per cent ownership of the broker in 1986 and to raise the stake further in due course. The firm is one of the best in the gilt-edged market and boasts the nearest that London has to a market guru: Gordon Pepper, who pioneered techniques of monetary analysis in the days when influential economists argued that money didn't matter.

Royal Bank of Scotland	—		Charterhouse Group, 100%	The Scottish bank looked south to supplement its fee income with this £152m acquisition that includes second rank accepting house Charterhouse Japhet. The seller: Jacob Rothschild.
British merchant banks				
Mercury Securities/ S. G. Warburg	Rowe & Pitman (Aug 84) Mullens (Aug 84)	Akroyd & Smithers, 29.9% (Nov 83)	—	An ambitious merger in which a new holding company will control investment banking interests covering the full range of wholesale services in both domestic and international markets. Charter Consolidated, a British affiliate of the South African mining finance group Anglo American, originally took a 29.9 per cent interest in Rowe & Pitman, but then diluted its interest when confronted with the Mercury-Warburg master plan. City verdict: the bank most likely to — but at what cost?
Kleinwort Benson	Grieveson Grant, 5% (June 84)	Charlesworth & Co, 29.9% (June 84)	—	As well as being a top broker in gilts and equities, Grieveson Grant, for which Kleinwort will pay £44m on completion, has significant international business. Kleinwort has also acquired ACLI Government Securities and part of Virginia Trading in the US, together with broking and market making interests in Australia. Tokyo is another key focus of attention. In pursuing this grand international strategy Kleinwort starts with the advantage of being London's biggest merchant bank.

Ultimate owner	Stockbrokers	Jobbers	Banks, discount houses, other	Comment
Morgan Grenfell	Pember & Boyle, 5% (Oct 84)	Pinchin Denny, 29.9% (April 84)	Target Group, 19.9% (May 1984)	Less obviously ambitious than Warburg and Kleinwort, this other member of the top triumvirate in British merchant banking is nonetheless worth watching. It expects to take 100 per cent of its broker and jobber when rules permit. Pinchin is a medium sized jobber, while Pember & Boyle is one of the biggest brokers in the gilt market. The interest in the Target life assurance and unit trust group is a more surprising move towards retail finance.
Schroders	Helbert Wagg & Co, Anderson Bryce Villiers 29.9% (Aug 84)	—	—	A respected bank that has chosen to grow its own securities operation, Schroders already makes a market in Hong Kong securities in London. International ambitions will be helped by recent divestment of controlling shareholding of US commercial bank subsidiary – the wrong sort of bank for the securities-related business of the 1980s and 1990s and one which inhibited the development of Schroders' investment banking activity in the US.
Hill Samuel	Wood Mackenzie, 29.9% (June 84)	—	—	Wood Mackenzie is one of the success stories of British stockbroking, having moved part of its operations from Edinburgh to London and found favour with the big institutions. Well known for its research and investment performance surveys, the firm's high proportion of non-commission income should stand its new merchant bank partner in good stead when it raises its stake to 100 per cent in the year of the Big Bang.

Bank				
Hambros	Strauss Turnbull, 29.9% (March 84)		—	Strauss Turnbull is best known for its joint Eurobond activities with state-owned French bank Société Générale; Hambros for its lucky escape when its shipping magnate client, the Norwegian Hilmar Reksten, went down. A vital cushion was provided by the bank's highly successful investment in Mark Weinberg's Hambro Life, which was recently sold at a huge profit to BAT Industries.
N. M. Rothschild	Scott Goff Layton, 5% (Dec 84)	Smith Bros, 29.9% (Dec 83)	—	N. M. Rothschild is one of 5 members of the London gold market; Smith Bros are leading jobbers in gold shares. Smith was the buyer of the stake in Scott Goff Layton.
Baring Bros	Henderson Crosthwaite Far East, 79% (May 84)	Wilson & Watford, 29.9% (Dec 84)	—	Henderson Crosthwaite is a useful addition to Baring's growing international fund management business. With restricted access to outside capital Barings is unlikely to take Wilson & Watford, one of the smaller gilt jobbers, too far out of its depth in the new gilt-edged market.
Guinness Peat	—	White & Cheeseman, 29.9% (April 84)	Britannia Arrow, 28% (Jan 85)	After a long period of internal strife Guinness Peat has taken a small plunge into the City Revolution with the purchase of shares in a jobber specializing in foreign bonds and shares. The group owns a small accepting house, Guinness Mahon, and did not receive a rapturous welcome when it bought into Britannia Arrow, which controls another small accepting house, Singer & Friedlander.

Ultimate owner	Stockbrokers	Jobbers	Banks, discount houses, other	Comment
Other British purchasers				
Mercantile House	Laing & Cruickshank, 29.9% (May 84)	—	Alexanders Discount, 100% (Feb 84) Jessel Toynbee & Gillett, 100% (Feb 84)	With origins in money broking Mercantile House has its eye on a full international investment banking role. Laing & Cruickshank is expected to cost £25m on completion of the purchase, while the two discount houses cost £29m and an estimated £21m respectively. Mercantile House already controls US broker Oppenheimer and has significant money broking interests in Japan, where it is looking to expand further. Merchant bank competitors question whether money broking is a solid enough base on which to build such an ambitious securities operation. But as one of the City's more successful exponents of growth by acquisition, Mercantile House should not be dismissed lightly.
Exco International	Galloway & Pearson, 29.9% (May 84)	—	—	Among British financial houses, Exco has one of the larger securities firms in the Far East, in the shape of Wico (formerly W. I. Carr), which is being merged with Galloway & Pearson. Another money broker that has widened its horizons.
Britannia Arrow	Heseltine Moss, 29.9% (Nov 84)	—	Singer & Friedlander, 85% (April 84)	Original link with provincial broker Heseltine Moss unwound – an early casualty of the City Revolution.
Save & Prosper	Montagu Loebl Stanley, 5% (June 85)	—	—	The big unit trust and investment group is to take 100 per cent of the broker's private client business, while hiving off its small institutional broking arm.

114

Edinburgh Financial Trust	Wishart Brodie, 10% (Nov 84)	—	The Scottish end of the revolution.
Lancashire & Yorkshire Investment Co	Battye Wimpenny & Dawson, 25% (Aug 84)	—	Another stake in a provincial broker.
Refuge Assurance	—	Leopold Joseph, 29.9% (May 1984)	Rather surprising link between Manchester-based insurer known for its industrial (ie, door-to-door) life assurance business and a small London merchant bank.
Granville & Co	R. A. Coleman, 29.9% (June 84)	—	Granville, which runs its own over-the-counter market outside the Stock Exchange, buys into a small Welsh broker as a springboard for bigger things.
North American commercial banks			
Citicorp	Vickers da Costa, 29.9% plus 80% of Far Eastern operations (Nov 83) Scrimgeour Kemp-Gee (Sept 84)	Seccombe Marshall & Campion, 98% (Feb 85)	The two broking firms are being merged to form part of a fully integrated investment banking operation backed by £25m of capital; Citicorp will own 100 per cent. Seccombe provides an entrée into the restructured gilt-edged market. An enormously powerful grouping that can be relied on to stay in the race however high the initial cost.
Chase Manhattan	Simon & Coates (Nov 84) Laurie Millbank (Nov 84)	—	Chase plans to take 100 per cent of these two medium sized firms. Laurie Millbank's money broking operation was not included in the purchase – it was snapped up by Exco International.

Ultimate owner	Stockbrokers	Jobbers	Banks, discount houses, other	Comment
Security Pacific	Hoare Govett, 29.9% (June 82)	Charles Pulley, 5% (April 84)	—	Security Pacific intends to increase its holding in Hoare, one of London's biggest brokers with an attractive Far Eastern business, to 80–90 per cent when rules permit and to take full or majority ownership of the small firm of Charles Pulley.
North Carolina National Bank	Panmure Gordon, 29.9% (Dec 84)	—	—	North Carolina National Bank is the only US regional bank to chance its arm on the City Revolution. Though Panmure is not in the big league in equity and gilt dealing, it is known for its strong corporate finance arm.
Royal Bank of Canada	Kitcat & Aitken, 29.9% (Feb 85)	—	—	The stake in Kitcat was bought from Charterhouse J. Rothschild by Orion Royal Bank, the London merchant bank subsidiary of Royal Bank of Canada. There were longstanding links between bank and broker.
Other US financial institutions				
Shearson Lehman-American Express	L. Messel, 5% (July 84)	—	—	Big US financial conglomerate proposes to increase stake to 100 per cent when rules permit. Messel is known for its gilt business and a useful list of corporate finance clients.
Dow Scandia	Savory Milln, 29.9% (Sept 84)	—	Arbuthnot Latham, 100% (Nov 81)	Dow Scandia is 52 per cent owned by the US industrial giant Dow Chemical, with the rest being jointly owned by 3 Scandinavian banks. It proposes to take 100 per cent of Savory when rules permit.

Prudential Bache	PB Securities, Down de Boer and Duckett, 29.9% (July 84)	—	Pru-Bache was set up from scratch by defecting partners from James Capel. A very modest flutter in London for this US life insurance colossus, which has no connection with the British Prudential, but does have connections with Hambros. Prudential plans to move to 100 per cent.
Merrill Lynch	—	A. B. Giles & Cresswell, 29.9% (June 85)	An even more modest flutter by the biggest US broking house, which is buying into one of the smaller jobbers in the gilt-edged market with a view to taking 100 per cent ownership. In announcing the deal Merrill confirmed that it was still more anxious to buy in people than to buy out firms in building up its British securities operations.

Continental European banks and insurers

Deutsche Bank	—	Morgan Grenfell, 4.99% (Nov 84)	A small but intriguing move by one of Europe's most successful universal banks into one of London's more impressive merchant banks.
Union Bank of Switzerland	Phillips & Drew, 29.9% (Nov 84)	—	The big British broker is well known for its large fund management operation as well as its research – both appealing characteristics for Switzerland's biggest banking group.
Credit Suisse	Buckmaster & Moore, 29.9% (Jan 85)	—	Buckmaster is a medium sized broker that ranked Lord Keynes among its clients and once employed pro-Labour economist Lord Balogh (plain Mr at the time) as a researcher. Rather dwarfed by the London operations of Credit Suisse First Boston, the Eurobond offshoot of Switzerland's third largest bank and one of Wall Street's leading investment houses.

Ultimate owner	Stockbrokers	Jobbers	Banks, discount houses, other	Comment
Banque Bruxelles Lambert	Williams de Broe Hill Chaplin, 29.9% (July 84)	—	Henry Ansbacher, 29.9% (May 84)	The Belgian bank, which has close links with US broker Drexel Burnham Lambert, plans to take 66.7 per cent in Williams de Broe and 100 per cent of Ansbacher, a small merchant bank which has seen a shake-up after a loss-making venture into the US firm Laidlaw Adams (now sold).
Skandia	Quilter Goodison, 29.9% (April 84)	—	—	Swedish insurer with existing interests in the British life assurance market buys into medium sized broker headed by Stock Exchange chairman Sir Nicholas Goodison.
Banque Arabe et Internationale d'Investissement (BAII)	Sheppards & Chase, 29.9% (Feb 85)	—	—	A European–Arab consortium bank based in Paris buys into medium sized broker.
Crédit Commercial de France	Laurence Prust (June 85)	—	—	Nationalised French bank plans to take 100 per cent of Prust's institutional and corporate finance business, together with a 28 per cent stake in the quoted Framlington unit trust group, which was hived off from Prust in 1984 but retains close links.

Other international banks

Hongkong and Shanghai Banking Group	James Capel, 29.9% (Aug 84)	—	—	One of London's biggest institutional brokers, Capel also has a sizeable international business with obvious appeal for a former British overseas bank that now controls Marine Midland Bank in the United States. Hong Kong and Shanghai will move to 100 per cent when rules permit.
Australia and New Zealand Banking Group	Capel-Cure Myers, 29.9% (July 84)	—	—	Australia and New Zealand Banking Group recently acquired another former British overseas banking group Grindlays, through which the stake in Capel-Cure was purchased. It plans to own 100 per cent of this medium sized firm which has a significant private client business.

laid particular stress in a television interview on having sought a partner who was 'wholly British'. Many potential mergers were also beset by tax problems.

Who ended up with who

The outcome of the lottery can be seen in the preceding pages. By then every major Stock Exchange firm had been accounted for bar one: Cazenove. Such was this firm's strength in corporate finance, where its ability to distribute shares in even the most indigestible issue was legendary, that splendid isolation remained an option that the firm could afford to keep open even at that late stage. For the rest, all the top five jobbers had been accounted for, as had virtually every other broker with a claim to strong links with the big investment institutions. Around thirty-four of London's eighty-eight broking firms had found potential partners; a majority of those that remained employed fewer than fifty people apiece.

There are no precise estimates of how much the buyers laid out in this extraordinary spending spree. One of the stranger features of the Revolution was that many purchasers felt a stronger obligation to preserve secrecy for the millionaires they were creating in broking and jobbing firms than to reveal to their own shareholders how much they were spending on these very intangible assets. The figures are in any case complicated because part of the consideration for the purchases was in the form of shares. But on the authors' own crude calculations, taking the value of the shares at the time the deals were announced, the ultimate price agreed for the purchase of Stock Exchange firms alone would probably come to not much under £¾ billion. By the time the new owners had pumped fresh capital into their new subsidiaries, the overall tally would comfortably pass the billion mark.

These are undeniably big figures; but they need to be put firmly into an international perspective, since the Bank of England's aim in opening the way to the City Revolution was to project the Stock Exchange's leading firms back to the top of the international securities business. In fact the cream of British stockbroking and stockjobbing had been knocked down for less than a third of the market capitalization of a single American broker, Merrill Lynch, at the time of the Parkinson deal. This is a measure of the uphill task that British securities firms faced under their new, and in many cases cosmopolitan, owners.

5

The Race to the Big Bang

Why was it that so many were prepared to pay so much for so few, in the face of so much uncertainty about the future? That fundamental question about the City Revolution will continue to haunt some of the City's big spenders for the rest of the decade. Once the initial euphoria had worn off, none of the explanations looked quite as convincing as they had done at the time the commitments were entered into.

One reason advanced by many of the buyers of broking and jobbing firms was that they were really taking out an option, or making a down payment, on the right to whatever was likely to be profitable in the new deregulated climate. Much of the thinking was defensive: if one bank had bought a broker or jobber, its competitors had to ask whether they could afford to be without one. While some players in the market had clearly defined, hard-headed objectives, such as the acquisition of experienced management or a strong position in a given area of the securities business, others were swept along without making realistic appraisals of the risks they were running. Financiers have always been prey to fashion and tend to move in herds. The herdlike behaviour was accentuated on this occasion because it was provoked by sudden regulatory change. But for a more detailed explanation of the buyers' motives, it is necessary to take a closer look at the thinking of some of the leading banks, including those already touched on in Chapter 4.

The thinking at Barclays

The strategy that Barclays evolved under Andrew Buxton and Lord Camoys, the two youngest members of Barclays main board, was essentially international. Its aim was to give corporate clients a full range of services in the international capital markets by establishing a strong presence in New York and Tokyo. But the starting point was London; and by March 1984 Barclays had bought a 29.9 per cent interest in one of the two biggest jobbing firms, Wedd Durlacher Mordaunt, for £29.9 million, and a 5 per cent interest in a major broker, de Zoete & Bevan for £2.5 million. Together this valued the two firms at £150 million. A year later the bank had concluded that it would need to put in further capital to take its total investment to £200 million or more to get the new international securities and investment banking group off the ground. This was needed to support a comprehensive wholesale banking operation, which was to take in basic lending and market making in a range of instruments including gilt-edged securities and Eurobonds, new forms of commercial paper such as note issuance facilities, international and domestic equities, together with primary dealing in the United States government bond market. A heavy initial investment in computers was also called for. Barclays agreed to restrict its ultimate shareholding in these acquisitions to 75 per cent in order to leave the existing partners with a continuing commercial interest in the business.

As well as being involved in corporate finance Barclays proposed to develop its international fund management activities both in the United States and in Japan, where in 1985 it applied for a licence to run a trust bank. Japan's trust banks shared with the insurance companies a lucrative monopoly of the management of domestic pension funds. The big British bank was also keen to develop de Zoete's international broking and research activities with a view to capitalizing on the huge potential investment flow both in and out of Tokyo. And it was on the lookout for corporate clients that were likely candidates to issue securities on the international markets. Then, at a much later stage, there was the possibility of distributing shares through the branch network to personal customers in Britain. Barclays was thus moving closer to the continental model of the 'universal' bank offering a full range of financial services. To round off its gameplan it brought in a new chairman for its investment banking subsidiary Barclays de Zoete Wedd in the shape of Martin Jacomb, previously a vice-chairman of Kleinwort Benson. Jacomb, one of the most respected merchant bankers in the City, played a prominent role on several of the City's self-regulatory committees. He immediately became a force to be reckoned with as a deputy chairman on the main board of a bank that had hitherto given the top jobs to members of the original banking families that combined to form the group.

This was an intensely ambitious programme, but one that Barclays felt it had little option but to pursue. It was a defensive move, in that the bank would not have been able to offer a proper service to its big corporate clients in the new era without embarking on its investment. But the bank also saw opportunities. Lord Camoys, the chief executive in charge of day-to-day management, told the authors that he expected Barclays de Zoete Wedd to be making at least £50 million before tax within five years, or two to three times as much as the firms had made when they were separate.

For the group the investment of £200 million was well within the bounds of prudence in relation to a capital base of £2.6 billion, provided that the bank was able to establish tight control over the risks inherent in market making and in integrating all the activities. Barclays was nonetheless reckoned to have spent more than £100 million in cash on goodwill alone, of which around four-fifths related to Wedd Durlacher. Any difficulty in seeing the merger through would still lead to embarrassment.

Warburg's grand strategy

At Warburg the choices looked rather different. There was little interest at the bank in retail finance and some scepticism about the ease with which wholesale and retail operations could be successfully integrated. The question was more one of whether to offer a full, integrated range of merchant banking services or to pursue a speciality in a particular area of the market. Since Warburg had always been interested in providing a broad service to international users and suppliers of capital, its past pointed firmly towards an integrated approach rather than a policy based on exploiting specialist niches.

In pursuit of this grand strategy, Warburg's parent company, Mercury Securities, snapped up 29.9 per cent of the share capital of one of Britain's two biggest jobbers, Akroyd & Smithers, for nearly £41 million in cash. Shortly after this deal Akroyd and Rowe & Pitman, one of the biggest brokers, announced that they proposed to combine their international equity-related research, distribution and trading activities in a joint venture. It was not long before the partners of Rowe & Pitman had decided to throw in their lot with Warburg. All saw the logic of combining forces immediately in the attempt to establish a stronger position in twenty-four-hour trading of equities across the globe. Warburg was strong in international bond markets but weak in equities because it had lacked the freedom to operate in its own home base. Rowe & Pitman's inability to make markets in the United States meant that US investors were tempted to use its services without giving it commensurate orders in return. Akroyd's US operations had been hampered by an inadequate flow of orders. It was hoped that a merger would help to make good all those shortcomings. Over the longer run there was considerable scope for integrating the firms' corporate finance activities. The combination also looked an exceptionally powerful one in terms of market making and broking in the domestic equity and gilt-edged markets after the Big Bang.

This acquisitive strategy was rounded off by the purchase of one of the oldest and most venerable broking firms in the market, Mullens. Since 1786 Mullens had had the distinction of sporting a senior partner who was, to give him his full title, Broker to the Commissioners for the Reduction of the National Debt. The government broker's job was to act on behalf of the Authorities (the City's rather Kafkaesque name for the Bank and the Treasury) in the gilt-edged market. He also advised the Bank of England on other Stock Exchange matters. Far from presiding over a reduction in the national debt the GB, as he is known in the market, had profited in the 1970s from an explosion of debt which he and his predecessors had done well to persuade investors to absorb.

But now the government broker, Nigel Althaus, was to be

taken into the Bank of England on the introduction of a new gilt-edged dealing system. And while Mullens claimed to derive the greater part of its revenues from non-governmental business, it was not one of the more attractive brides on the marriage market. It is widely known in the City that what really persuaded Warburg to take Mullens aboard was a powerful nudge from the Bank, on whose Court Warburg's chairman, David Scholey, sat. After nearly two hundred years of loyal service to the Bank, in which its special relationship imposed heavy constraints on the expansion of its non-official business, Mullens could not be left on the sidelines. Warburg's graceful intervention spared the Bank embarrassment and provided Mullens' partners with paper valued at the time at £8.6 million for a firm that had made profits of £1.5 million in its last full year.

Merger risks and non-risks

Warburg's competitors argued that this comprehensive merger of a merchant bank, two brokers and a jobber involved an investment in goodwill well in excess of £100 million and amounted to what Americans refer to as 'betting the bank' – that is, risking the future of the whole business on one throw of the dice. Yet this is probably the wrong way to describe the nature of the risk. To start with, only £41 million of cash was laid out on the merger, and all of that sum was retained in the enlarged firm to swell the capital. The remaining consideration for the interest in Akroyd, Rowe & Pitman and Mullens was in the form of shares and stock in Warburg's parent, Mercury Securities. No goodwill was likely to find its way into the balance sheet. The terms of the deal did, however, point to a fair amount of risk, as the underlying figures indicated.

In effect the shareholders of Mercury Securities were exchanging 100 per cent ownership of their existing company for just short of 59 per cent of the new, merged conglomerate in which the former owners of the three Stock Exchange firms were to have the remaining 41 per cent. The rise in net asset value from £170 million to £246 million on the merger (figures which exclude Warburg's hidden reserves) was not enough to compensate Mercury shareholders for the dilution in their share of those assets. And there were big question marks over the ability of the newly acquired firms to sustain the level of profitability they were enjoying at the time of the merger, since those profits had not only been earned in bull market conditions, but constituted the last monopolistic fruits of the fixed-commission system.

The risk can be seen more directly by looking at the dynamics of a single firm in the merger. At the time when the formal documents announcing full details of the terms were published, in October 1984, the price paid for Rowe & Pitman was equivalent to £42.5 million. The last recorded profit, on the accounting basis that would apply after the merger, amounted to £6.6 million. Assuming a standard tax charge, Mercury was paying thirteen times the last year's exceptionally buoyant earnings. Looked at another way, Mercury was buying £9.6 million of hard assets and £32.9 million of goodwill. The goodwill represented the premium Mercury was prepared to pay to acquire the skills, knowledge and client contacts of the individuals who comprised the broking firm. What no one knew for certain was how much those advantages would count for after the Big Bang; or, indeed, whether the individuals concerned would stay with the enlarged company.

These points could equally have been made of Barclays' acquisitions (or almost any of the others that took place in 1983 and 1984). But in Warburg's case there was a further consideration. Did the new grouping have enough capital to support its international aspirations? Much of the quarter of a billion of capital in the enlarged balance sheet was already committed to existing banking activities. As for the combined enterprise's ability to exploit the opportunities for cross-selling services and extracting synergy from the different components of the group, it was all heavily dependent on a regulatory structure whose details had yet to be revealed by the government. Equally important, it was anyone's guess how clients of the various firms would react to potential conflicts of interest. Warburg intended to keep the enlarged investment management activities in separate companies within the group, kept apart by so-called Chinese Walls. These consisted of self-imposed barriers to the exchange of price-sensitive information between one part of the business and another.[1]

With its experience of providing an integrated capital-raising service in the Euromarkets Warburg nonetheless looked better equipped than many more heavily capitalized competitors to take on these risks. And it carried some good wishes with it. The verdict of one competitor was that Warburg had better management and better ingredients in its new grouping than most. 'If they can't make a good cake out of that,' he said, 'it will be awful for the rest of the industry when the thing doesn't succeed.'

The gospel according to Citicorp

In terms of sheer scope, perhaps the most ambitious of the investment banking operations that emerged in 1984 was the one outlined by Citicorp. The background to the American giant's moves in Britain was that the bank had been forced to reformulate its international strategy after Mexico announced in 1982 that it was unable to meet its debts. Having been one of the most active lenders to Latin America and other Third World countries in the period of petrodollar recycling, Citicorp concluded that it had neglected markets in the developed world. A further change in emphasis was signalled in 1984 by the arrival of a new chairman. The successor to Walt Wriston, who had been a vociferous apologist for the rush into Latin America, was the head of the bank's retail operations, John Reed. Retail banking had traditionally played Cinderella to the more glamorous corporate business. It was also a predominantly domestic activity. Yet Reed, with a reputation as a young whizz-kid with a fascination for new technology, had taken the unusual step of building an international retail strategy.

---

[1] A full definition given in the government's Licensed Dealers (Conduct of Business) Rules 1983 runs as follows: 'A Chinese Wall means an established arrangement whereby information known to persons in one part of a business is not available (directly or indirectly) to those involved in another part of the business and it is accepted that in each of the parts of the business so divided decisions will be taken without reference to any interest which any other such part of any person in any part of the business may have in the matter.'

Enthusiasm in New York for the British operations of the bank had waned when Labour was in power between 1974 and 1979. But after the Mexican crisis Citicorp's top management saw Mrs Thatcher's Britain in a new light. The other main focus of its attention was the Far East, where it was particularly anxious to make inroads into Japan. Paradoxically, the US bank's first move in the City Revolution had little to do with what the Revolution was initially all about. It started to negotiate its 29.9 per cent stake in Vickers da Costa before Cecil Parkinson's announcement because it was attracted by the firm's operations in the Far East, which constituted the greater part of its business. When the process of deregulation set in, the Americans suddenly realized that Britain had, in the words of Citibank's Kent Price, 'become a very interesting crucible in which to develop a broader franchise than in the United States'. Or, to put it another way, London was turning into the adventure playground of the international financial system, in which an American bank could experiment with all the different combinations of financial services that were prohibited in the tighter regulatory climate back home.

Vickers, with its position in securities trading in Japan and a presence in Hong Kong and Switzerland, fitted neatly into plans to undertake global investment banking in what is now called the 'golden triangle' of New York, London and Tokyo. But it was not a particularly significant broker in the London market. So Citicorp turned to Scrimgeour, Kemp-Gee, reckoned to be one of the most profitable of all the broking firms in London. As well as having a lucrative business in equities, Scrimgeour was no laggard in the gilt-edged market; and its information technology systems were reckoned to be more advanced than any other British broker's.

Scrimgeour's partners had brought in Baring Brothers to sort out the suitors, who included such heavyweight British contenders as National Westminster Bank. But the firm finally opted for Citicorp because of its size and staying power. At close to £50 million the price, which was not publicly disclosed, was below the highest offer. But the sellers were convinced that, when it came to a price war after the Big Bang, the aggressive American bank was one of the few that could afford to back the firm all the way through the bad times to the profitable new dawn that they expected would follow.

To round off the picture Citicorp spent £7 million buying one of the smallest discount houses, Seccombe Marshall & Campion. Seccombe had long acted as the Bank of England's eyes and ears in the discount market, and its sale represented a historic step towards the liberalization of one of the City's most esoteric banking fraternities. Since Seccombe was another loyal servant, like Mullens, it is tempting to speculate that Citicorp was required to offer a *douceur* to the Old Lady in exchange for access to the club.

The underlying thinking in all this was that Citicorp itself had a good list of corporate customers (though one that it intended to enhance) from which to promote the issue of securities. Scrimgeour, Kemp-Gee and Vickers would bring capability in underwriting, distribution and research. Seccombe, meantime, was to bring trading skills, notably in the gilt-edged market. Kent Price was not unduly concerned at the lack of a jobbing firm in the line-up because Citicorp had never had any problems in market making: taking risks was very much part of the bank's corporate culture.

With a capital of $6½ billion and total assets of $150 billion Citicorp undeniably did have the muscle to become one of the most formidable investment banking operations in London. The unusual feature of its plans, which were expected to take some five years to implement in full, was that they envisaged the total integration of its wholesale and retail business. At the time of the British Telecom issue the bank asked itself whether it would be possible to organize and underwrite the issue of British Telecom shares and then distribute them along a chain running through Scrimgeour, Kemp-Gee to the holders of Diners' Club cards, in which Citicorp was a joint owner with National Westminster. This proved impracticable at the time. But Citicorp had every intention of selling stocks in due course, through the medium of an integrated investment banking operation direct to private investors who held its plastic cards. The cards were also intended to provide a vehicle for the sale of insurance products, since Citicorp's move towards conglomeration included both life assurance and insurance broking companies in the United Kingdom which already worked in tandem with its retail branches around the country.

Mixed motives in more marriages

Other American participants were similarly tempted by the freedoms offered by London from tough barriers between commercial banking and investment banking which had been interposed by the Glass-Steagall Act in the United States. But they were also responding to a harsher competitive climate at home. Security Pacific became the first to take a 29.9 per cent stake in a leading broker, Hoare, Govett, partly because, like other US banks, it had seen the margins on its basic lending business shrink and was anxious to build up its fee income. Will Richeson, head of Security Pacific's capital markets division in Los Angeles, told the authors that his company had been attracted by Hoare's research in Far Eastern markets as well as its position in London. The Californian group, he said, was keen to become 'a sizeable factor' in underwriting, broking and research in the United States, London and Far Eastern markets.

The same search for worldwide fee income was a high priority for commercial banks of whatever nationality. It was certainly true of Chase Manhattan, the ultimate purchaser of stakes in Simon & Coates and Laurie Millbank, and Hongkong and Shanghai Banking Corporation, which bought into James Capel, one of the oldest and biggest firms on the Exchange. Union Bank of Switzerland felt that it could not afford to be without a London-based securities operation and took the opportunity of its purchase of a stake in Phillips & Drew to castigate the Swiss authorities for making their domestic fiscal climate inhospitable to international operations.

As for the British clearing banks, none were prepared to embark on commitments of the scale undertaken by Barclays. But National Westminster's merchant banking subsidiary, County Bank, shared the same global aspirations and bought into brokers Fielding Newson-Smith, together with the jobbing firm of Bisgood Bishop. Midland stopped short at the purchase of Greenwell. And Lloyds, interestingly, refrained from joining the throng, arguing that the risks in these acquisitions were disproportionate to the likely rewards and that it made more sense to do the job in-house, with the additional help of new recruits from outside. Yet it lacked a merchant bank subsidiary of comparable significance to the other three on which to build, having taken a similarly aloof view of earlier clearing bank moves to set up half-autonomous merchant bank subsidiaries.

For the independent British merchant banks the choices were much more difficult because a worldwide presence was not easily reconciled with slender capital resources. The top end of the accepting houses committee was dominated by a triumvirate of Kleinwort Benson, Morgan Grenfell and S. G. Warburg. The biggest of them, Kleinwort, did succeed in purchasing a US primary bond dealer, ACLI Government Securities, as well as committing itself to the £44 million purchase of Grieveson, Grant, along with the small jobbing firm of Charlesworth. Its competitors wondered how easily it would control the risks in the United States where small bond dealers had been known to crash, leaving behind what were – by British standards – staggeringly large losses. Even Kleinwort, which considered it had enough experience of market making in-house to be able to cope, had to admit that it had a long way to go before it could be considered a significant force in North America.

Morgan Grenfell, 24 per cent of whose shares were owned by insurance broker Willis Faber, bought into Pinchin Denny, one of the big five jobbers, and Pember & Boyle, a leading broker in the gilt-edged market. It also brought in a new outside shareholder with enormous financial resources and competence in universal banking, West Germany's Deutsche Bank. In contrast Schroders chose to grow from within by resurrecting the old broking name of Helbert Wagg. This new firm, in which Schroders held 29.9 per cent, was to complement Schroders existing international operations in Europe and the Far East. Others, however, were precluded from setting up new firms because the Stock Exchange moved in July 1984 to reinforce its residual monopoly in relation to the membership by prohibiting outsiders from holding more than 10 per cent of newly established firms until after the Big Bang. Apart from Schroders only Pru-Bache, the big US insurance and broking conglomerate, succeeded in slipping through the net.

Outside the accepting houses' ranks the most plausible global investment banker was Mercantile House, which committed around £75 million in total to brokers Laing & Cruickshank and to two discount houses, Jessel Toynbee & Gillett and Alexanders Discount. With the US firm of Oppenheimer under its belt Mercantile was keen to expand into Japan. The rest of the field, meantime, nurtured more modest aspirations. Of the larger accepting houses Hill Samuel, which linked up with the aggressive, information technology-conscious Scottish firm of Wood Mackenzie, chose to play down its international aspirations. And family-controlled banks such as N. M. Rothschild, Baring Brothers and Hambros pursued less ambitious niche strategies. One, Lazard Brothers, a subsidiary of Lord Cowdray's S. Pearson empire which owns a collection of interests ranging from Château Latour to Madame Tussaud's and the *Financial Times*, let it be known that it thought the prices being paid for brokers and jobbers nonsensical. It simply chose to strengthen existing links with Lazard Frères in Paris and New York. Then, at the rear, came a rag-tag-and-bobtail army of foreigners, insurers, fund managers and rank outsiders on whom the City Revolution exerted a compulsive fascination. And finally, in a category all his own, came Jacob Rothschild.

Second thoughts of a self-confessed revolutionary

Rothschild had been one of the earliest in the field with his purchase of a 29.9 per cent stake in brokers Kitcat & Aitken. He had gone on to buy Charterhouse Group, which owned one of the second-rank accepting houses, Charterhouse Japhet. On the international stage he had made his big move into the United States with the acquisition of 50 per cent of L. F. Rothschild, Unterberg, Towbin and forged links with Nikko Securities of Japan to handle international investments for US pension funds. This left him with an empire that struck many analysts as less than convincing. On the positive side it contained most of the components of a global investment banking house; yet it could equally be regarded as a ragbag of diverse interests run by an entrepreneurial financier whose formidable talents were not of a kind to bring about the successful integration of these rapidly assembled acquisitions.

Rothschild promptly put a new complexion on the matter by seeking a merger with Mark Weinberg's highly successful direct selling insurance and financial group Hambro Life. In April 1984 Charterhouse J. Rothschild, as his group was then called, announced that it was to buy nearly 25 per cent of Hambro Life from the Hambros banking group for shares and cash. In the press release the two men were quoted as saying that the deal constituted 'an engagement between CJR and Hambro Life which we hope and trust will lead to a marriage between the two companies'. They believed that a merger would create a British-based group with the financial strength and management resources to compete with the major American and Japanese houses.

The marriage never came about. For while there was some superficial logic in putting together Hambro Life's earning power with Charterhouse J. Rothschild's assets, the scope for synergy was far less than had been assumed at first sight. The Rothschild interests were predominantly wholesale, whereas the Hambro Life business was retail from top to toe. When it came to examining the potential benefits from integration this combination turned out to be singularly unfruitful for the profits of the combined group. And the stock market took a strong dislike to the whole idea. Both Rothschild and Weinberg were forced to concede that, if they merged, the sum of the enlarged group would be valued at less than the parts.

Soon after the full-scale merger was called off Hambro Life found a new partner in BAT Industries, which paid a handsome £664 million dowry for a company with assets of little more than £100 million. The sale left Weinberg with £8–9 million for his personal stake in the business and made many members of his sales force, who held many of the shares, very rich. And Jacob Rothschild had second thoughts, as he took a profit on his shares, about the whole revolution. It was not just with Hambro Life that he was up against problems of integration: melding together the wholesale businesses in his empire was also problematical. The City was rife with rumours of mutiny at Charterhouse, where the old guard was having difficulty adapting to Rothschild's freewheeling style of operation. In the event Baring Brothers, who acted as advisers to the

Royal Bank of Scotland, read the signs right and approached Rothschild with a view to buying the accepting house for its client. A deal was quickly struck. Later Rothschild shed his stake in Kitcat & Aitken to Orion Royal Bank, an offshoot of the Royal Bank of Canada. And the deal with Nikko Securities was unwound within a year of its inception. All in all Rothschild had accumulated a cash mountain of £600 million whose future disposition became a subject of constant speculation in the financial press.

To the City there was something faintly shocking about the way in which Jacob Rothschild spat out these recent acquisitions in short order, especially in the case of Charterhouse, which was a member of one of the City's oldest clubs. It also raised questions for his institutional backers, who were left to ponder what kind of animal they had invested their money in. The answer was that Jacob Rothschild, for all his early revolutionary rhetoric, was first and last a dealmaker. He recognised that the component parts of his new financial empire were simply not of adequate quality to project him into the top league of international investment banking. First-hand experience of putting together an international financial conglomerate had no doubt taught him that more money could be made from the revolution by sitting on the sidelines watching for opportunities to redeploy his £600 million as longer-lived revolutionaries struggled to pull all the disparate pieces together.

6

Fall-out

If Jacob Rothschild had been the only absentee from the party, those who were pumping more than £1 billion into London's new securities business would have had little to worry about. Unhappily for them some of the most powerful players chose not to join the melee – notably the big American investment and brokerage houses. The fact that Merrill Lynch failed to participate in the buying spree for British brokers left some of the City's new hybrids with the uncomfortable feeling that what they were witnessing was a little like Macbeth without the lady – yet they knew that this crucial omission would unquestionably be made good, for want of a better phrase, after the Big Bang. No one drew consolation from Merrill's belated decision in mid-1985 to buy the small gilt-edged jobbing firm of A. B. Giles & Cresswell (in which it is tempting once again to see the hand of the Bank of England). The American giant, like its opposite number in commercial banking, Citicorp, was one of the few international houses that had the ability to run an integrated wholesale and retail financial operation. Its claim to be regarded as the most dangerous competitor in the London securities business was enhanced when it recruited one of the Eurobond market's seasoned veterans, Stanislas Yassukovich, to become chairman of Merrill Lynch Europe. Yassukovich, who came from European Banking Co., a consortium of seven European banks including Britain's Midland Bank, let all concerned know that he had a mandate to build up a big position in the newly liberalized domestic markets in the Square Mile.

All the other big US investment houses in London, though open to friendly conversation, chose not to spend their petty cash on the acquisition of British firms. Instead they dipped into the labour market for the whole range of stock market skills running from research to market making. This indicated that London was importing a phenomenon that had characterized Wall Street since the second half of the 1970s. In the tough competitive climate that had followed the abolition of minimum commissions on the New York Stock Exchange in 1975 a marked shift in the balance of power from corporations to individuals had been noted. Wall Streeters became aware that some of the best-known investment houses often owed their continuing (or new) prominence to a handful of individuals. Deregulation in the British stock market might have been expected to have the same result over a period of time, but the much more comprehensive nature of the upheaval in London accelerated the process because everyone on the Stock Exchange was forced to make a hard-headed appraisal of their own market value in the eighteen months that followed the Parkinson deal. The resulting labour mobility spawned a whole new vocabulary of mixed metaphors ranging from the mobile marzipan layer to the golden handcuff and the golden hello.

The mobile unrewarded

The marzipan layer consisted of people just below the level of partnership who were deprived of the icing on the cake when the bidders struck their deals with the existing partnership, but provided much of the expertise on which the goodwill was based. A number of merchant bank acquisitions were short-sighted, in that they offered little incentive to the marzipan layer to stay put; the partners, meantime, could rest content in the knowledge that even if they were immobilized by golden handcuffs – that is, an incentive to sit tight because their payoff would be cut if they left in less than three to five years – their retirement would be comfortable regardless of the firm's fortunes after the Big Bang. In many cases the partners became employees with little real incentive of the kind they had previously enjoyed to build up the business. The marzipan layer, meantime, was, as the press headlines put it, on the move; and since there were numerous new entrants in the market searching for scarce broking and market-making skills, many started to ask potential employers for a 'golden hello', which amounted to no more than a down payment for services as yet unrendered.

Even those who had been munificently rewarded were sometimes tempted to incur the penalty involved in departure on the basis that another firm offered more challenging opportunities, more capital to support a dealing operation or simply a more congenial environment. By the middle of 1985 some serious defections had taken place and the trade was very much a two-way street. Barclays was badly shaken, for example, when Wedd Durlacher lost a team of eight top dealers to Kleinwort Benson, including two senior partners who had been involved in negotiating the original link with Barclays. The golden handcuffs proved ineffective when set against Kleinwort's golden hello. Another of Wedd's top partners left to set up a gilt-edged dealing operation at Merrill Lynch while its European equity trading team defected to brokers Savory Milln. On the broking side de Zoete & Bevan poached the whole Far Eastern section of Lawrence Prust and seduced a much respected Japanese expert from Grieveson, Grant to set up a new Tokyo office. With so much attention devoted to the new international market in equities, the trade was particularly active in Far Eastern and continental European specialists. Warburg was no more fortunate since Rowe & Pitman was another to suffer from, *inter alia*, the defection of its Japanese team. It did, however, succeed in winning over a top expert in the Japanese market from Merrill Lynch.

A clash of cultures

A constant subject of conversation in the Square Mile in 1984 was culture shock. 'Culture' was the management consultant's vogue word for the feel and management style of an organization. Few things contrasted more sharply than the respective cultures of commercial banks, merchant banks, brokers and jobbers. Commercial banks and merchant banks tended to be budget-conscious, risk-averse and, in another management consultant's phrase, committee-driven. Within that constellation merchant bankers tended to see clearing bankers as the civil servants, while merchant banks stood for private sector dynamism. Stockbroking culture was more sales-oriented: most brokers lived a short-term existence in a world dominated by the rhythm of the two-week Stock Exchange account. This fact, together with the cumbersome ownership structure – the unlimited liability partnership – made it difficult for brokers to develop what the average quoted company would regard as depth of management or adequate financial and strategic planning. Jobbers were instinctive gamblers, whose job had more in common with a racecourse bookie's than a broker's. They were also alleged to be less cultured, in the general sense, than all the others.

Not surprisingly, the cultures clashed when the attempt was made to integrate the separate businesses into one. The plethora of committees formed by Barclays to implement its plans for Barclays de Zoete Wedd became a City talking point. Rumours abounded of strains at Warburg, where the gentlemanly English style of Rowe & Pitman and Mullens was having to be accommodated within one of the City's more cosmopolitan banks with a notoriously spartan culture. Warburg was famous for running two lunchtime sittings for entertaining clients, at which beer and water were usually served. The clashes were exacerbated by problems of remuneration. While merchant bankers often had weighty social aspirations, their remuneration was very small beside that of the biggest broking firms in a good year.

Some banks, such as Barclays, tried to get round the problem by limiting their stake in the new investment conglomerate to 75–80 per cent in order to give the brokers and jobbers a continuing interest in the profitability of the firm. In contrast Mercury-Warburg insisted on 100 per cent ownership on the ground that anything else was potentially disastrous: a recalcitrant minority, with all the attendant conflicts of interest, could turn management of an integrated firm into a nightmare. As for jobbers, it was said that the wives were being instructed to bring their jewels out of their safe deposit boxes so that bankers would be left in no doubt, over the dinner table, as to the style of life that the jobbing fraternity took for granted.

Merchant bankers were prone to insecurities of their own.

Some were conscious that the growing emphasis on securities trading in the big investment houses on Wall Street had caused a shift in the balance of power away from the old-style corporate financier. The lesson had been rammed home by an infamous board room putsch at Lehman Brothers in New York, where the highly respected Pete Peterson, who had had a long and distinguished career at the firm, had been unceremoniously ousted from the top job by a man who stood for all the new and abrasive values of the dealing room, Lewis Glucksman.

The biggest threat to the new banking and securities firms, however, came from the possibility that the Stock Exchange would lose much of its more lucrative business before the Big Bang took place. This was not simply because American houses were dealing increasingly in British shares such as ICI, Glaxo and British Telecom outside the Stock Exchange. Robert Fleming, a member of the accepting houses committee, started in late 1984 to make a market of its own in British electrical shares in direct competition with the Stock Exchange.

Fleming takes on the Exchange

Fleming's market-making activities in London typified the informal way in which many merchant banks' business strategies evolved, and are worth tracing not just because of their impact on the revolution, but because of the light they throw on London's position in international securities markets. Best known for its investment management activities and its controlling interest in the Save and Prosper unit trust group, the bank had a small sideline in the 1960s and 1970s making a market in premium dollars, the scarce pool of currency available for the purchase of foreign assets when exchange controls were still in force. When exchange controls were lifted, Fleming had to decide what to do with the dealers who were left without a function. Its small trading team did some research on potential new areas of activity; and it was natural that they should look at Far Eastern securities since Fleming had a successful 50/50 joint venture with Hong Kong-based Jardine Matheson, which undertook merchant banking and stockbroking in Japan, Hong Kong and Singapore. The traders came back with the suggestion that there was an obvious gap in the market in Japanese convertible stocks – that is, fixed-interest debt securities which carried the ultimate right to convert into equity shares in the company concerned. They started to make a market in convertibles and also in Japanese bonds with attached warrants, which constituted a right to subscribe for equity shares of the company on agreed terms at some future date.

Fleming soon became a leading London dealer in these securities and in due course started to trade in the underlying bonds and equities. At the same time the bank put its Far Eastern expertise in broking to good use in London: it advised institutional investment clients on the purchase of Far Eastern Securities and executed the transactions on their behalf. In effect, the bank was acting as a broker, a jobber and an investment manager in the international markets. Yet it was precluded from membership of the Stock Exchange. When the revolution came, Fleming was disinclined to pay out large sums for the goodwill of existing firms. And following the halving of stamp duty in the 1984 budget, it noted that the disincentive to make a market outside the Stock Exchange (where jobbers enjoyed exemption from stamp duty) had been greatly reduced. As a family-dominated bank, Fleming lacked the capital resources to make a market in all the leading British stocks and shares. So it decided to make a market in twenty or so leading electrical shares, on the ground that international interest in British companies such as British Telecom, Plessey, STC and Racal was likely to be high.

Unlike many of the US investment houses making markets outside the Stock Exchange, Fleming committed itself to making two-way prices in fair weather and foul. According to Fleming's director David Pearson, the bank was not worried about making losses initially, because they represented a sounder investment in the future than would an expensive purchase of goodwill in an existing firm. The idea was to build up experience in market making, researching and distributing British stocks and shares and, by cutting out the broker, to establish a fair-sized market share. The subtlety of the scheme lay in the fact that there was nothing that the Stock Exchange's brokers and jobbers could do, as Fleming built up a clientele at their expense, until the Big Bang took place.

Fleming was thus a thorn in the Stock Exchange's side and the Council was greatly irritated that the Bank of England raised no objection. The Bank's decision to approve the Fleming move was a signal that the Old Lady had come a long way from its former tolerance of monopolies and cartels. But it had not gone the whole way because the competition was carefully managed. Fleming was encouraged by the Bank to make a public announcement that it intended to join the Stock Exchange when rules permitted (unless, of course, the terms proved to be prohibitively expensive). The merchant bank also agreed with the jobbers that it would not try to undercut their spreads – the margin between the buying and selling price – since it was making use of the Stock Exchange both to acquire shares and to unwind its positions. And it showed its rules governing the handling of conflicts of interest to the Bank of England for approval. Its own discretionary investment clients were given a choice of whether or not to allow Fleming's investment managers to put business in their own market makers' direction; if they gave the go-ahead, it was on the understanding that the fund managers would only deal in-house if it provided the best terms available. Ironically, Fleming's own huge investment subsidiary, Save and Prosper, was unable to deal directly with the Fleming market makers because its trust deeds required it to deal only through the Stock Exchange.

By early 1985 Fleming was reckoned to have won anything up to 10–15 per cent of the market in electrical shares. As well as extending the number of companies in which it dealt to around thirty, it talked of doing the same with pharmaceutical shares. In some companies it was able to deal in larger sums than on the Stock Exchange itself. Even merchant bank competitors, including S. G. Warburg, were prepared to trade through it to reduce dealing costs and gain experience of operating under dual capacity conditions. In 1985 Fleming's example was followed by European Banking Company, which announced that it was to start making a market in chemical and pharmaceutical shares. Other outsiders talked to the Bank of England about making markets in British equities.

Not unnaturally, all those financial institutions that had bought into Stock Exchange firms were angry and began to lobby both the Bank of England and the Department of Trade, demanding that a stop be put to the activity outside the market. All they got in return was a commitment from the government to look into the question. In spring 1985 the Bank of England carried out a survey of institutional investors which suggested that the problem had been greatly exaggerated, and so no immediate action was taken. But the authorities did recognize that the problem was likely to become worse as the Big Bang crept up. So they began to give serious consideration, at least in private, to bringing forward the date of the Big Bang. Yet this posed enormous problems for the Stock Exchange.

Towards a screen-based dealing system

Throughout 1984 the Stock Exchange was involved in protracted consultations with its members over a new dealing system to cope with the brave new world ushered in by the abolition of minimum commissions. It opted for a system of competing market makers, in which members could decide whether they wanted to act as agent, principal or both. The scheme was modelled on NASDAQ's system in the US over-the-counter market and was screen-based: dealers could decide for themselves whether to transact their business on or off the trading floor. The basic rules required market makers to maintain two-way prices, that is to say, to be prepared to deal continuously, come fair weather or foul, on a new Stock Exchange automated quotations system to be known as SEAQ; broker–dealers were required to go to the market maker offering the best price, unless they could deal at a more advantageous price for their client by dealing as principals or by matching business directly between clients. All transactions had to be reported immediately to the central market authority and a system of electronic surveillance would allow the policing of the best execution rule, which required broker–dealers to go for the best price, by permitting the authorities to reconstruct the pattern of quotations in the market at any given moment so that they could be examined in detail.

One of the many advantages of the system was that it was

ideally suited to international twenty-four-hour trading. But it represented a huge leap for the Exchange – far greater than anything that had been attempted, for example, on the New York Stock Exchange. The London Exchange's chairman, Sir Nicholas Goodison, was widely admired both in the Bank and in the City at large for the skill with which he pushed through reforms to which there was initially considerable resistance among the membership. But there were limits to what he could do to cope with the technical problems of the new system: the computer people were fully stretched to meet the October 1986 deadlines proposed for the Big Bang. If the deadline was brought forward before the new computer systems were in place, investor protection would be rudimentary, so leaving the way open to scandals.

The waters were further muddied by a fresh challenge to the exchange from Reuters, which declared its intention of setting up an electronic stock market dealing system in London. The system, known as Instinet, had long been in use in the United States. Reuters, which had the marketing rights outside the United States, was to all intents and purposes telling the Stock Exchange that if it continued to develop its own dealing system, Instinet would be used to make a market in leading British shares in competition with the Exchange. Since it could be introduced long before the Big Bang there was scope, as with Robert Fleming, for a further loss of business to the Exchange. So the Exchange was obliged to consider some form of cooperation with Reuters in introducing its new dealing system.

In one respect, at least, Fleming and Reuters were doing the Stock Exchange Council a service. For by demonstrating that the Exchange no longer enjoyed a monopoly right to investors' business in equities, it helped to strengthen Sir Nicholas Goodison's hand in selling his package of reforms to the more recalcitrant members of the Exchange before they voted on 4 June 1985. While it may be too Machiavellian to assume that Fleming was put up to it by the Bank, the authorities were privately delighted at the demonstration effect of the accepting house's market-making activity.

The coup of the century

For those who had spent £¾ billion mainly on goodwill in broking and jobbing firms it was another matter. Firms such as Mercury Securities and Mercantile House, for whom the revolution was very significant in relation to their whole business, had seen their share prices fall sharply: the market's verdict on the whole thing was damning. Investors, including the fund management arms of many of the merchant banks that had bought into brokers and jobbers, were saying that the purchasers had grossly overpaid for what they had got. Most outside observers concurred. Members of the Stock Exchange's larger firms had almost certainly pulled off one of the greatest financial coups of the century: they had persuaded some of the most sophisticated financiers in the world to stump up premium prices that reflected inflated profits just when future profitability was threatened as never before. Whatever its critics may have thought about the Stock Exchange's failure to serve the national interest in international markets, there could be no doubt at all that it had brilliantly served the commercial interests of the larger members of the club. By levering up fixed commissions on equities in 1982 in the teeth of hostility from some of its biggest customers and in the midst of the battle with the Office of Fair Trading, the Council had ensured that firms reaped the maximum benefit from the bull market that followed. The brinkmanship paid off as a new set of proprietors rushed to compensate larger firms for their loss of a waning monopoly and to take over the enormous uncertainties they faced in the more competitive climate that would inevitably follow the Big Bang. And by moving in 1984 to prevent outsiders from taking 29.9 per cent stakes in new partnerships formed by ex-partners in established firms the Stock Exchange helped those firms that enjoyed an institutional clientele extract the highest possible price for their stake in that same declining monopoly.

Those that had made the biggest acquisitions could no doubt console themselves that they would still be left with some good people and some market share at the end of the day. The problem was mainly one of overpayment. For some the numbers involved were small in relation to their 'war chests' –

the resources set aside for takeovers. For the rest, in mid-1985 a director of one of the top merchant banks summed up the situation for the authors like this:

> The extent of the enthusiasm to buy second-tier brokers at huge sums beggars credibility. They've been paid fifteen to twenty times their average annual earnings, when they've no obvious future. There was no real equity in most of them anyway – yet they managed to sell themselves on a multiple of earnings that could only have made sense if life was going to go on as before.

Life was clearly not going to go on as before. And when one of the authors asked Sir Nicholas Goodison where the profits were going to come from to justify the high prices that had been paid to his members, his response was brutally succinct: 'Where indeed?' was all he had to say.

In the gilt-edged market it is generally considered that brokers and jobbers between them were earning around £100 million a year before tax and expenses. In June 1985 the Bank of England announced that thirty-one financial groups had applied to become dealers in the restructured market in which investors were to have the freedom to approach market makers direct, who in turn would have direct access to the Bank of England. The total capital of the thirty-one, which was expected to amount to £600–700 million, was required by the Bank to be used solely for gilt-edged dealing. This was universally regarded by market practitioners as being excessive. The market makers had been required to reveal to the Bank their target market shares, which added up to between 150 and 200 per cent of the available cake. Only if turnover increased spectacularly could they hope to make a return on all this capital. Not surprisingly some took fright and started to think again about their decision to play the new gilt-edged game.

The safest prediction in the City about the gilt market, however, was that the number of participants would be thinned out in a price war in which the Bank of England would not hesitate to encourage people to withdraw if they appeared to be running excessive risks or failed to match up to the Bank's exacting requirements for liquidity. One leading broker pointed out to the authors that of thirty-six primary bond dealers in the equivalent market in the United States, only five or six counted for much – yet the US market was around ten times the size of the one in London. Those with ambition, a long purse and real skill who stayed the course could expect good profits in the end, he argued, but the drop-out rate would be high and some of the survivors would probably do little more than potter along. Whereas the Bank of England had organized rescues for discount houses that had overstretched themselves in the gilt market in the past, there were to be no automatic bale-outs in future.

Lessons from America

The revenues provided by the London equity market are substantially greater, but there, too, many participants predicted a profits crunch. In part, this judgement was instinctive. But it was also supported by research carried out by the management consultants McKinsey in the United States, which cast the whole City revolution in an interesting perspective. McKinsey looked at the impact of deregulation on five major industries – securities broking, airlines, trucking, railroads and business terminal equipment. Despite the very different nature of the industries concerned, a number of common features recurred when they were subjected to a process of liberalization. In heavily regulated or cartelized industries, firms competed over a narrow range of products and services. They sought to differentiate themselves from the competition by offering higher- or better-quality levels of service. When traditional pricing arrangements broke down, new products and services proliferated. Then new, low-cost competition invariably came into the marketplace. Whereas competition in protected markets focused on extras such as brokers' research or airline meals, the range of price and service options offered to the customer quickly multiplied on the introduction of free competition. The new discount firms were able to undercut traditional operators who laboured under a burden of historic structural costs. Finally, the introduction of new technology intensified: whereas the technology was used in protected markets to attract customers through better service, in a more competitive environment it offered a means of reducing costs.

One outcome was concentration: a small number of big, broad-based firms tended to move into a dominant position. On Wall Street price deregulation led between 1973 and 1978 to an increase in market share for the top twenty-five US brokerage firms from 48 per cent to 71 per cent of the industry's total revenue; and within that twenty-five the top ten rapidly gained market share at the expense of the other fifteen. And as well as 'no frills' discount operators, a group of specialist firms usually survived on the basis of offering a less cost-sensitive product to a particular part of the market.

What, then, should British firms have done when confronted with deregulation in the British securities markets? A key rule, according to consultants at McKinsey in London, was to avoid thinking of acquisitions as the answer to the problem. They had a way of proving expensive, especially in periods of rapid regulatory change, and the participants too often assumed that fruitful management synergies would material- ize unprompted after the change of ownership. A second key rule was to refocus corporate strategy on the customer.

What the customers weren't asked

This highlights one of the more bizarre features of the City revolution, which is that the customers played a very limited part in influencing the whole outcome. Had more time been spent canvassing their opinions it is conceivable that doubts about the changes would have multiplied even further. Alan Clements, finance director of ICI, told Channel Four's *Business Programme* late in 1984 that many of the new conglomer- ates were not natural groupings as far as he was concerned because they cut across ICI's existing banking and broking relationships. Those relationships took years to build and Clements did not intend initially to upset them. His words carried a strong hint that synergy was indeed going to be hard to extract from all the mergers and acquisitions, especially if other finance directors took a similar view. As for investors, most of the insurance companies, pension funds and other institutions welcomed the removal of fixed commissions on gilt-edged dealings. Larger ones, such as the Prudential, felt they could look after themselves when dual capacity came in and were delighted with the prospect of not having to pay for unwanted research that came as part of the brokers' overall fixed-commission package. But Michael Newmarch, in charge of the Prudential's investment portfolios, told us that it was most unlikely that the Pru would change its allegiances in international markets from the big US and Japanese brokers to much smaller British firms.

There was similar scepticism lower down the institutional scale. Robert Walther, investment manager of Clerical Medical & General Life Assurance Society, argued that there was little point in his company dealing in IBM stock through one of the new City groupings rather than a New York broker unless the former was giving a service on the whole US securities market. He was also concerned about the potential conflicts of interest. Under the old system no one was allowed to run the whole gamut of fund management, corporate finance, stock-broking and market making under one roof. The investor could rely on the broker, acting as agent, to look for the best price for a purchase or sale of stocks and shares. Good service was rewarded by patronage: institutional investors steered their business, and thus commission income, towards the efficient. Efficiency was measured in terms of the quality of research, advice and ability to execute transactions effectively.

Under the new system institutional investors had to ask whether they should do more research in-house and whether they should set up dealing desks to negotiate the best prices. Clerical Medical & General was instinctively unhappy about doing so because additional dealers were expensive and the benefit they brought was hard to measure. Yet with brokers acting as principal as well as agent, and with the new hybrid firms running investment management operations themselves, it would become more important to check that fair prices were being obtained.

Such was the concern on these issues at Clerical Medical & General that its managers were not content to rely on the British Insurance Association alone to make the case. It wrote direct to the Bank of England and the Stock Exchange to express its fears, emphasizing that its willingness to deal with the new hybrid firms would depend on the tightness of the arrangements to pre-empt trouble arising from conflicts of interest. These concerns were widely shared by all but the biggest and most self-confident insurance companies and pension funds. Matthew Oakeshott, investment manager of Courtaulds' pension fund, went so far as to say publicly that under the new regime the pressure for short-term profits would be so great that stockbroking firms would be out to 'get profits quickly and the devil take the hindmost'.

These criticisms were especially worrying to merchant banks, which had enjoyed considerable latitude in relation to potential conflicts of interest in their investment management activities. The presence of Chinese Walls meant, for example, that Warburg felt free to hold on its clients' behalf nearly 10 per cent of the share capital of its parent, Mercury Securities, at the time it was proposing to issue shares to buy into Rowe & Pitman, Akroyd & Smithers and Mullens. The existence of this shareholding was not widely known in the City. But it was a fair assumption that such arrangements would be viewed in a more critical light, in the new deregulated climate, by some of Warburg's clients.

Brokers were no more sanguine about the way the market was likely to evolve. Some were prepared to admit that the world was likely to be chaotic in the immediate aftermath of the Big Bang. John Brew, chief executive of Grieveson, Grant, predicted 'a very messy period of evolution' as people adjusted to the new dealing system, about which he had strong personal reservations. He believed that the new automated structure based on America's NASDAQ system did not make it easy for institutional investors to reward brokers for good service. For the broker, he argued, the key to success would lie not in the acquisition of jobbing skills but in the traditional virtues of marketing good ideas to customers and executing transactions efficiently. It would also be vital to master the new art of managing risks on a scale none had experienced before. As for the abuse of conflicts of interest, Brew bluntly asserted that there would be little problem in the gilt-edged market because it was a market for professionals who could look after themselves; but in equities the obvious way to compensate for a loss of income on the introduction of negotiated commissions was for broking firms to take positions in the shares that their analysts were about to recommend. Some analysts were already complaining in 1985 that they were beginning to come under pressure from their new potential owners in the banking sector to say the right thing about the banks' corporate clients.

After deregulation, re-regulation

This raises one of the most fundamental questions about the whole City Revolution and the City's relations with government. For the history of regulation in financial markets since World War II is about the tension between two conflicting demands: on the one hand the need to avoid excessive controls that strangle innovation, and on the other the need to protect individual investors and preserve wider confidence in the integrity of markets. Not unnaturally, the Bank of England, the Stock Exchange and other City clubs were anxious to retain maximum freedom of manoeuvre. They believed that the postwar growth of the City's international business was a direct reflection of the light regulatory environment in London, and they bolstered their case by pointing to the growing competition from other financial centres which were deregulating markets fast in order to win a bigger share of international business.

Yet a number of their own constituents were genuinely worried about the ability of self-regulation to cope with an influx of foreigners, who were less likely to subscribe to the City's club ethic, into domestic securities markets. Those markets were moving to an American-style system of dealing without any of the prohibitions imposed on conflicts of interest by America's Securities and Exchange Commission. Most of the conglomerators in the City, with encouragement from the Bank of England, wanted to go on with informal arrangements such as Chinese Walls; but as the Big Bang came closer, their customers' scepticism grew. David Hopkinson, the outspoken chairman of M & G Investment Management who combines a role as a Church Commissioner with a realistic view of human nature, raised the question in its most simple form. If Chinese Walls *really* worked, he asked, what was the point of combining broking, jobbing, banking, corporate advice and investment management in the first place?

This debate took place against the background of the first comprehensive review of securities legislation since the 1930s. For over the previous decade and a half the self-regulators had, in fact, been fighting a losing battle. Some of the City's self-regulatory agencies, such as the Takeover Panel and the Stock Exchange, had relatively successful records. Others, such as the Council for the Securities Industry, had failed to make any real mark. None of the effective ones had a mandate in those areas of the markets where a rising tide of scandals caught the attention of Westminster and Whitehall.

Successive insurance scandals, culminating in the collapse in 1971 of Vehicle & General Insurance, a member of the British Insurance Association, had already led to very detailed insurance company legislation and to a rare increase in the regulatory staff of the Department of Trade and Industry. The secondary banking crisis had brought about the Banking Act of 1979. And in the early 1980s a growing number of scandals in the securities and commodity markets had put Mrs Thatcher's government under increasing pressure to overhaul the whole regulatory structure for the capital markets.

These scandals took place outside the Stock Exchange, which had its own compensation fund and a sound record on investor protection. The worst of them concerned the commodity markets, which an Old Bailey judge not so long ago described as 'a jungle suitable for hunting for large and experienced animals but one in which the small animal is at very serious risk'. This revealed, so the judge said, 'a most perilous state of affairs which merits attention by Parliament'. But a number of the scandals also concerned securities dealers directly licensed by the Department of Trade. Most embarrassing, from the point of view of the Bank of England, was the collapse in questionable circumstances of Norton Warburg, a licensed securities dealer which had invested substantial sums of money for some of the Bank's own staff.

Self-regulation within a statutory framework

The government's response was to call in a distinguished legal authority, Professor L. C. B. Gower, an adviser on company law to the Department of Trade, to review the general framework of investor protection and to advise on the need for new legislation. In an initial discussion document in 1982 Gower pointed out that the existing system of statutory and non-statutory regulations was really a non-system, and that enforcement of the regulations left much to be desired. He favoured a comprehensive statute to replace the Prevention of Fraud (Investments) Act, which would seek to bring everyone professionally involved in the investment business under regulation, while leaving the day-to-day task of making rules and monitoring them to be handled by self-regulatory bodies in the City.

These proposals provoked howls of protest from many of the City's more influential bodies, which preferred their self-regulation undiluted. Gower had not endeared himself to them, either, by letting it be known that he had never seen a Chinese Wall without a grapevine trailing over it. But by the time he produced his full report in January 1984 attitudes were beginning to change. They were coloured not only by the changes on the Stock Exchange but by the explosion of scandals in the Lloyd's insurance market, which cast undiluted self-regulation in an unflattering light.

Professor Gower urged a new Investor Protection Act whose administration would be handled either by the Department of Trade or by a self-standing commission answerable to the Secretary of State – in other words, a quango, or quasi-autonomous non-government organization. Within the new legal framework self-regulatory agencies such as the Stock Exchange would continue to enjoy rights and privileges, provided that their rules complied with basic principles laid down in the new act. Gower's guiding principle was not to protect the foolish and greedy from their own folly, but to ensure that reasonable people were not made fools of.

Neither the Bank of England, nor Sir Nicholas Goodison at the Stock Exchange, relished the prospect of a commission. The mere mention of the word raised the spectre, in the minds

153

of suspicious City folk, of the American Securities and Exchange Commission which they regarded as an over-legalistic, bureaucratic and over-zealous watchdog. An enlarged role for the government appeared to them equally unpalatable. Yet Gower had put ministers at the Department of Trade on the spot by defining the argument in terms of these twin poles. While the debate raged in and out of the City, and the government wondered how to respond to Gower's report, the Bank of England decided that the onset of the Big Bang called for urgent measures. In what subsequently turned out to be a crucial step in relation to the City's freedom of action, Robin Leigh-Pemberton announced in May 1984 that he was inviting a group of ten wise men from the City to advise him on the structure and operation of the City's self-regulatory agencies. The chairman was Martin Jacomb, then still at Kleinwort Benson. Since the Bank had no interest in the life assurance and unit trust area, which was also covered by Gower's legislative proposals, the Department of Trade felt obliged hurriedly to put together a similar body under the then chairman of the Life Offices Association, Marshall Field.

Instead of sticking to their brief the Bank's ten wise men looked at the question of whether there really should be a commission. They concluded that it would be preferable to have the government delegate powers to a private City body resembling a more powerful version of the existing Council for the Securities Industry. The Bank of England then pressed this solution on the government, where the Department of Trade was anxious to produce a White Paper offering a package acceptable to the government and the City, which would be presented as carrying their joint imprimatur.

This was easier said than done. For while the Secretary of State, Norman Tebbit, and the Corporate and Consumer Affairs Minister, Alex Fletcher, were anxious to keep the City happy, they had simultaneously to cope with complex constitutional issues, placate their own backbenchers and ensure that the City would be willing to pay more for its own regulation. In a Commons debate in July 1984 the government had been taken aback at the strength of feeling on the Tory backbenches about the need to avoid minimalist solutions to the problem of conflicts of interest in the new City climate.

Both Professor Gower and the Department of Trade lawyers pointed out that there was no constitutional precedent for delegating powers in this way to purely private bodies in the City of London. And Sir Nicholas Goodison let it be known that since his members already paid £4 million a year for an existing system of investor protection run by the Exchange, he saw no reason why they should pay more to bring order to the affairs of other bodies which were competing with them.

By the time a long-delayed White Paper emerged – and its gestation was not helped by the bombing at the 1984 Tory party conference in Brighton where the unfortunate Norman Tebbit was badly injured – by no means all the issues had been resolved. But the Bank had, once again, successfully muscled its way back into the argument, for the government did propose the setting up of a new private City watchdog called the Securities and Investments Board; and, since something had to be done about insurance and unit trusts, it also proposed a second body called the Marketing of Investments Board.

Under the new legislation the government proposed to seek parliamentary approval for regulatory powers to be given to the Secretary of State for Trade. He would then delegate the powers to the new City bodies, provided they could satisfy him, among other things, on the following points.

– Their rules for authorizing investment businesses were fair and reasonable.
– There was a 'fit and proper' test for practitioners.
– The rules afforded adequate protection to investors.
– Procedures and resources were adequate to ensure proper monitoring and enforcement of the rules.

The new City watchdogs were, in turn, expected to delegate day-to-day powers to self-regulatory agencies such as the Stock Exchange or the National Association of Securities Dealers and Investment Managers, once they were satisfied that their rules complied with basic principles of investor protection enshrined in the new Act. These were to cover such things as the need for fair dealing, disclosure to cope with conflicts of interest and duties of skill, care and diligence to be exercised by the agencies' members towards their clients.

Alternatively, individual investment businesses could seek to register directly with the new watchdogs.

At first sight the new regime appeared tough, in that it cut the role of the self-regulators down to size. Their rules would have to comply with very specific statutory requirements designed to prevent conflicts of interest being exploited and to inhibit other abuses. For newer self-regulatory agencies, such as the National Association of Securities Dealers and Investment Managers and the Association of Futures Brokers and Dealers, the requirements were onerous and potentially expensive to satisfy. The Secretary of State, advised by the Director General of Fair Trading, was to retain the power to amend any rules that were detrimental to competition beyond the needs of investor protection – so Sir Gordon Borrie, the Stock Exchange's old adversary, was not wholly removed from the picture.

Gilbert and Sullivan to the rescue

Yet for all that, the City had won a considerable victory. As the White Paper pointed out, it was unprecedented for a statutory power of authorization and regulation to be given to a private sector body, which was allowed to make rules with the force of law and to make businesses comply with them. The Bank of England had also won the battle for control over the membership of the Securities and Investments Board (the SIB) by striking a compromise with the Department of Trade whereby the Secretary of State appointed the chairman with the agreement of the Governor of the Bank of England; and the Governor appointed the other members with the agreement of the Secretary of State.

This was pure Gilbert and Sullivan, as the financial editor of *The Times* acutely observed, and it enraged Labour spokesmen in the Commons who saw it as an attempt to protect the Securities and Investments Board from interference by a future Labour government. The oddity of the arrangement was underlined by the way the wise men of the insurance industry acquiesced meekly in the appointment of all the Marketing of Investments Board's members by the Secretary of State. The impression that the new watchdogs had been captured in advance by the people they were supposed to regulate was reinforced when Sir Kenneth Berrill, a former head of the government's 'Think Tank' who had moved to the City to run Vickers da Costa, was appointed chairman of the SIB. At the press conference announcing his appointment he conveyed the impression that he was no poacher turned gamekeeper and saw himself in a more ambassadorial role, putting the City's case to the outside world. Similar concern was voiced when Mark Weinberg, the insurance super-salesman, was appointed part-time chairman of the MIB.

The City also took satisfaction in the limited nature of the boards' accountability under the White Paper's outline. While the new boards were to prepare a report for parliament, the White Paper said nothing about any debate on the contents. The Secretary of State was to be accountable to Parliament only in the very general sense that he had to justify any decision to delegate or, in the event of scandal, any failure to withdraw delegated authority. His powers to amend the rules of the new body were few, and tightly circumscribed.

At the end of the day, despite the rather chaotic nature of the proceedings, the Bank of England probably felt that it had some cause for satisfaction in the City Revolution. At a time when it had suffered heavily at Mrs Thatcher's hands for its role in the conduct of monetary policy, and had been savaged by the Treasury for an alleged failure of supervision in relation to the collapse of Johnson Matthey Bankers, it managed to set in train a reform of the City structure pretty much on its own terms. It had helped steer the securities business towards a sophisticated new dealing system that compared more than favourably with those in other major financial centres and was compatible with what the Bank perceived to be the wider national interest. It had watched over the establishment of a number of big new domestic securities firms. It had extended its own authority outside the banking area. And the Bank had won a greater degree of autonomy for practitioners in the City markets than had seemed likely when Professor Gower produced his report.

Winners and losers on the Stock Exchange

Sir Nicholas Goodison also emerged with more than he might have dared hope in the days when Sir Gordon Borrie was casting a critical eye over his club's rules. From his point of view the only sour note was struck by the small firms. They rightly diagnosed that the big names, amply represented on the Stock Exchange Council, had been handsomely compensated for the loss of their waning monopoly while the smaller fry faced a problematical future with no marriage and no dowry. And they recognized that their best hope of winning a consolation prize lay in extracting some value from their shares in the Stock Exchange itself. Each member held a single share in the Exchange, whose chief tangible assets were the Stock Exchange Tower, in the books at £90 million, and its electronic gadgetry.

Liquidating those assets was simply not practicable. But in an attempt to cope with the small firms' grievance the Stock Exchange Council proposed that each member's share should be split into five so that individuals would be able to keep one share and sell off the rest to the newcomers to the Exchange, who were to be required to buy whatever number of shares the Council stipulated. Under the watchful eye of the Bank of England, the Council put a fixed £2000 ceiling on the price of the shares to ensure that prices did not soar to a level that deterred outsiders from completing their takeovers of broking and jobbing firms or from setting up new member firms from scratch.

In a rearguard action partners in the Exchange's smaller firms whipped up opposition to this fixed-price ceiling. Realizing that it would be immensely difficult to win the requisite 75 per cent support for the rearrangement of the shareholdings, Sir Nicholas concluded that the ceiling would have to be removed to allow a free market in the Stock Exchange's own shares. Yet the Bank of England was strongly opposed to anything that risked alienating potential new entrants to the market, or which threatened to fragment the central market by giving people an incentive to deal outside the Exchange. In the end the Bank reluctantly conceded the point to Goodison. But the concession was not enough to win the day. When it came to the crucial vote in the first week of June 1985, a majority of the membership gave the green light to a motion to bring in outsiders; but the motion to alter the ownership structure of the Exchange fell just short of the 75 per cent support that it needed.

This meant that the new outside members and owners were disenfranchized, but it also had the effect of preventing the small firms from extracting value for their shares. On balance all the bigger participants in the revolution concluded that the failure of the less important of the two motions would do little to stop the reform of the Exchange. At the end of the day even Sir Nicholas's opponents were inclined to acknowledge that he had done a remarkable job in bringing one of the nation's most conservative institutions to accept such drastic reforms to the membership and the dealing system. Few previous Stock Exchange chairmen had shown anything approaching the analytical ability or political skill of this former scholar of King's College, Cambridge; or, indeed, his extraordinary energy. It is worth putting on record the fact that in this period when he was doing battle with the Office of Fair Trading, seeking to reform the Exchange and trying to preserve its right to perform its own self-regulation, Sir Nicholas himself submitted a PhD thesis in architecture and the history of art, brought the Scandinavian insurer Skandia into his own firm, Quilter Goodison, as a 29.9 per cent stakeholder, and lived a protean existence as one of the great and good of the arts world, being an honorary Keeper of Furniture at the Fitzwilliam Museum in Cambridge, a member of the executive committee of the National Arts Collection Fund, chairman of the management committee of the Courtauld Institute of Art, vice-chairman of the English National Opera, honorary treasurer of the Furniture History Society, a director of the City Arts Trust, and an editorial director of the *Burlington Magazine*.

The one job that Sir Nicholas did not take on in this period, despite pressing invitations, was that of top regulator in the new legal framework for the securities business. It probably looked a thankless task – for it is a moot point how long the new Securities and Investments Board will be able to preserve the degree of freedom that the City managed to win from government in the debate over the Gower Report. To be effective the new bodies (which everyone expects to be merged in due course) would have to be expensively staffed with able people. They will be required to apply the same statutory standards to the barons of the Stock Exchange, who have long experience of regulating markets, as to new bodies such as the National Association of Securities Dealers and Investment Managers and the Association of Futures Brokers and Dealers, who have very little. If anything goes wrong, the fundamental weakness in the government's legislative blueprint will quickly be exposed: the government's only real sanction is its right to withdraw delegated powers from the City bodies and have the Department of Trade regulate investment markets directly. Yet the Department's record in regulating securities dealers and insurers, with its relatively slender staff resources in these areas, is less than impressive; and it will have reduced its staff considerably on the basis that day-to-day regulation will have been passed over to the new bodies after delegation has taken place.

Sir Nicholas Goodison makes no secret of his fear that a statutory commission will not be long in coming. And it would not be surprising if he had concluded that the Stock Exchange's interest lay in distancing itself as far as possible from the new Board and the newer self-regulatory agencies whose ability to police their memberships is untried. The challenge to what remains of self-regulation in the City will come from scandals in the newer markets – and in the City's other great club, Lloyd's of London, where the 1980s saw the eruption of what was probably the biggest financial scandal of the century.

7

Counter-revolution at Lloyd's

The Society of Lloyd's, whose members include some of the wealthiest individuals in the country, has, in common with so many City institutions, been run for centuries as a gentlemen's club. Now the insurance market at Lime Street has been undergoing a transformation every bit as far-reaching as the one at the Stock Exchange. However, if the developments at Throgmorton Street can be described as a revolution, those at Lloyd's constitute, if anything, a counter-revolution.

The contrast between the changes at the two institutions could hardly be starker. At the very moment that the distinction between the roles of principal and agent was being cast away at the Stock Exchange, Lloyd's was rooting out owner-ship arrangements which created potential conflicts of interest in the market. While dual capacity in the nation's capital market was being given the full blessing of the government, Lloyd's brokers were being compelled as a result of parliamentary legislation to divest themselves of their long-standing interests in agencies which manage the insurance undertaken at Lloyd's by its members. So, as the doors of the one club were being prised open to all comers, the doors of the other were being slammed shut.

The paradox of the apparent contrary thrust of government policy towards Lloyd's and the Stock Exchange has not been lost on the City. There is a further ironic twist to the tale: the counter-revolution at Lloyd's is expected, like the revolution at the Stock Exchange though on a much smaller scale, to make many of the professionals working in the market even richer than they already are.

If a number of members of Lloyd's fail fully to savour this irony, they may perhaps be forgiven. For this development is occurring in the wake of what were undoubtedly the most serious financial scandals in the City since the war. Thousands of members of the Society have been milked of up to £100 million by a number of their fellow members working as professionals in the market. This 'plunder' – to use the description given to the scandals by the man brought in to clean up Lloyd's, Ian Hay Davison – took place within the club. In the words of one leading figure at Lloyd's, 'it was the rape of the greedy by the very greedy'.

For over a thousand individuals who had undertaken insurance through an agency owned by a leading Lloyd's broker, Minet Holdings, the experience of being a member of Lloyd's has been doubly traumatic. Not only have they lost heavily as a result of the misappropriation of their funds which is alleged to have been perpetrated at their expense by Peter Cameron-Webb and Peter Dixon, the professionals who formerly controlled the agency; in May 1985, they learnt that they were also liable for catastrophic trading losses, estimated to amount to £130 million. These losses were the worst to affect a single group of members in Lloyd's long history. The most illustrious of those affected was the Duchess of Kent. However, her share of the losses was in fact extremely small; by contrast several medical and legal luminaries were said to be liable for amounts of up to half a million pounds each. A number stared bankruptcy in the face. Many considered that these losses were not the consequence of misjudgement on the part of the agency's professional underwriters, but were directly related to the previous troubles that had beset the agency. At the time this book was going to press a steering committee under the honorary chairmanship of Lord Goodman was considering bringing civil proceedings not just against the agency and Minet Holdings, but against Lloyd's itself. A driving force on the steering committee was Keith Whitten, an executive headhunter, who himself stood to lose over £100,000. The walls of his West End office are hung with prints of hunting scenes, and it was clear that Whitten was now seeking to adorn them with City scalps.

Lloyd's: a unique institution

This prospect was causing nothing short of panic at Lloyd's, an institution whose very bedrock is the commitment by each of its members to pick up the bill for losses arising from insurance undertaken in his name. On this basis, Lloyd's can boast that in nearly three hundred years of history it has always paid up; all legitimate claims by policyholders have been honoured. Now, however, members affected by the financial scandals which had occurred at the Minet agency were challenging this cardinal principle of unlimited liability. The situation threatened to put the entire institution in jeopardy. The gravity of the crisis demonstrated – if further proof were necessary – the imperative need for reform at Lloyd's.

The need to stamp out the conditions which fostered financial scandals is the key reason why Lloyd's has introduced changes so diametrically opposed to those of the City revolution. The counter-revolution has not been confined to the question of divestment, which forms so striking a counterpoint to the tune of 'Here Comes the Bride' at the Stock Exchange; the sale of agencies owned by brokers forms part of a much wider set of reforms transforming the insurance market at Lime Street. The mainspring of these changes has been the need to modernize Lloyd's historic system of self-regulation to an insurance market which had grown in spectacular yet topsy-turvy fashion in the 1970s; and which in the process had spawned one abuse after another.

The programme of reforms at Lloyd's may thus be regarded as a counter-revolution in another sense. It forms a regulatory response, driven by the hot breath of financial scandal, to revolutionary changes which had already occurred in the 1970s. For, unlike the Stock Exchange, Lloyd's has not stagnated as a domestic backwater in the past fifteen years; instead it has seized many of the opportunities which have arisen as a result of the expansion of international insurance.

The Bank of England has been keeping a close eye on events at Lloyd's, for in the outcome of the reform programme there is much at stake, and not just for Lloyd's: further misdemeanours could besmirch the reputation of the entire City as an honest place to do business. At the same time, any hint of failure by the new regime could fatally weaken the Bank's hand in any further battle fought with Whitehall over the question of self-regulation in the Square Mile. However, the significance of the reforms is even greater for the City. For by its very nature, the counter-revolution at Lloyd's calls into question the wisdom of the entire City Revolution.

The first key question, then, about the reforms at Lloyd's is simply whether they will work. Will the new regime at Lime Street succeed in extirpating the roots of potential financial abuses? In order to assess the prospects of the reforms, it is vital to understand why the need for them arose in the first place. This may in turn provide an answer to the second key question: whether the City is about to go down a path which led to disaster at Lloyd's, or whether the experience of the insurance market is *sui generis*.

The source of the problems which have plagued Lloyd's over the past few years lies in certain characteristics which make it a unique institution. In an insurance world dominated by companies, Lloyd's is a Society of individual insurers. Each member undertakes insurance in his own name and accepts unlimited liability for any claims that ensue. The Society is organized along the lines of a club. And in marked contrast with insurance companies, which are subject to extensive government regulation, Lloyd's has long enjoyed the privilege of self-regulation. This unique structure only exists today because of Lloyd's long and chequered history.

Individual underwriters

In the sixteenth and seventeenth centuries, long before insurance companies had been set up, the expansion in Britain's overseas trade created a pressing requirement for protection against peril at sea. This demand was met by rich merchants and other wealthy figures, each of whom would take on a portion – or line – of the risk being insured in return for a similar share in the premium being paid by the shipowner. The individuals who did this came to be called underwriters because they would sign their names at the bottom of the policy describing the nature of the risk and the terms of the insurance.

Until the mid-eighteenth century such underwriting was

generally no more than a sideline for the individuals concerned. Samuel Pepys, for instance, sometimes had the odd flutter in insuring a ship while he was Secretary to the Navy. His diary entry for 23 November 1663 reveals that the potential which insurance affords for sharp practice is nothing new. He recorded that on this occasion he had been trying with no little difficulty to arrange insurance on a supply ship which was overdue from Archangel. The entry continues:

> Called at the coffeehouse and there hear by great accident that a letter is come that our ship is safe come to Newcastle. With this news I went like an asse presently to Alderman Blackwell and told him of it. . . . Now what an opportunity had I to have concealed this and seemed to have made an insurance and got £100 with the least trouble and danger in the whole world!

Individual underwriters were able to prevail over subsequent competition from companies in the field of marine insurance primarily through exclusive access to shipping intelligence, the lifeblood of marine underwriting. This was the key reason why Lloyd's coffee house became the principal centre where they gathered. Edward Lloyd is known to have established a coffee house by 1688, and by the time he died in 1713 it had already become one of the main auction rooms in the City of London for ships and their cargoes. However, although it is reasonable to assume that some underwriting was carried out there, it was by no means the principal centre for this activity. The success of Lloyd's in prevailing over its rival coffee houses was due mainly to the enterprise of a later proprietor, Thomas Jemson, who in 1734 founded *Lloyd's List*, one of the world's oldest surviving newspapers. Jemson had begun the tradition, which continues to this day, that the most up-to-date marine intelligence is to be found at Lloyd's. As a result, by the mid-eighteenth century the coffee house had become the undisputed centre where private underwriters would gather to carry out their business.

The club is formed

It was scandal which led to Lloyd's being organized along the lines of a club. In the 1760s, anyone could turn up at the coffee house and anything could go on there; and in the slack years for insurance which followed the Seven Years' War, just about anything did go on there. Gambling fever had broken out in London; and in 1768 the *London Chronicle* carried a leader criticizing 'the introduction and amazing progress of illicit gambling at Lloyd's coffee-house'. Particularly distasteful were the wagers being made on the chances that well-known personalities who were ill might die within a specified period of time. Eventually a group of underwriters decided that this betting shop atmosphere was bringing their business into disrepute. They seceded from the coffee house, and in 1771 seventy-nine of them subscribed funds and elected a committee to find a permanent home for the market. Lloyd's destiny no longer rested in the hands of the owner of a coffee house; instead the market was now to be run by the committee on behalf of the subscribers.

After this first step, the development of Lloyd's into a fully fledged club was both gradual and faltering. A century later, the committee's powers had extended beyond the question of premises to the admission of members. But it had no right to regulate the behaviour of members. Once again, financial scandal was the spur to change. An underwriting member had accepted a premium on a ship which was thought to be severely damaged but which he privately knew to be intact. Samuel Pepys would have been proud of him, but the rest of the market was not. However, when he was expelled by the committee, a High Court found that it had exceeded its powers. Lloyd's decided that it must establish a formal constitution for the club by sponsoring a private Act of Parliament.

This Act, passed in 1871, formed the basis on which Lloyd's was to run its affairs until the beginning of 1983. Lloyd's was established as an incorporated Society; the Corporation of Lloyd's was henceforth responsible for the administration of the market. Although the Society was now a corporate body, this did not alter the principle of unlimited liability for its underwriting members. Under the Act, an elected committee was responsible for managing the affairs of the Society, formulating rules, admitting members and regulating them. However, legislative powers and disciplinary functions were still vested in the membership through the holding of general meetings. For example, the passing of bye-laws required the approval of two general meetings. This meant that the committee, which was the effective ruling body, was forced to run Lloyd's to a large extent on an informal basis. This formal restriction on the authority of the committee was to play an important part in its failure to supervise the market effectively in the 1970s.

The privilege of self-regulation

The prime purpose of the 1871 Act was to provide Lloyd's with a constitution which would enable members to run the club in a manner which would protect their own financial interests. However, the key regulatory problem raised by insurance as an industry concerned the interests of innocent policyholders, who can be ruined through the collapse of an insurance enterprise, whether through fraud or mismanagement. This led to extensive government regulation of the insurance industry existed therefore from an early stage. Not the least remarkable chapter in the Lloyd's story was its achievement in winning exemption from outside regulation.

In the early years of the twentieth century, a financial scandal in which a number of members of the Society were made bankrupt drew attention to the fact that there were no controls over the use to which an underwriter put the premiums he was receiving, nor indeed of his overall solvency. This led members to agree, in 1908, that premiums should be held in trust; and that a regular audit of an underwriter's accounts should be carried out to confirm his solvency. The existence of these rules meant that Lloyd's was able to gain exemption from legislation which was passed a year later by Parliament to regulate fire and accident insurance: the ambit of the 1909 Assurance Companies Act did not extend to Lloyd's. In a speech delivered in early 1985 on 'The Auditor's Role at Lloyd's', Ian Hay Davison described this as 'the genesis of the self-regulatory status that we at Lloyd's enjoy today'.

Strengths and weaknesses

So by World War I, the basic characteristics of the modern Lloyd's had taken shape. A group of individual underwriters had staked out a pitch in the insurance world where they could compete with companies; they had organized themselves along the lines of a club; and they had won the right to self-regulation. While this peculiar – some would say eccentric – structure has certain inherent advantages, it also imposes on Lloyd's a number of serious handicaps.

It has two drawbacks compared with an insurance company; the first of them concerns capital. The conduct of underwriting on the principle of unlimited liability has cut Lloyd's off from the capital markets which are open to insurance companies. Instead it has had to rely on the collective wealth of its individual underwriting members. The second drawback turns on the question of winning and managing business. As a market of individual underwriters, Lloyd's has been unable to set up sales and marketing arms in the same way as a company. At the same time, its underwriters have lacked the skills and resources needed to manage a large underwriting operation. Instead they have had to rely primarily on the brokers who bring business into the market to provide these services.

To set against these disadvantages, Lloyd's has had three strong cards to play. The first has been the security of a Lloyd's policy, which rests, together with other safeguards, on the entire personal fortune of the underwriting member. The second has been the readiness of individual underwriters to innovate and to be entrepreneurial, in contrast with the generally more bureaucratic and hidebound behaviour of company insurers. And the third has been the relatively lower cost in running the operation of underwriting centralized in one main building, without the heavy managerial and administrative expenses entailed in the organization of an insurance company.

Lloyd's performance

In some respects, the performance of Lloyd's today might suggest that these advantages have counted for less than the disadvantages. Lloyd's now has less than 1 per cent of the total world insurance market. What is more, its share is estimated to have declined consistently since the war. In 1983 the premium income of the market amounted to about 15 per cent of the worldwide business of British insurance companies. Using premium income as a yardstick, Lloyd's remains larger than any one single British insurance company. However, it is somewhat smaller than two of the UK's biggest insurance companies, the Royal and the Commercial Union, put together.

This relatively small size may be attributed directly to the weaknesses of Lloyd's structure. Life insurance comprises about half the total premium of British companies. Lloyd's is excluded from the bulk of this business because it has taken the view that the length of the obligations made in life insurance requires corporate entities to honour them. Lloyd's other main weakness is that its underwriting operation is physically confined to London. This means that its underwriters must rely on overseas business to be brought to the market at Lime Street. By contrast, the insurance companies have been able to set up overseas establishments, which in 1983 accounted for about a half of their general (non-life) business. In the case of the Royal, 42 per cent of its general insurance in 1984 came from its American affiliates.

The performance of Lloyd's today may, however, be viewed in a more favourable light. It may have experienced a relative decline, but in absolute terms it has grown by leaps and bounds. The most graphic evidence of this is that the expansion of the market has already forced two moves earlier in this century to more spacious accommodation. The third – in 1986 to a new building which has been constructed at a cost of £165 million and is nicknamed the Refinery – trebles the available underwriting space.

Lloyd's particular significance

Lloyd's also continues to play a more important role in insurance than its mere size might appear to warrant. Only a small portion of total world insurance is transacted across frontiers. According to one estimate, Lloyd's has about a quarter of this market in international insurance. Together with the companies in the City, it forms the 'London market' which makes the Square Mile the world's leading international insurance centre.

The Society's importance stems in the first instance from its continuing grip on marine insurance, the bulk of which is now foreign business as a result of the decline of the British shipping industry. A continuing edge in shipping intelligence continues to play a part in this achievement. Every day the *Blue List* is published, a unique shipping index which charts every single movement of oceangoing vessels around the world.

However, Lloyd's no longer relies exclusively on marine insurance, which now forms only about a third of its business. Its primary role, and half its total business, has changed to that of a reinsurance market in which insurance companies, principally foreign ones and in particular American ones, lay off some of the risks on policies they have accepted. Most of this reinsurance is done in the non-marine business into which Lloyd's first started to diversify a century ago under the lead of the pathfinding underwriter Cuthbert Heath. Heath came to be called 'The Father of Modern Lloyd's' for the example he set in steering the market away from its former marine dependence. He pioneered a whole range of non-marine policies, including a number, such as catastrophe and excess of loss reinsurance, which were to prove particularly attractive to American clients. Altogether some three-quarters of Lloyd's present business comes from abroad.

Lloyd's significance today also stems from the particular role that it plays in the international insurance market: its underwriters enjoy a reputation for undertaking new sorts of risks. Lloyd's pioneered the insurance of aviation before World War I, and is today at the forefront of satellite insurance. On the marine side, Lloyd's was the first to insure offshore oil drilling and container ships.

The other major reason why Lloyd's continues to exercise an influence disproportionate to its size is that it is a 'lead' market. This means that its senior underwriters are prepared to provide the first line of an insurance policy which others in the international insurance market will then follow. In other words, brokers can look to Lloyd's to set a price on risk. David Palmer, chairman and chief executive of Willis Faber, one of Lloyd's most blue-blooded brokers, says that 'Lloyd's provides a lot of strong leads for virtually every class of business'. This is not to say that the underwriters in companies do not perform a similar function. According to Alan Horsford, chief executive of Royal Insurance, companies provide the main leads in general liability business, employers' liability, commercial motor and big commercial fire risks. Be that as it may, Lloyd's clearly plays a particularly significant role as a 'lead' market, particularly in marine and aviation insurance.

Two key changes at Lloyd's

Evidence of Lloyd's continuing importance is the sizeable contribution it makes to the balance of payments. In 1983 it earned £564 million in overseas income, a figure which was equivalent to 10 per cent of total invisible earnings from UK financial institutions. Clearly Lloyd's has only been able to achieve this degree of success by overcoming the weaknesses inherent in its structure; this has involved the acceptance of major changes, the pace of which has quickened so markedly in the past ten to fifteen years that the market has virtually been transformed.

The revolution has been driven by the spectacular growth of the international insurance market as multinational companies have increasingly sought to organize cover on a worldwide basis. The risks for which protection has been sought have become larger and larger. For example, an oil rig in the North Sea could well be insured for £1.5 billion; a fully laden jumbo jet could well entail a liability close to £1 billion. Such risks are now dealt with in a vast international market in which broking companies operating on a global scale raise business from clients on one side of the world and place it with insurers on the other side.

This development has led to two major changes at Lloyd's. First, the Society has had to recruit new non-working under-writing members on an unprecedented scale. These external Names, as they are called, do not themselves work in the market, but put their entire fortunes at the disposal of the professional underwriters in return for a share of the profit – or loss. This recruitment drive has been necessary in order to provide the ever-increasing amounts of capital required to meet both the soaring size of individual risks and the general increase in the size of the international insurance market. The second important change is that a select group of Lloyd's brokers, which have succeeded in establishing their operations on a worldwide scale, have won more and more power in the market. They have achieved this primarily by becoming the essential conduit between the underwriter at Lime Street and the international insurance market.

Names, syndicates and agents

The influx of new members into Lloyd's in the 1970s was certainly a watershed. Yet it was one of degree rather than of kind. For over a hundred years Lloyd's has allowed a profes-sional underwriter to undertake insurance not just for himself, but also for non-working members willing to entrust their personal fortunes in his hands. The syndicate provided a convenient vehicle for this kind of participation in the market. Syndicates had themselves emerged in the early days of Lloyd's as a means of spreading risk among the underwriting mem-bers. The essential characteristic of the Lloyd's syndicate is that it provides a means by which insurance can be conducted jointly without jeopardizing the principle of individual under-writing.

Each person on a syndicate commits himself to a certain level of underwriting which is defined by the amount of premium income he agrees to accept. This line determines his portion of the total insurance undertaken by the syndicate. Profits and losses are allocated to each person solely according to his share of the business. A member has no right to any profits, and no responsibility for any losses, arising from the insurance accepted by other members of the syndicate. This key principle is summed up in the phrase 'Each for his own, not one for another'. A syndicate thus differs from a partnership or a company in that its members do not have joint liability for any losses that may arise.

It was not until the twentieth century that the involvement of non-working members in the market was put on a formal footing through the emergence of underwriting agents. The impetus for this development arose from the growth in the size and number of syndicates. In contrast with the structure of syndicates, agencies were allowed to take the form either of partnerships or of limited liability companies. By the 1970s two types of agent had emerged: managing and members' agents. Although an agent could act in just the one capacity, most of them combined both functions.

Managing agencies were established in order to look after the general administration of syndicates. A managing agent can run one or more syndicates. It chooses the underwriters and is responsible for preparing syndicate accounts. The agent's principal reward comes from commission on the profit generated by the syndicates it is managing. A bone of contention in recent years between some agents and their Names has been the absence of what is called a 'deficit clause': its omission means that an agent running one syndicate at a profit, and another at a loss, does not have to offset the one against the other when calculating the profit commission from Names on both syndicates.

The other kind of underwriting agent, the members' agent, is the direct link between non-working members and the market. It acts for members in all respects other than the management of syndicates. Such an agent directly represents the Name's interests; it advises him which syndicates to join and supervises his affairs. The role of members' agent, too, has been controversial in the past few years. Many Names feel that they have not received the quality of independent advice to which they are entitled.

The position in 1970, then, was that Lloyd's already consisted of two types of underwriting members: professionals working in the market, and non-working members. Of the 6000 members in that year, about 4000 were external Names. The system of underwriting agents formed the formal bridge between these two categories. However, the introduction of new members into Lloyd's was essentially casual and informal. In the twenty years from 1951 to 1971, the size of the club had gradually doubled. Yet Lloyd's remained a close circle of members of some of the most wealthy City dynasties and landed families in Britain. At its disposal was the wealth of the establishment. Informal links between external Names and the professionals in the market therefore remained strong. Many of the non-working members were friends and close acquaintances of those working in the market. Lloyd's remained a club in spirit as well as in form.

The recruitment drive

It was against this background that Lloyd's took the crucial decision to embark on a deliberate recruiting drive for new members. This policy stemmed from growing fears in the late 1960s that the market was doomed to stagnate through shortage of capital. A special working party was set up under Lord Cromer, the former Governor of the Bank of England, to examine how Lloyd's should overcome this problem. The committee accepted a principal recommendation of the Cromer Report, that Lloyd's should expand the capacity of the market by making it much easier to become a member. The doors of the club were opened for the first time to overseas citizens and to women: and the means test for Names was considerably reduced.

The effect of the recruitment drive was startling. Within ten years, membership more than trebled to reach a figure of 18,643 in 1980. The rise in the number of Names was particularly marked in the late 1970s. It was during these years that the sports personalities, the pop stars and other celebrities joined Lloyd's. Membership became *de rigueur* for the *arriviste*.

Attractions of membership

The startling success of the recruitment drive was due to the many advantages which membership confers on the rich – and now not so rich. There is no beating of the breast at Lloyd's at the idea of a means test; a Name must possess a minimum

£100,000 in unencumbered assets, excluding his or her principal residence. All prospective new Names have to be interviewed by the rota committee – composed of members of the committee – the main purpose of which is to make sure that the applicants are fully aware that, by joining a syndicate at Lloyd's, they put their entire personal fortune at risk, down to the last legendary gold cufflink. However, such were the advantages thought to be conferred by membership that the principle of unlimited liability did not act as a deterrent.

Lloyd's generally argues that the chief attraction of membership is the fact that it provides a means of making one's capital work twice. Suppose, for example, a Name puts £100,000 of his wealth at the disposal of four or five syndicates at Lloyd's. Under the arrangements in force in 1985, he must put £50,000 into a deposit fund held by Lloyd's, as one of the lines of defence in the event of losses arising from the underwriting undertaken in his name. This will entitle him to accept £200,000 of premium income in the insurance done by his syndicates. He will naturally expect to make a profit on this business, which will itself comprise two elements. The first will consist of the balance between premium income and claims, the straight underwriting profit. The second will consist of the profit derived from the investment of premiums held by the syndicates. This component has become exceedingly important in recent years as a result of high interest rates and has generally compensated for losses on the straight underwriting. However, in addition to the total profit generated in these two ways, the member will at the same time be earning interest or dividends on his original capital of £100,000, including the funds held on deposit at Lloyd's.

This 'double your money' mechanism was undoubtedly an important reason why so many people joined Lloyd's in the 1970s. However, an even more compelling attraction was the opportunity that membership afforded prospective Names for avoiding the depredations of the Inland Revenue. The premiums taken in by syndicates can be invested in such a way that it generates capital appreciation rather than investment income. This benefits top-rated taxpayers, since capital gains tax is limited to 30 per cent. Losses arising from underwriting can be offset against taxable income. Furthermore, the Lloyd's three year accounting system allows Names to enjoy a tax holiday, by deferring taxation on members' profits for over three years. This feature of membership was particularly important in the late 1970s, when high rates of inflation virtually halved the tax liabilities of members. The massive influx of members which occurred as a result of these inducements transformed the Society. Within just ten years Lloyd's ceased to be a club where underwriters in the market wrote for themselves, their families and a close circle of friends and acquaintances. Instead it had become a two-tier Society. There was now a yawning gulf between the professionals in the market and the non-working members who participated essentially in the capacity of investors, and this sea change clearly called for major reforms at Lloyd's. It was the failure to make such changes that was to lead ultimately to many of the difficulties that have plagued the Society in the past few years.

The rise of the big brokers

However, this expansion of membership was only one of the ways in which Lloyd's has been transformed in recent years. The other important change has been the rising power and influence of Lloyd's brokers, and in particular the top dozen broking companies. The market has had to accept this development because of its dependence on brokers to provide the sales and marketing arm and the managerial skills which the Society would otherwise lack. For it has been the success of its brokers that has enabled Lloyd's to overcome this second in-built disadvantage.

Lloyd's brokers are those companies on which Lloyd's confers the right of access to the underwriting room. Underwriters in the market will not accept business from other brokers. In return for this privilege, they submit to the regulation of their affairs by the Society. Since many of the leading figures in these companies are Names, Lloyd's brokers can participate in the affairs and politics of the Society, even to the point of becoming chairman – witness Peter Miller who has held the post since 1984. Throughout the 1970s, about 25 per cent of the members of the committee were brokers.

However, in the past fifteen years or so a major change has occurred in the nature of the Lloyd's broking community. A dozen or so companies have cut loose from the pack and have become major multinational corporations. The Sedgwick Group, for instance, has developed through successive mergers into a company operating on a large scale across the world. After its acquisition of Fred S. James, the sixth largest American broking company, in 1985, the company was worth £1.5 billion and was expected to handle about £6 billion a year in premiums.

The prowess of these companies has been crucial in the success of modern Lloyd's. They have brought to the underwriters sitting in their boxes in the underwriting room at Lime Street business scoured from all quarters of the world, and in this way have enabled Lloyd's to overcome the difficulty that a market of competing underwriters – unlike a company – faces in winning business. However, Lloyd's has had to pay a price for this solution to the problem: by the late 1970s the balance of power in the market which had formerly characterized the relationship between brokers and the underwriters had disappeared. The age of the 'broker barons' had arrived.

The power of the large brokers stemmed in the first place from the sheer concentration of business in their hands. By 1978, eight broker groups out of a total of 167 accounted for 60 per cent of the total premium placed at Lloyd's. The top three companies accounted for no less than 40 per cent. The clear danger presented by this development was that an underwriter might accept certain business on terms which were disadvantageous to the Names on his syndicate just in order to keep one of the big brokers sweet.

However, there was a further way in which the major brokers could be said to exercise undue influence in the market. As a result of their long-standing involvement in the market, they had come to own many of the underwriting agencies. They were uniquely placed to provide the management, capital and back-up office skills required. Broking firms had a hand in setting up five of the first six limited liability companies in the 1930s. After 1945, brokers acquired agents which had formerly been owned by underwriters when they had to be sold on their deaths in order to pay estate duty. As a result, by the end of the 1970s 45 per cent of the total underwriting capacity at Lloyd's was managed by agencies which were directly controlled by brokers; a further 6 per cent was managed by agents in which brokers had an ownership stake. All in all, brokers controlled or had a hand in just over half the total underwriting capacity of the market.

Abuses surface

By the late 1970s, then, Lloyd's had been transformed by the upsurge in broker power and by the admission of new members on an unprecedented scale. However, despite these momentous changes the Society continued to be governed and regulated under the 1871 Act which had been drawn up for a small club of individual professional underwriters. This failure to modernize the regulatory system was the fundamental reason why abuses began to surface at Lloyd's in the late 1970s.

Probably the first inkling the public received that all was not well was in 1978 when Conservative MP Jonathan Aitken raised in Parliament the question of the *Savonita* affair. The *Savonita* was a ship on which a fire had broken out while it was carrying some Fiat cars reinsured at Lloyd's. The broker responsible for placing this reinsurance refused to claim the loss from the underwriters because he believed it was fraudulent. The *Savonita* affair turned in the first instance on the dispute that resulted from this action. However, the issues that it was ultimately to raise were whether the big brokers were wielding excessive power at Lloyd's, whether the committee was showing sufficient regard for the interest of the Names, and whether the regulation of the market accorded with the ethical standards of the modern City.

Questions in Parliament about Lloyd's were uncomfortable enough for an institution which had always resented any outside scrutiny of its affairs. However, much worse was to follow. By late 1979 the Corporation of Lloyd's was involved in bitter litigation with a number of Names who were contesting some £20 million of losses that had arisen on the Sasse syndicate. In 1975 the underwriter Tim Sasse had committed his syndicate to an arrangement which resulted in its members underwriting a large amount of low-quality property business in the United States. The resulting avalanche of claims led to extensive losses for the 1976 and 1977 account years. Some of the Names on the syndicate disputed their liability for these losses on two main grounds.

They argued firstly that there was no authority for the underwriting because it had been conducted in breach of Lloyd's own rules, and secondly that the committee had failed in its duty to enforce proper regulation of the market. Eventually the Corporation and the Names reached an out of court settlement in which the bulk of the losses was met by the Corporation through a special charge on the whole of the market.

The Sasse dispute was altogether more serious than the *Savonita* affair for it focused attention on the unsatisfactory relationship which now existed between external Names and the professionals working in the market. The illusion was shattered that non-working members could rely on the informal sanctions of a gentlemen's club to protect their interests; the essential bond of trust between the external Names and the market professionals was severely weakened; and the legal battle challenged the very foundation stone of the Society, the acceptance by Names of the principle of unlimited liability. Even more than the *Savonita* affair, the Sasse dispute highlighted the deficiencies in the committee's supervision of the market.

In the late 1970s a further cause for concern on this score was the prospect of takeovers of the big Lloyd's brokers by a number of large American broking companies which supplied them with much of their all-important American business. The committee feared that this development would greatly weaken its ability to regulate the market, which had always rested to a large extent on the force of informal undertakings. In April 1978 the committee tried to block one imminent takeover by imposing a 20 per cent limit on the shareholding in any Lloyd's broker by insurance interests outside Lloyd's. However, because of Lloyd's reliance on the American connection it was clear that this could only be a stopgap until a longer-term solution to the general problem of supervision was found.

Fisher to the rescue

As a result of these developments the committee – nudged along by pressure from the Bank of England which was increasingly concerned at the direction events were taking at Lloyd's – took a crucial decision. A working party was set up under Sir Henry Fisher, a former High Court judge, 'to inquire into self-regulation at Lloyd's'. The purpose of the exercise was made explicit in the terms of reference: to head off any prospect of outside intervention in the affairs of Lloyd's, by modernizing its system of self-regulation. Of the seven members on the working party three, including Sir Henry, were outsiders, and the remainder were working members of Lloyd's. Significantly only one of the professionals was a broker; from that perspective, it was very much 'an underwriters' committee', to quote one of the participants. It was the recommendations of this working party that were to lead to the Lloyd's Act of 1982 under whose aegis the counter-revolution was instigated.

The Fisher Report's central conclusion was that Lloyd's could no longer continue to regulate its affairs under the 1871 Act. The existing constitution prevented effective supervision of a market which had been transformed by the growth of power of the big brokers and the influx of new members. Action was necessary to reduce the direct influence of brokers. And Lloyd's needed to give much more protection to the interest of the non-working members of the Society. However, to achieve this the ruling body of the market needed itself to be reinforced in its authority, which was unduly limited under the 1871 Act.

The central recommendation of the Fisher Report that sprang from this analysis was that Lloyd's needed a new constitution. Sovereignty should no longer be vested in the general meeting of members but in a new Council, which was to be given wide-ranging powers to enable it to regulate the market effectively, including effective disciplinary machinery. In exercising that supervision, it was to undertake an 'overall responsibility' towards Names. Members of the Council would be chosen by a system of dual electorates, reflecting the two-tier nature of the new Lloyd's. Professionals working in the market, including both underwriters and brokers who were Names, would vote for sixteen members of the Council. Non-working members would elect a minority of six onto the Council; in addition there would be three outsiders, who would gain their place through nomination by the Council and approval by the Governor of the Bank of England. The passing of bye-laws by the Council would require a majority from each of these two sections.

The underlying purpose of the Council was clearly to give some redress to the imbalance of power between the external Names and the market professionals. Yet in this respect the proposal was something of a *trompe-l'œil*. Non-working members were to win their representation on the new body at the sacrifice of their existing voting rights which gave them a potential, if wholly unrealized, ability to win power on the committee. At the same time, the sixteen working members of the Council were to continue to form the committee of Lloyd's. The Fisher Report clearly envisaged that the Council would delegate considerable power to the committee, including the right to make investigations and to formulate many of the rules.

If the proposed new Council did not mark as clean a break from the past as it might have appeared at first sight, the same cannot be said about the other main recommendation of the Fisher Report, which concerned the controlling interests of brokers in managing agencies. A majority of the working party felt that there was an unacceptable conflict of interest between on the one hand the broker's duty to his client, the assured, and on the other hand the duty of the managing agent, controlled by that broker, to the Names on his syndicates. Accordingly it proposed that the Council should be given the power to compel such broking companies to divest themselves of their interests in managing agents within a period of five years.

The Lloyd's Act

Lloyd's accepted the recommendations of the Fisher Report and sponsored the private parliamentary bill which was necessary in order to give effect to them. After protracted proceedings in both Houses, the new Act was eventually passed in 1982. In most essential respects it followed the draft bill which had been drawn up in the Fisher Report; however, there were three important changes. The divestment measure was made mandatory rather than at the discretion of the Council. Parliament also insisted that there should be more non-working members on the Council. Under the Lloyd's Act there were accordingly sixteen working members, eight non-working members and the three outsiders, making a Council which was twenty-seven strong. Finally Lloyd's was given immunity from any lawsuit brought by a member of the Society. The Fisher working party had not explicitly recommended this; however, the committee believed that without this protection it would not be able to exercise its duty to police of the market effectively.

The Lloyd's Act, which came into force in January 1983, had received the royal assent on 23 July 1982. It was not a moment too soon. Only a few weeks later, the storm broke with allegations of a major financial scandal in the market. The accusations were of such gravity that, had they been made earlier, it is doubtful whether Lloyd's would today be enjoying the right to run its affairs which had been re-established and reinforced by the 1982 Act.

The Alexander Howden scandal

The allegations were made by the American broking company Alexander & Alexander Services, and resulted from its purchase of the Alexander Howden Group, a Lloyd's broker which owned one of the largest underwriting agencies at Lloyd's, Alexander Howden Underwriting. One of the Group's directors was Ian Posgate, also the leading underwriter for Alexander Howden Underwriting. As a result of 'a fair value audit' of the Alexander Howden companies, Alexander & Alexander had made an unpleasant discovery. This was broadcast to the public at large when it submitted a report, as it had to do under American law, to the Securities and Exchange Commission in Washington. In this document, the American company alleged that $55 million of funds had been diverted from Howden companies and the underwriting syndicates that its agency managed into offshore companies owned by four former directors of Alexander Howden: Kenneth Grob, Ronald Comery, Jack Carpenter and Alan Page. The document alleged that funds taken in by these offshore companies 'were used in part for the personal benefit of the four individuals and Mr Posgate'. Funds in one of the offshore companies, Southern International Re (SIR) were directed to be 'used on behalf of the four and Mr Posgate to purchase a substantial interest in the Banque du Rhône et de la Tamise SA from Howden at a time when they and Mr Posgate were directors of Howden. Neither the four nor Mr Posgate disclosed the interest to Howden.' Alexander & Alexander announced that it was suing the four directors for breach of fiduciary duty and misrepresentation, and breach of a settlement agreement which they had reached with them for the return of some of the funds; in a separate action it was also suing Posgate for breach of fiduciary duty and misrepresentation.

These allegations hit the market like a bombshell. The accusations against Posgate were particularly startling. He was the market's most celebrated underwriter, and had been dubbed 'Goldfinger' because of his prowess. Names had flocked to join his syndicates, which were among the largest and most profitable at Lloyd's. Posgate immediately denied all the charges, announced that he was defending the action, and started proceedings against Alexander & Alexander for wrongful dismissal. Quite separately the other four directors, who had predictably acquired the sobriquet of 'The Gang of Four', also denied the charges, and announced their intention to defend themselves.

In April 1984 Alexander & Alexander Services and the four former directors reached a final settlement, under which they returned various further assets and the company stopped its suit against them. In mid-1985 the company and Posgate were, however, still involved in litigation; the case was due to be held in October 1986. Meantime, a Lloyd's disciplinary committee set up under the Lloyd's Act acquitted Posgate of the serious charges of involvement in the misappropriation of funds from the Alexander Howden Group and the syndicates run by its agency. He was acquitted of knowing who owned SIR and of being party to the misuse of funds placed with it; and of being a party to the plundering and syphoning of funds from the Alexander Howden Group for his personal benefit. However, he was found guilty of accepting the secret gift of a Pissarro painting from Kenneth Grob, in his capacity as chairman of the Alexander Howden Group, and of realising that this was given to him with the intention of influencing him as an underwriter to act for the benefit of the Howden Group. He was also found guilty of a failure to disclose his interest in the Banque du Rhône et de la Tamise.

The PCW scandal

The investigations into the affairs of Alexander Howden led to a further startling revelation in late 1982. As a result of these inquiries, a query had arisen over some reinsurance contracts which had been routed through Alexander Howden; they had come from the syndicates managed by PCW Underwriting Agencies, which was owned by another important Lloyd's broker, Minet Holdings. Investigators later established that between 1968 and 1982 the agency's underwriting executives, Peter Cameron-Webb and Peter Dixon, had placed nearly £40 million in the form of reinsurance premiums – broked primarily through Alexander Howden Insurance Brokers Ltd – with offshore companies which the two men secretly controlled. In December 1982 PCW Agencies – which now had a new management team – issued a writ against Cameron-Webb and Dixon for the return of profits made from this reinsurance and for damages for breach of duty in their former capacity as directors of the agency. Both men defended the action, though neither was still living in Britain, Cameron-Webb having moved to the United States, and Dixon to Marbella in Spain. In points of claim pursuant to the writ, the agency, which in 1983 was renamed Richard Beckett Underwriting Agencies (RBUA), later alleged that the two individuals had 'each improperly made for themselves very substantial personal benefits at the expense of the Names'. Investigators appointed by the agency estimated that through the use of funds in these offshore companies Cameron-Webb had benefited to the tune of £6.5 million, and Dixon to £8.4 million. Money was said to have been spent on executive jet aircraft, yachts and the purchase of property, amongst other things. Racehorses in Kentucky had been purchased, and a soft porn film called *Let's Do It* had been financed out of money which belonged to the Names on the syndicates. A subsequent investigation by the top City accountants Price Waterhouse estimated that Names were owed a further £32–40 million in interest which had accumulated on their funds in these companies.

The first Minet disclosures in late 1982 led to a decisive development. The Bank of England became worried about the damage that the apparently unstoppable spate of scandals at Lloyd's was doing to the image of the City. At the behest of the then Governor, Gordon Richardson, Lloyd's was forced to accept the appointment of a complete outsider as an independent chief executive. Ian Hay Davison, a leading partner in the accountancy firm Arthur Andersen, was chosen as the white knight. Davison enjoyed a reputation for not suffering fools gladly, and quite how his abrasive executive style would go down at Lloyd's remained to be seen. He took up his appointment on 14 February 1983, St Valentine's Day – a coincidence which led people in the market to think of the St Valentine's Day massacre rather than the patron saint of true love.

The Council's reform programme

The Council which met for the first time in January 1983 differed, therefore, from what both the Fisher Report and Parliament had envisaged. There was now to be a further outsider with the key post of independent chief executive. More importantly, the reforming brief of the Council had become wider and more urgent. Not only did it now have to eliminate the weaknesses in the regulation of Lloyd's which had been pinpointed by the Fisher Report in the wake of the difficulties which had emerged in the late 1970s. Most pressing of all, the Council had to restore the good name of Lloyd's by stamping out the conditions which had fostered the financial scandals that had come to light in late 1982.

So reforms at Lloyd's are a combination of measures stemming directly from the Fisher Report and further steps which have been seen to be necessary in the wake of the financial scandals. The counter-revolution has been underpinned by the determination of the new Council under the direction of Ian Hay Davison to assert its full authority and independence. On this basis, the Council has unveiled a reform programme which falls under four principal headings: the establishment of effective machinery for policing the market; a policy of enforcing the fullest possible disclosure on the part of market professionals; the implementation of the divestment of the ownership interests of brokers in managing agents; and proposals, which in mid-1985 are still being worked out, to regulate Lloyd's brokers.

Establishing the Council's authority

The most pressing task for the new Council has been to re-establish the very credibility of self-regulation at Lloyd's, for the confidence of the non-working members and the outside world in the Society had been stretched to near breaking point. It has therefore been of paramount importance to assert the full authority of the Council. In particular, it has been vital to demonstrate that working members no longer dominate the running of Lloyd's through the old committee.

The main way in which Ian Hay Davison claims this has been achieved has been by setting up a number of standing committees which report directly to the Council on the crucial regulatory issues. Of the ten committees established for 1985, seven were chaired by non-working members. The old committee continues to have important responsibilities. It supervises the admission of members and the regulation of underwriting agents. However, early fears that it might continue to exercise powers to make rules and investigations have been assuaged by the establishment of two independent committees, each chaired now by nominated members of the Council. The Rules Committee was chaired in 1985 by Ian Hay Davison himself, and the Investigations Committee by Edward Walker-Arnott. Ian Hay Davison regards these changes as a major achievement. In February 1985 he reviewed the progress of the reforms at Lloyd's in an important speech delivered to a conference on the future of Lloyd's organized by the Risk Research Group. He claimed that 'the Council is clearly seen as

the governing body despite early concerns that it might delegate most of its functions to the Committee'. He suggested that
this was a principal reason why 'the isolation and exclusive-
ness of the old Committee has given way to the wider perspective of the new Council'.[1]

Discipline

A priority for this new regime has been to establish a fair and
rigorous system of self-policing which would command the
respect of both those working in the market and the outside
world. Discipline was accordingly the first front which the new
Council opened in its war against the old customs of Lloyd's.
The Council quickly passed bye-laws to establish disciplinary
machinery over the membership, and the Investigations Committee mentioned above was set up to supervise the policing of
the market. Charges brought by the Investigations Committee
are heard by the Disciplinary Committee which was established to act as the 'court' of Lloyd's.

These committees have not been short of work: up to
mid-1985 there have been between ten and twenty investigations. For a variety of reasons long delays have been experienced in the hearings. The most important case which had
been published by the end of 1984 concerned the use which
underwriters Raymond Brooks and Terence Dooley had made
of a Bermuda-based offshore company, Fidentia Marine Insurance, which Brooks effectively controlled and in which both
men had an interest. Investigators ascertained that over a
period of thirteen years Fidentia had gained £6.2 million
through its transactions with the syndicates run by the two
underwriters. Because this interest was not disclosed to or
agreed by members of the syndicates, the Disciplinary Committee found that Brooks, the active underwriter, had conducted insurance business in a discreditable manner. He was
found guilty on six charges in all, and as a result was expelled
from the Society. Dooley, the deputy underwriter, was also
found to have failed to disclose or seek the consent of syndicate
members to his interest in Fidentia. However, because the

[1] *The Future of Lloyd's* published by the Risk Research Group, 1985.

committee felt that his responsibility for the relevant defaults was less culpable – though still extremely serious – than that of Brooks, his sentence was less severe. He was suspended from the Society for twenty-one months.

Disclosure

If the creation of disciplinary machinery was the principal work of 1983, then disclosure was above all the theme of 1984. It was clear that the cloak of secrecy which enveloped the operation of underwriting syndicates had to be stripped away. Greater disclosure is the key reform made by the Council to protect Names from possible malpractice on the part of professionals in the market. Ian Hay Davison's pet phrase is: 'When the sun shines, the mists clear away'; it is certainly true that under his direction the mists of secrecy have been dispelled to a far greater extent than was ever envisaged in the Fisher Report.

The principal thrust of this new regime of disclosure has been to bring the accounting of syndicates into line with that of limited liability companies. Under the new rules, underwriting agents must draw up comprehensive standardized annual accounts and reports for their syndicates. Starting in 1985, they have been required to provide 'true and fair' accounts, which means that they must now reach the same standard of accounting as that which applies to limited companies. And since August 1984 the reports have been open to public scrutiny.

The Council initially took the view that disclosure would be sufficient to stamp out the key abuse of 'related party' underwriting – the placing by underwriting executives of reinsurance contracts with insurance companies which they owned or controlled. The bye-laws passed in 1984 made it mandatory for agents to disclose in their reports any interests in insurance and reinsurance companies; however, this policy was widely criticized as insufficient to deal with the problem. In early 1985 Lloyd's responded to this pressure and made it known that it intended to take further action. Agents would no longer be allowed to hold any interest in outside insurance companies; a code of conduct would also be issued spelling out the fact that another abuse, 'preferred underwriting' – the placing of more profitable business with a 'baby syndicate' composed of a few professionals in the market – was contrary to the law of agency.

Divestment

As well as asserting discipline and introducing this general policy of disclosure, the Council has also had to execute the task of divestment which Parliament had imposed on the Society in the Lloyd's Act. In his speech to the conference organized by the Risk Research Group in February 1985, Ian Hay Davison stated that the removal of ownership from brokers would affect managing agents handling over 70 per cent of the syndicates at Lloyd's. In his view, the change was 'as far-reaching as the changes currently occurring at the Stock Exchange'.

In carrying out divestment, the Council has had two goals in mind. The first has been to ensure that the new ownership arrangements will not create conflict with the duty of agents to their Names; the second, to ensure that the new agencies attract as much capital, managerial expertise and resources from outside as possible. The difficulty is that these two goals are inherently opposed, since the first requires restrictions on ownership and the second requires the provision of as wide a market as possible. The Council's method of resolving this dilemma has consisted of a somewhat comic compromise. Strict restrictions have been imposed on the provenance of the directors and the ownership of the agents. All directors must be members, associates or subscribers of Lloyd's, and two-thirds must be professionals working in the market. At the same time, two-thirds of the voting shares in a managing agent must be restricted to the Names represented by that agent, and working members of the market. However, a coach and horses has then been driven through this regulation by a provision which allows holders of non-voting shares the right to hire and fire directors.

Despite the existence of this loophole, the broad effect of divestment has been to create sales on terms which have greatly favoured the purchasers. The underlying value of the agencies being divested, although difficult to determine precisely, is certainly not high. Adam Broadbent, a director of the merchant bank J. Henry Schroder Wagg, estimated in early 1985 that the total value of the 114 agencies affected by divestment was £70 million. However, since most of them were combined management and members' agencies, this figure includes the value of members' agencies which brokers may retain under the Lloyd's Act. An exact breakdown of the separate value of the two types of agent is not available, but informed estimates suggest that it is therefore unlikely that the total value of the managing agents being sold exceeds £50 million.

Although it may be difficult to estimate the exact value of the agents, what is beyond doubt is that they are being sold at knockdown rates. As one senior figure in a major broking company said bitterly, 'We're being robbed; because of these forced sales we're having to sell at half the true value.' Those who particularly benefit are those underwriting executives who are striking hard bargains through management buy-outs.

Regulation of brokers

This embarrassing side-effect of the divestment programme is not stopping the Council from pressing ahead with further plans for brokers. The aim of these reforms is to introduce effective regulation of Lloyd's brokers. Even before the formal issuing of the rules in early 1986 the Council clearly intended to regulate Lloyd's brokers in three main ways.

The first of these is financial. Rules are being established for the solvency of Lloyd's brokers. The aim of this measure is to ensure that underwriters may be certain of receiving the large amounts of credit which brokers owe them through premiums they have received from their clients for policies that have been underwritten at Lloyd's.

The second concerns the structure of ownership, specifying in particular the extent to which insurance companies may hold shares in Lloyd's brokers. The essential problem this poses concerns the extent to which Lloyd's can exert regulatory control over brokers which are owned by outside insurance interests. Added urgency has been given to this issue by the merger which took place in 1985 between the Sedgwick Group, Britain's largest independent broking firm, and Fred S. James, a US insurance broker. This left the former owner of Fred S. James, Transamerica, an American conglomerate with extensive insurance interests, owning 29 per cent of the voting shares and 39 per cent of the equity of the Sedgwick Group.

The third main way in which the Council is to regulate brokers is by issuing a code of conduct by which all employees and directors of Lloyd's brokers will have to abide. Lloyd's will monitor the behaviour of brokers in the market and bring disciplinary proceedings against individuals who breach the code. Furthermore, Lloyd's will not hesitate to implement the disciplinary machinery in the event of complaints about brokers' behaviour in other markets. The argument is that, if an individual can be shown to have behaved unacceptably in any market, his behaviour presents a danger to the underwriting members of the Society.

The cost of the reforms

These reforms clearly constitute a full-blooded attempt to make self-regulation work at Lloyd's. The contrast between the position in 1985 and that in 1982 at the time of the passage of the Lloyd's Act is dramatic. However, there are many members of the Society who remain far from happy. Predictably, market professionals are already concerned about the cost of the new system of self-regulation. The new regime imposes a double burden: the spending by the Corporation on the government and policing of the market, and the expense incurred by syndicates in complying with the new rules. Many underwriters are also worried about the effect of the new regime on the spirit of enterprise at Lloyd's: they are worried that the culture which has fostered innovation may be stifled by the new regulations. In his speech of early 1985 Ian Hay Davison acknowledged 'the fear that we may be tying up the underwriters in so much red tape that they will be unable to maintain their enviable reputation for flexible and innovative underwriting'.

The question of broker power

Scepticism has also been expressed within the market about whether the reforms offer a real answer to the issue of broker power. The source of this is the concentration of business in the hands of a small number of huge broking companies, one or two of which are regarded by underwriters as 'steamrollers'. Stephen Merrett, one of the most respected underwriters at Lloyd's, refers to 'the huge power of pocket' that they hold in the market, particularly over the small underwriter. Divestment by itself therefore offers no solution to this problem. Many inside the market believe that it is futile to pretend that the Council can exercise any real control over such large companies, whose activities span the world and many of which are themselves now owned by big American companies. Critics argue that the Council's right to regulate Lloyd's brokers simply gives it responsibility without power. Robert Kiln, a former member of the committee, says that Lloyd's cannot win, since it will be held to account for scandals or difficulties which it has no way of preventing. As he wrote in *Lloyd's Log* in 1983, 'We must stop pretending to regulate areas that we cannot. It is surely questionable whether Lloyd's should or could regulate these financial empires. Should we not confine our regulation to their conduct in our market and leave the rest to outside bodies?'

The real brake on the power of brokers is likely to come from an unintended and unexpected side-effect of divestment: the emergence of a handful of large underwriting agents controlling the bulk of the underwriting capacity of the market. This development is already taking place as a number of agents use the opportunity afforded them by divestment to increase their share of the market. Sturge Holdings' purchase of the Edwards & Payne underwriting agency from the Sedgwick Group brought its share of capacity in 1985 to about 9 per cent. Merrett Holdings' purchase of the agency interests of Stewart Wrightson brought its share of the market to about 6 per cent. Other major agencies seem certain to emerge.

The relationship between Names and agent

The rise of the 'underwriting barons' may curb the power of the brokers, but it is likely to create a fresh set of regulatory difficulties for Lloyd's. The problem presented by this development is that there is a conflict between the duty of a managing agent to Names on the syndicates which it runs on the one hand, and on the other hand its interest in keeping shareholders happy. Quite apart from this, the key relationship between Names and their agent remains unsatisfactory, in the view of many, for all the Council's reforms.

Their most fundamental criticism concerns the issue of information. Proper accounting procedures may now have been set in train; however, many Names complain that they are still denied sufficient information for them to make rational investment decisions. League tables are now published on the profit and loss performance of syndicates, thanks to the initiative of the founders of the Association of Lloyd's Members, a group of about three thousand external Names (but no thanks to the former committee which initially tried to prevent the venture). However, this analysis is only really a starting point. Names need to know much more about the potential risks and rewards entailed in the various classes of business conducted by Lloyd's syndicates; above all, they need much more information about the way in which syndicates set aside reserves to meet future claims. It was the need to increase such provision that led to the huge losses which the Names on the Minet syndicates are now facing. In early 1985 Michael Hesketh, an insurance analyst at the stockbroking firm of Rowe & Pitman, addressed the conference organized by the Risk Research Group on the future of Lloyd's. He drew attention to the surprising lack of any recruitment drive by agents among the newly enriched partners of the Stock Exchange – on Lloyd's very doorstep. 'Perhaps that is because the agents fear that, notwithstanding recent improvements, their standards of disclosure are still grossly inadequate by Stock Exchange standards – and they would be right.'

One of the fiercest critics of the existing relationship between an agent and its Names is John Rew, the driving force behind the Association of Lloyd's Members. Rew's owlish appearance and mild manner bely his passion to force further change on Lloyd's. His West End flat is the first port of call for the growing band of Names who feel they have not just been hard done by, but downright cheated. Rew believes that at present all the cards are stacked in the agent's favour. For example, aggrieved Names can only sue an agent as a group of individuals, not as a collective body in the form of the syndicate; this makes it very difficult to organize legal action against an agent.

Rew believes that it would be possible to give some measure of collective power to Names on a syndicate without broaching the cardinal principle of 'each for his own and not one for another'. In particular he believes that there should be emergency powers whereby members of a syndicate in which trouble has erupted – such as the PCW syndicates – could have the power to bind themselves to act collectively. At the same time, he believes that syndicate members should have the power to appoint auditors, whose failure to prevent the scandals was the subject of a stinging rebuke in a speech made by Ian Hay Davison in Paris in early 1985.

There are obvious difficulties arising from Rew's proposals. It is clear that the interest of a Name facing losses of £100,000 in collective legal action is very different from that of a Name facing losses of just £1000. Lloyd's certainly takes the view that such changes would move the structure of syndicates dangerously close to the principles of joint liability. However, it is clear that the present balance of power between Names and agents is unsatisfactory. To that extent, Rew certainly has a point when he says that the reform programme at Lloyd's has done no more than 'paper over the cracks'. He argues that the whole structure of syndicates, and indeed the cherished principle of unlimited liability, should be re-examined in the light of the troubles that have assailed Lloyd's in the past ten years.

Doubts about discipline

Considerable scepticism is also voiced about the value of the disciplinary machinery which has been established. Several of the key cases have dragged on for years, and such delays have meant that at a critical stage Lloyd's has been unable to demonstrate its full commitment to police the market and to impose penalties on wrongdoers. A further problem is that Lloyd's sanctions are necessarily limited. The punishment of expulsion is hardly relevant to those who no longer work in the market. Somewhat unfairly, Lloyd's has attracted flak for the lack of any action on the part of the Director of Public Prosecutions (certainly until July 1985 when this book went to press). That of course is a separate – and much remarked upon – issue. Yet the feeling persists that Lloyd's disciplinary proceedings are 'laudable but irrelevant', in the words of one agent who should know. Somewhat incongruously, the disciplinary office is sited in a Portakabin on the roof of the Lloyd's building. The location seems curiously appropriate; in the view of many observers, the much trumpeted new disciplinary machinery has been precisely that – out of sight.

The constitution of the Council

Another fundamental doubt about the new regime of self-regulation concerns the nature of the Council and the extent to which it can really be expected to look after the interest of non-working members. For all the attempts made by the Council to provide for fair treatment of external Names, it can be argued that the reforms are being made under a constitution which is fatally flawed. The external Names at Lloyd's are effectively the investors in the business conducted at Lloyd's, yet in the last resort they do not call the shots in the regulation of the Society. Non-working members are of course now present on the Council. However, it is widely felt that they can exert little influence when set against the professionals with all their expertise and experience. Furthermore, the committee of working members still has important powers including the regulation of underwriting agencies. In the future, when the present rumpus has died down, it is thought likely that they will end up chairing most of the standing committees which have been established. At the same time, the Lloyd's Act stipulates that it is from their ranks that the key post of chairman must be filled.

The running in the reform programme has been made by the nominated outsiders under the direction of Ian Hay Davison.

The reason for this is clear: Davison and the other three nominees are backed by the authority of the Bank of England. This outcome was certainly not intended by Parliament. It must be questionable whether it is the best way to regulate Lloyd's, since the Bank of England, unlike the Department of Trade, is simply not equipped with the resources and expertise necessary to monitor the insurance market.

Lloyd's gravest crisis

At the beginning of 1985 Ian Hay Davison himself attempted to assess the reform programme in the speech he delivered to the conference on the future of Lloyd's. His verdict was favourable. He argued that Lloyd's had showed a commitment to change which press critics in particular had doubted was possible at the time of his appointment. His judgement was one of 'considerable progress'. At about the same time Lloyd's chairman, Peter Miller, made an upbeat speech in which he pointed to the buoyant future which lay ahead for Lloyd's as a result of the improving fortunes of the world insurance industry. He predicted that the necessary surge in applications for 1986 to enable Lloyd's to have the capital to meet the upturn in the insurance cycle would be forthcoming. The purpose of the speeches was clear: the authorities were seeking to put the past behind them; but the attempt proved premature. Within only a few weeks Lloyd's was back in the headlines as the troubled affairs of the Minet syndicates took yet another turn for the worse. Names learnt that they faced prospective losses of £130 million for insurance conducted during 1979–82. Some of them soon made it clear that they were not going to take this lying down; a steering committee was set up, and the accountancy firm of Price Waterhouse was dispatched once again to probe into the affair.

The background to this development lay in the controversial offer which was made to Names by Richard Beckett Underwriting Agencies in June 1984. Names had earlier learnt that they were facing trading losses in 1984 of £37.9 million. They had also been informed that the misappropriation of their funds between 1968 and 1982 amounted to £38.9 million; £25 million of this money had been located in companies in

Gibraltar. Minet Holdings and Alexander & Alexander Services offered to top up the Gibraltar funds with a contribution of £13.14 million. Alexander & Alexander were involved because questionable reinsurance premiums made by PCW syndicates had been routed through Alexander Howden prior to their purchase of the company in 1982. The total offer made by the agency to Names thus amounted to just over £38 million. However, there was a crucial condition to RBUA's offer: Names had to waive legal rights against any parties to the affair, and assign them to Jufcrest, a joint company set up by Minet Holdings and Alexander & Alexander Services. The steering committee received clear advice from counsel that they should not give up their legal rights in this way; they also knew that if they accepted the offer they would gainsay nearly £40 million of interest which had accumulated on the funds. Under the pressure of Lloyd's annual solvency deadline, when Names must show that they can meet their underwriting obligations, almost all chose to follow the example of Lloyd's chairman Peter Miller, himself a Name on one of the syndicates, and accept the offer. Keith Whitten, a leading member of the steering committee, maintains that a key reason why Names accepted the offer was the assurance given them by RBUA that they should expect no more than a small loss on the non-marine syndicates the following year.

By 1985, however, many of them were bitterly regretting their decision. The agency informed them that because of a 'disastrous deterioration' in underwriting results in the last quarter of 1984, Names now faced prospective losses of £130 million for the years 1979–82. These losses resulted primarily from US casualty business, particularly in the field of liability insurance, under which companies get cover from claims resulting from deficiencies in their products and in their manufacturing processes. The losses were concentrated on 350 members of syndicates 918 and 940 which had specialized in this line of business. They faced heavy claims, for example, on asbestosis and Agent Orange, the chemical defoliant used extensively by the United States in the Vietnam War. Such insurance is called 'long-tail' because claims typically continue for many years after the policy has originally been taken out. As the Minet Names had painfully discovered, such business has a sting in the tail. However, because the anticipated £130 million losses were expected to arise from claims stretching over a period of as long as twenty years, the actual call on Names in 1985 was for £60 million. This was the present value of the £130 million losses, taking into account the interest that would accumulate on £60 million over the next twenty or so years.

A number of questions arose. Why had the huge losses taken place? Were they simply the consequence, as the agency insisted, of the deterioration in underwriting results which had occurred in late 1984? Or could they be attributed in part, as the steering committee claimed, to the reserves being calculated on a different basis from the method used in the previous year? Why was there no adequate reinsurance cover for the syndicates most heavily affected? To what extent could the losses be linked, as the steering committee claimed, to the malpractices that had occurred before the new management took over at the agency? Finally, could Lloyd's itself (at a time when it did not enjoy immunity) be held responsible for a failure to regulate the market?

During the summer of 1985, Lloyd's came under heavy pressure to organize a market rescue for the beleaguered Names. However, the Council set its face firmly against any repetition of the earlier bail-out won by the Sasse Names. In a key speech delivered to the General Meeting of Lloyd's members in June, Peter Miller was adamant in his rejection of this course of action.

> The one thing the Council cannot do is to provide some sort of so-called financial lifeboat and thus depart from the principle that we each individually have to respond for our share of losses, if unhappily, they occur.

The only concession of note which Miller announced was the appointment of an independent committee of enquiry to investigate the conduct of the management of the syndicates while it had been in the hands of RBUA.

Lloyd's unyielding attitude could clearly only be justified if the emergence of trading losses was unrelated to the malpractices that had occurred at the agency before 1982. There were many, however, who argued that this position was untenable;

and it was soon under attack in Parliament itself. In July, Bryan Gould, Labour spokesman on Trade and Industry delivered a scathing speech in the House of Commons on the whole affair. His judgement was uncompromising.

> The truth is surely that these further losses arose, as did the earlier ones, which are plainly attributable to fraud, from one continuous course of conduct. There were fraudulent defalcations which had the inevitable consequence that the underwriters involved in that fraud were then compelled to give top priority to maximizing immediate premium income – irrespective of the nature of the business, the risk undertaken and the Lloyd's rules – with the prime and overriding objective of getting in the money so that they could conceal the fraud and escape detection for as long as possible

He sounded a warning to Lloyd's if it continued to 'bury its head in the sand' by failing 'to take responsibility for the fact that it has not carried out its supervisory duties effectively', this would discredit the principle of self-regulation. A future Labour Government would have to review Lloyd's regulatory powers.

Mixed prospects

The rekindling of the Minet affair showed that the past simply will not go away for Lloyd's; the prospects for its future are thus mixed. On the one hand, the market stands to benefit from the turnround in the underwriting cycle which has led to sharp increases in premium rates in the all-important US market. The heavy losses of the early 1980s are expected by some to give way to buoyant results from 1986 on. But Lloyd's will only be able to take advantage of these favourable conditions if it can continue to attract new Names into the society. The scandals did not deter a large number of Names from joining the Society in 1984 and 1985; but the effect of the huge losses on the Minet syndicates may prove otherwise in the years ahead. The apparent indifference of the Council to the fate of the members of the Minet syndicates cannot have acted as a good advertisement to join Lloyd's.

Lessons for the City

The eventual outcome of the reform programme may therefore be uncertain. What is clear is that the counter-revolution at Lloyd's does call into question the new regulatory regime which is being established elsewhere in the Square Mile in the wake of the City Revolution. Of course much of the recent experience of Lloyd's has been *sui generis*, yet it does seem to hold two crucial lessons for the new City of London. The first concerns the paramount need for disclosure in order to protect investors. The second is that insiders simply cannot be trusted to do the job of regulation solely by themselves. As Alan Horsford, chief executive of Royal Insurance, says, 'If we've learnt one thing from the troubles at Lloyd's, it's that the Society may have had a lot of fine traditions, but a lot of abuses were able to flourish in that club atmosphere.'

8

After the Revolution

After hubris, nemesis. Or, as that gloomy City luminary Dean Inge put it, if there is one safe generalization in human affairs, it is that revolutions always destroy themselves. The consummate irony in the City Revolution lay in the way disenchantment set in even before the Bastille had been stormed. By 1985, well in advance of the Big Bang, doom-laden forecasts had become commonplace in the Square Mile. Concern was mounting about the risks inherent in the new freedoms that had initially been embraced with so much enthusiasm.

The earliest intimation of these misgivings emerged in Jacob Rothschild's abrupt unscrambling in 1984 of the rather indigestible financial omelette that he had spent much of the previous two years concocting. Then in 1985 came the first of the potential marriages to be dissolved before it was consummated: Britannia Arrow, an investment, banking and unit trust group that had taken a 29.9 per cent stake in a provincial stockbroker, Heseltine Moss, joined its partner in announcing that the marriage was off. People also started withdrawing from the new gilt-edged market. Both Schroder's and Drexel Burnham Lambert decided that there was little hope of making an adequate return if thirty-one participants poured up to £600 million of capital into a market which had hitherto been dominated by just two big jobbers and enjoyed the support of only £100–150 million of capital. So they reduced the numbers to twenty-nine. Others who had hoped to become primary dealers in the new market, such as the big US securities house E. F. Hutton, did not bother in the end to make a formal application to join. For people in the securities markets who were about to return to the capital-raising and trading methods of the nineteenth century there was no consolation in the succession of bad news from Lloyd's of London, which appeared to be trapped in a nineteenth-century regulatory time warp.

The swing in mood from euphoria to gloom in the first half of 1985 was nicely caught by an article in the magazine *Institutional Investor*. Indelicately blazoned across its cover in February of that year was the blunt question: 'Has the City gone mad?' Inside, a number of alarming scenarios were painted – and not just for those who had money riding on the outcome. The magazine extended the debate into the political arena by asking: could Mrs Thatcher find her election campaign in 1987 embarrassed by City scandals in the aftermath of the Big Bang?

The government's purpose in fostering change in the Square Mile was originally to preserve the City's role as an international financial centre and to create new opportunities for British financiers. Yet senior officials at the Bank of England had been aware all along that domestic securities firms were a long way behind in the race and that the risks in the reform of the financial structure were enormous. They also knew that the outcome of the City Revolution would depend heavily on the way both the Bank and the practitioners in the markets handled those risks. The difficulty lay in the existence of powerful forces which were transforming the international financial system in such a way as to make risk management a nightmare.

Technology transforms the markets

The most important of those forces related to another revolution, the one in information technology. Not only did technology pave the way for the internationalization of the capital markets; it made physical trading floors potentially irrelevant to the conduct of business in financial markets. The most international of all the securities markets, the Eurobond market, is a telephone market in which the market makers give their prices to electronic information services such as those run by Reuters and Telerate; subscribers to their services can then obtain prices on a screen simply by using a keyboard. Similarly, the foreign exchange marketplace, whose technology was pioneered by Reuters in the 1970s, is wholly electronic. Both markets bear witness to the extraordinary power of technology to erase natural barriers and conventions. The hallmark of the financial world in the 1980s and 1990s will undoubtedly be the dealing room full of shirt-sleeved young men (and a growing band of women) confronting flickering screens, batteries of telephones and electronic press buttons.

The implications for the Square Mile, whose financial services grew originally out of the trade that passed through the port of London, are immeasurable. The link between City markets and trade in physical goods has, in fact, been weakening over a longer period than that dictated by technology alone. The Lloyd's insurance market diversified away from London-based marine insurance in the nineteenth century and considerably extended the scope of its activities into new types of risk in the twentieth. The commodity markets have long since switched from trading in goods to trading in claims on goods. On the Baltic Exchange, home of the London shipping fraternity, the postwar period has seen diversification from shipping into air freight; latterly the Baltic has set up a market in futures. By now the close proximity between the banking and securities markets on the one hand, and the insurance, shipping and commodities markets on the other, is a function more of history than of necessity. Even for those in banking and securities the need to be located physically in the City is diminishing. Many of the larger American financial institutions whose business is geared primarily to international markets have opted to do business from offices outside the Square Mile.

Far more important, advanced telecommunications are undermining the power of players in the financial markets to monopolize information. This development is dramatic because inside information has always been the key to making money in financial markets: the Rothschilds are supposed to have made a killing on the London Stock Exchange after the battle of Waterloo by obtaining advance warning of the outcome via carrier pigeons – though it should be said that some latterday Rothschilds hotly deny that profits were made from the information. The whole basis for Lloyd's of London's competitive advantage in world marine insurance markets was the information network it established for reporting on shipping movements around the globe. London's securities, insurance and shipping markets originally developed in coffee houses precisely because they were natural places in which to exchange information, gossip and rumour.

For much of the nineteenth century the London Stock Exchange did not have an exclusive monopoly over securities trading in the Square Mile. Only in the 1880s did it establish supremacy over rival dealers in the Bank of England and the Royal Exchange, so instituting a single, central securities market in London. It pulled off the trick by doing a deal with the Exchange Telegraph Co. by which the Exchange offered price lists for Exchange Telegraph's tape machines on condition that the company withdrew its service to outside brokers.

Since this information monopoly began to wane in the twentieth century there has been nothing to prevent people making markets outside the Stock Exchange, provided that they belonged to one of the other clubs that enjoyed exemption from the licensing requirements of the Department of Trade, or obtained a licence directly from the Department. And indeed the discount houses successfully established themselves as market makers outside the Stock Exchange in short-dated gilt-edged stock after World War II, which helps explain why this is the one area of the securities business where negotiated commissions prevailed long before the City Revolution. But until recently no one seriously challenged Britain's only recognized Stock Exchange across a wider range of securities. Even Ariel, the computerized trading system backed by top merchant banks, failed to undermine the Stock Exchange's competitive position. As explained in Chapter 3, this was largely because the Bank of England chose to give the Exchange a monopoly of dealing in gilt-edged securities; in leading equities the Stock Exchange's monopoly survived because Ariel was not sufficiently user-friendly, to use an apt piece of computer jargon, in a world where institutional investors needed a powerful incentive before they were prepared to desert the friendly broker who took care to keep them well dined and well stocked with research.

In the 1980s the position is rather different. The Bank of England is still keen to preserve a central market in government securities, though it would not hesitate to take the market away from the Stock Exchange if it became dissatisfied with the service that the Exchange provided. In a fully international equity market, with negotiated commissions and reduced stamp duties on share transactions, the Stock Exchange should in theory be less vulnerable to the erosion of its remaining business after the Big Bang, in that dealing costs will compare more favourably with those in other international financial centres. But technology could make it vulnerable in other respects, because investors no longer need a physical central marketplace. With the switch to a new, high-technology dealing system, most people in the City expect that business will ultimately disappear from the Stock Exchange floor to the broker–dealers' offices; the only question is: when? So the Exchange's remaining competitive advantage will lie in its own electronic gadgetry for communicating prices and settling transactions, together with the regulatory framework it puts in place to ensure an orderly market.

When it comes to providing information technology, outsiders have plenty to offer the Exchange's existing customers. Not the least among those outsiders is Reuters, which performs a function not unlike that of the Stock Exchange in the foreign exchange market, albeit without regulatory responsibilities. So it is hardly surprising that Reuters should have thrown down the gauntlet in 1985 by proposing to set up the American inter-active dealing system Instinet, for which it had acquired marketing rights in Europe, in direct competition with the Stock Exchange. No doubt its underlying assumption was that the world's capital markets were poised to emulate the foreign exchange markets in which trading follows the sun. At the time of writing the equity capital of around 250 companies is already traded around the world, with financial houses such as the American giant Merrill Lynch moving their equity book across from New York to Tokyo and on to London in the course of a full twenty-four-hour day. Such big international investment houses might not hesitate to use any system that offered low dealing costs if they were able to deal in size; and the absence of comprehensive regulatory back-up is not necessarily a disincentive to the giants of the business, who reckon to be able to look after themselves.

Information technology is putting the big commercial banks under similar pressure as financial data about their larger corporate clients is disseminated more widely. Information relating to the trading prospects of those same 250 companies is now simultaneously available on screens in the offices of institutional investors across the world. Since the commercial banks no longer automatically enjoy better access to such information than their competitors, they are losing business – and not just to their fellow bankers.

Tinker, tailor, banker, broker

This underlines a point that is fundamental to the City Revolution. All financial markets are a marriage of convenience between those who need money and those who are looking for a remunerative outlet for their money. Bankers have no divine right to act as marriage broker. In the Middle Ages the job was often done by scriveners who were able to offer their skills in documentation relating to all forms of paper money and credit. Then, and subsequently, goldsmiths were able to offer safe custody for bullion deposits, which put them in a position to advance credit on the security which they held. Cloth merchants such as Sir Francis Baring, who founded the bank of the same name in the eighteenth century, not only had cash but a range of business contacts across Europe. By extending his operations into banking this grandiose rag trader was doing no more than what a modern management consultant would call 'leveraging the customer base', by selling a wider range of products to an existing clientele – which is precisely what an equally successful latter-day rag trader, Marks & Spencer, has been doing with its recent move into financial services.

Today big multinational companies such as Exxon, ICI or British Petroleum use information technology in their treasury departments to reduce the cost of their borrowings. They have discovered that they can raise money through the wholesale markets that grew up in the 1960s and 1970s more cheaply than from any bank. And since many of them have more capital than the banks and are not overburdened with loans advanced to overstretched Latin American countries it may only be a matter of time before many in-house banking operations go out to take on the commercial banks more directly.

For the moment, however, the one thing that big companies lack is constant contact with institutional investors. So while they may be able to cut out the commercial banks in raising short- to medium-term finance, they cannot bypass the investment or merchant banks that have the ability to distribute their bonds and securities to longer-term investors. Whether that investment house is owned by a retailer (as Dean Witter Reynolds is owned by America's biggest retailer, Sears Roebuck), or by an insurer (as Bache is owned by Prudential Corporation of America), or by a commercial bank (such as Morgan Guaranty, Deutsche Bank or Société Générale) is a secondary consideration. Speed and skill in distribution remain the key to successful wholesale banking in the international capital markets and the key to the strategy of the main participants in the City Revolution.

That is not to say that big corporations are hostile to less powerful financial houses, if they are able to offer bright ideas on how to reduce their clients' borrowing costs. As developed countries open up their capital markets and the capital markets become more volatile, bankers and securities firms have had a field day. They can juggle endlessly with different currencies and different financial instruments to help reduce the borrowing costs of multinational corporations. Since borrowers have so greatly increased their power relative to the banks in the 1980s, international banks in London have fallen over themselves to innovate, offering the corporate treasurer a proliferation of products such as floating-rate notes, revolving underwriting facilities, interest rate swaps and note issuance facilities of the kind mentioned in Chapter 2.

This 'borrower power' is beginning to extend to the retail market, where individuals in developed countries will soon enjoy readier access to credit if they are willing to pay the international market price. One indication of this can be seen in the deals struck in the mid-1980s between the Bank of

Scotland and a group of American banks to increase the Scottish bank's mortgage lending in the British market. The Bank of Scotland found the borrowers, while the American banks found the money in the Euromarkets; the Scottish bank was thereby enabled to expand its fee income for acting as a middleman without taking assets or liabilities into its balance sheet. By keeping the business off the face of its balance sheet the Bank of Scotland avoided the risk that its capital ratios would press up against regulatory ceilings, so causing the Bank of England's eyebrows to twitch. For their part the American banks won new business in a foreign market where they had no costly investment in bank branches or branch staff.

Fiscal fair play and a welcome for new players

If technology is the main engine behind this redrawing of the financial boundaries, governments and central banks can promote and accelerate the process through deregulation. This can mean changing the tax structure to create an even playing field on which a given type of financial institution enjoys no discriminatory tax privileges against its competitors; or it can mean lifting direct controls on financial institutions, such as ceilings on interest rates or balance sheet ratios. In putting the banks and building societies onto the same tax basis in his 1984 budget the Chancellor of the Exchequer, Nigel Lawson, promoted more direct competition between the two types of financial institution. Similarly, his earlier move to abolish life assurance premium relief removed an important privilege enjoyed by Britain's insurance companies vis-à-vis other savings institutions. Mrs Thatcher's government is also anxious to broaden the range of services that different types of financial institution can offer to the consumer. In June 1985 the Economic Secretary to the Treasury, Ian Stewart, told the building societies at their association's annual conference that they would soon be empowered to act as estate agents, to offer insurance broking not only on home loan-related risks but on the whole spectrum of life and casualty insurance, and to become agents for the purchase of stocks, shares and other investments.

In the same month Social Services Secretary Norman Fowler

announced that the government was to abolish the state earnings-related pension scheme and replace it with private pension arrangements. His green paper on the reform of social security revealed that the resulting pensions business could be provided not only by private insurance companies but by banks, building societies, friendly societies and unit trusts. The announcement was greeted with undisguised delight by some of the bigger fund management groups in the City, which had no doubt at all as to who the chief beneficiaries of this proposed reform of the social security system were likely to be.

Also noteworthy – and perhaps even more surprising – is that the Bank of England did not stand in the way when Save and Prosper, the big investment and unit trust group, moved onto the clearing banks' patch by offering a high-interest current account in conjunction with its merchant bank parent and 58 per cent shareholder Robert Fleming. Once again the Bank appeared to be taking a step away from its traditional readiness to protect its flock from outside competition.

The message for financial businesses in and out of the City is a tough one. A pervasive feature of the brave new deregulated world of finance in the second half of the 1980s will be that everyone's customers will come to be regarded as someone else's fair game. And size will be a crucial factor in determining who comes out on top of the heap. One result of the abolition of fixed commissions on the Stock Exchange, for example, will be that banks and brokers are forced to unbundle services whose precise cost has not always been apparent to customers: in fund management the laurels will no longer go to those who are best able to conceal the extent of the charges they impose on the customers. Even before negotiated commissions came in, leading merchant banks felt obliged to raise overt management charges sharply. Stockbrokers, too, faced a similar problem in moving from a system of remuneration based on fixed commissions to one where pricing had to be more explicit. The beneficiaries of the change will be the big independent fund managers and the insurance companies who were previously unable to compete because their charges appeared high in relation to those of the brokers and bankers, even if the reality was otherwise.

Michael Newmarch of the Prudential argues that the Pru's

fund managers have, in the past, been too much in awe of their own size. Under the new deregulated regime size will be put to good use in the interests of the Prudential's customers; and because of the huge volume of funds it controls, overheads will be more widely spread, giving a competitive advantage in fund management. Pension funds at below top level may, according to Newmarch, find that they are understaffed to cope with the conflicts of interest in the new system and be tempted to turn to big independent fund managers that can afford to run not just more extensive dealing desks, but futures teams, research analysts, venture capital divisions and other activities that have the potential to enhance returns. He is one of many in the financial community who believe that investors' tolerance of Chinese Walls will wane in the new climate and that merchant banks may be forced to hive off their fund management divisions to retain their clientele.

Beggar thy neighbour – or else

The hunt for other people's customers will be every bit as competitive in the retail area, where the boundary between City and non-City will become more blurred. Recognizing the need to recoup their heavy costs by pumping more products through their branch networks, the clearing banks have been building up their insurance broking sales at a spectacular rate from a very low base. Using a simple computerized service, the Royal Bank of Scotland is underwriting motor insurance in its own name for private car owners. In due course Barclays and Lloyds, which have substantial life assurance subsidiaries, will almost certainly sell their policies much more actively through their branches, as the Trustee Savings Bank already does with considerable success. And in the first half of the 1980s Lloyds has moved from nowhere to become the biggest residential estate agent in the country.

The building societies, too, are extending their ambitions in advance of the changes in the law that are intended to permit them to broaden their horizons. Where the societies have been unable, owing to regulatory constraints, to offer the fuller banking and insurance service that they might wish, they have simply teamed up with bankers and insurers in joint ventures to offer a package of complementary services to the customer. Nationwide, for example, is eating into insurance territory with a pensions policy whose benefits are linked to the retail price index. The pension contract is underwritten by the Abbey Life insurance group, while Nationwide manages the underlying fund which is invested in index-linked mortgages. In due course the building societies may be tempted to abandon mutual ownership and team up with other types of financial institutions. It is no secret that some top executives at the Prudential would see great attraction in a closer link with a building society because the societies have a strong grip, as do the clearing banks, on the young end of the savings market. This big insurer also revealed in 1985 that it proposed to buy into a small estate agent, so following Lloyds Bank's example.

Finally, outsiders are being tempted into the financial services sector by forecasts of above average growth. Some, like BAT Industries, bring capital to the business, in this case through the purchase of Eagle Star Insurance and Hambro Life. Others, such as the retailers, bring customers. The Debenhams store group derived more than half its 1984 profits from its Welbeck financial services subsidiary and now markets insurance and investment products provided by Hill Samuel. Marks & Spencer started to offer a credit card in its 264 stores in April 1985 and in no time acquired 600,000 card holders. The card will ultimately be used as a medium to deliver a range of financial products and services. Leading financial institutions have, predictably, been knocking at this big retailer's door in the hope of providing it with insurance and investment products. Tesco, meantime, has invited Midland Bank to set up shop in its own stores.

Open season for conglomerates

In a financial world with no boundaries, the dominant species will inevitably prove to be the international conglomerate, and among those conglomerates one of the most eye-catching will almost certainly be Citicorp, the New York-based bank holding company which no longer thinks of itself as a mere bank. Since Citicorp comes closer than most to the hydralike giant that Jacob Rothschild so graphically outlined in his speech heralding the onset of the City Revolution, it is worth looking again at the strategy of one of the few, or perhaps the only, bank holding company in the world that has a credible global strategy covering banking, securities, insurance and the sale of information technology. It explains a great deal about how the international financial game, in which the City is trying to maintain its competitive position, is evolving.

Citicorp's global gameplan is really a response to two key problems discussed earlier. The first stems from the disappearance of two of its biggest groups of customers. Not only are big corporations finding that they can raise money more cheaply for themselves in the markets; Third World countries can no longer provide international bankers with profitable growth in sovereign lending in the aftermath of Mexico's financial crisis in 1982. The second problem arises from the increase in the cost of attracting deposits with which to finance bank lending. Inflation in the United States and elsewhere created pressure for regulatory ceilings on bank interest rates to be lifted, since depositors were unwilling to park their savings with banks that offered only a negative real return. Depositors took their money to so-called 'non-banks' such as the giant investment and brokerage house Merrill Lynch, which cleverly promoted money market funds that offered rates of interest more closely tied to those in the wholesale markets. A huge chunk of America's savings fled from the banks and from savings and loan associations (equivalent to Britain's building societies) to this less heavily regulated haven. When deregulation came and banks were able to compete with non-banks on a less uneven footing, the margins between the interest rates at which they borrowed and lent were inevitably squeezed. By the mid-1980s basic lending was simply not a profitable business for many American banks; and with consumers becoming more demanding in other developed countries the pattern was being repeated in banking systems around the world, including Britain's.

In the Third World the boom days for wholesale lending will not come back for some time, but in the case of the big corporate customers in developed countries Citicorp and others are hoping to defend their existing relationships and find new ones by offering clients the benefit of a wider package of financial services. At Citicorp a crucial part of that package is technology; and within the international banking market it is probably true that the bigger US money centre banks have a technological lead over the Europeans, mainly as a result of a weakness imposed on their own banking market by regulation. Because the big banks' operations in the United States have been largely confined to a single state of the union, customers whose operations run across state boundaries have been forced to establish relationships with a whole string of banks. Technology was developed by the banks to overcome the problems arising from such a fragmented market, and then extended to cope with the needs of multinational companies. Citicorp, which spends close to $100 million a year on developing its technology, claims to offer the only worldwide electronic financial network covering all commercial currencies and is the exclusive provider of on-line corporate banking services in a number of the less sophisticated national markets. At the same time it has invested heavily in computer systems to reduce its costs in what has hitherto been a very low-productivity industry.

Another strand in Citicorp's attempt to make money out of the corporate sector is the move to build up the investment banking operations of the group. As corporate treasurers turn to the markets for their money, the bank aims to advise on and facilitate the issue of commercial paper and to offer its services in foreign exchange dealing. The object is to produce fee income and dealing profits to supplement the diminishing or non-existent margin on bank lending. Today Citicorp claims that less than a third of the profits made by its corporate arm come from direct lending. A complementary aim is to win new customers to whom access has hitherto been barred by either regulatory or national barriers. In the United States that has meant exploiting every possible legal loophole to establish a presence outside its home state of New York and to sell new non-banking services in its branches. Overseas Citicorp is the only US bank to have a comprehensive retail banking strategy. It is pushing into insurance, which stakes an even bigger claim on the public's savings than does the banking sector, in both Britain and the United States. The Federal Reserve Board recently gave permission for Citicorp to write life assurance in

Britain, and in 1984 its British operation also moved into insurance broking. A final element of the plan is the sale of economic, financial, marketing and regulatory information that it picks up in the course of doing its own business. Joint ventures have been set up with Reuters and Dun & Bradstreet, two of the world's biggest providers of business information, to package and sell these information offcuts. Interestingly, Citicorp expects one of its key competitors in the 1990s to be the international computer giant IBM.

For conglomerates such as Citicorp, the City Revolution presented a golden opportunity to try out the new financial games of the future, from which they were debarred in their home market. London is being used as the testing ground for a financial services operation that runs the whole gamut from satisfying the borrowing requirements of countries and multi-national corporations to selling stocks, shares and savings accounts to private individuals. But will Citicorp's gigantic experiment in diversification pay off? And how far can its fellow travellers in the City Revolution expect to emerge from their own attempts at diversification without costly mishaps?

These questions scarcely lend themselves to comforting answers. For one of the problems inherent in financial con-glomeration – and one of the paradoxes of the wider interna-tional financial services revolution – is that most of the players in the game inevitably start from a position of weakness. In the United States, where the enthusiasm for hybrid mergers has been especially pronounced, Sears Roebuck was attracted by a large-scale move into financial services because its own main-stream retailing business had grown so big that it could no longer escape the vagaries of the US economic cycle. For American Express comparable factors were at work in the purchases of the Fireman's Fund insurance group, the Wall Street firm Shearson and the international financial concern Trade Development Bank. The core business of American Express, travel-related services, was relatively mature. Simi-larly, though with less obvious business logic, the American steel giant Armco moved into insurance because it wanted to find a new source of income to plug the earnings gap that always opened up when the steel cycle turned down. As for the commercial banks, they were anxious to move into investment banking, securities broking and insurance because their core lending business was becoming unprofitable for all the reasons that have been seen.

The lessons of this headlong rush into the full range of financial services have been salutary for all concerned. The new entrants found that financial services income is cyclical and of relatively low quality – that is to say, not very durable. It also entailed high risks. Insurance proved a serious Achilles heel for Armco and American Express, which discovered that very different management skills were required in insurance than in their main businesses. The securities industry proved no easier for Sears Roebuck. While its Dean Witter Reynolds subsidiary successfully drummed up a huge increase in its personal clientele through gaining access to Sears Roebuck's 40 million customers, the securities firm's wholesale business deteriorated badly as key personnel struggled unhappily to come to terms with an owner whose culture was both bureaucratic and retail-oriented. The Dean Witter acquisition came just before a sharp downturn in activity on Wall Street, which led to substantial losses at a psychologically difficult time for the firm.

There were similar culture clashes at American Express in trying to absorb Trade Development Bank, which had been built up by an individualistic entrepreneur, Edmond Safra; and the investment in Shearson was by no means trouble-free. The American Express management was widely criticized for its failure to integrate fully the operations of these and numerous other acquisitions. In the case of the commercial banks, it proved difficult to make the jump into investment banking in international markets because of the very different pay scales and attitudes that prevailed in the different types of activity. If there were conspicuous exceptions – such as Morgan Guaranty, which has been highly successful both in Eurobonds and in international equity business – this may simply be because the bank has long been a predominantly wholesale concern with a style of management closer to that of an investment bank than to a conventional US money centre bank.

Winners and losers

What, then, are the lessons for the City Revolution? The first is that there are bound to be upsets for individual players in the revolutionary game as they move from familiar ground into new and dangerous territory that calls for different managerial skills. A large capital base will be essential for most of those who aspire to the top rank in the wholesale international financial game. This provides both a safety cushion and an opportunity to exploit the economies of scale which are largely absent in broking but extremely important where financial institutions act as principal in issuing, distributing and trading in securities.

But capital alone will not be enough. The other essential ingredients are an ability to distribute huge issues of securities and the skill to do so in a way that simultaneously minimizes risk and impresses the multinational client. Experience in the Eurobond market suggests that only a handful can establish and maintain the ability to distribute securities on the required scale. The giants of the corporate world have no wish to deal with second-best. Similarly, the giants of the investment world are bound to gravitate towards those houses that offer the finest dealing terms. In international equities and bonds only those who run a 24-hour book will enjoy a sufficient volume of business to pare their margins accordingly. A high degree of concentration in international investment banking is thus inevitable. Hence the conviction of some leading British bankers that the number of British-owned firms that make it to this select band may, at best, be no more than one or two.

Such a tally might seem a poor outcome, given the Bank of England's desire to promote strong British securities firms, and a poor reward in view of the turmoil through which the City went after the government struck its deal with the Stock Exchange in 1983. Yet the Bank could console itself that the Revolution had at least enhanced London's attractions as an entrepot centre for foreigners. And if performance in the Eurobond market is any guide, it would have been unrealistic to hope for anything more. As it is, a great deal of City money and goodwill is riding on that Euromarket success story Mercury Securities, parent of S. G. Warburg – despite its relatively small capital base. Yet Mercury faces an enormous management challenge in merging the components of its new business, as do clearing bank runners in the race. Of the Big Four, only Barclays and perhaps National Westminster look ready to take on the international giants. Whether they can overcome the problems of culture and remuneration in their revamped investment banking operations remains an open question. Their less than inspiring performance in the Euro-bond market suggests that it may take time for them to establish themselves as credible actors on the international securities stage.

The revolution also poses a harsh test of will and endurance. How long will European banks, without the benefit of such strong economies and currencies behind them, be willing or able to sweat it out against the Americans and the Japanese, whose financial institutions have shown a readiness in the past to soldier on regardless of costly mistakes? Some US bankers in London admit to grudging respect for Barclays, which is no mean tribute. But it is also worth noting that the long-standing tradition of universal banking in continental Europe should give the French and more particularly the Germans an advantage in the post-revolutionary climate. Deutsche Bank has long experience of the securities business, widely respected management, a powerful position in the Euromarkets and a conspicuous will to win. Of all the European participants in the international corporate finance and securities business this West German giant would pose a serious threat to the American and Japanese competition.

At the retail end of the City Revolution capital is probably less important than strategy. And in the view of Mark Weinberg, the insurance entrepreneur, no one can afford to opt out of the revolutionary game. Until the early 1980s Weinberg firmly believed that his company, Hambro Life, should stick to its last. But as the barriers began to crumble he concluded that outsiders were likely to pour onto the insurance companies' home patch. Both the clearing banks and the building societies seemed certain to attack the British insurers' customer base as they confronted problems in their own core business. And they were in a position to undercut those insurance companies that spent heavily on armies of salesmen and brokers, because they could spread the existing costs of running their branches over newer products such as life and casualty insurance. This would leave the insurers with no alternative but to retaliate by spreading their own marketing costs over a wider range of financial products, including interest-bearing accounts, credit cards and the rest.

With everyone actively cross-selling financial services in this way the key to success, says Weinberg, will be to foster an existing competitive edge. For the clearing banks, that consists of a firm hold on several million customers for whom the geographical spread of bank branches is a considerable convenience – though the mere existence of those customers and branches has arguably blunted the banks' competitive edge because they have not had to fight for customers. The big insurance companies have the marketing skills of their sales forces and contacts with brokers. Retailers have customers and the convenience of their location; but when it comes to selling financial services inside stores these will not be enough. The quality of the salesman is more important than location in selling investment and insurance products, argues Weinberg. The American (and indeed Scottish) banks have the advantage that they are not saddled with expensive branches all over the country. Electronic methods of delivering financial products to the customer may therefore provide them with a potential edge.

It would not be surprising, however, if there is a painful learning curve in retail financial services as institutions that have been hidebound by regulation and custom move into unfamiliar territory. Within the clearing banks, insurance-broking staff are some way from being treated with the deference that the logic of the financial services revolution requires. As a result of recent tax changes in mortgage-related endowment policies (known as MIRAS), which gave a strong incentive to home-owners to take out more insurance, building societies may well have gained a misleading impression of the ease with which life assurance can be sold. And in retailing it is hard to believe that all those who are selling financial services in their stores – which implies that they cannot find a more profitable use for the space selling the products they know and understand – will stay the course. Only Marks & Spencer, with its great credibility in the public eye and an impressive management, looks as though it could pose a real threat to the banks. Yet Marks & Spencer rarely rushes its fences and it remains to be seen how big a force in consumer finance it really wants to be.

The limits of popular capitalism

Perhaps the greatest conundrum of the retail financial services revolution in the 1980s and 1990s is whether attempts to bring the private investor back to the stock market in strength succeed. Citicorp's urge to sell shares to the holders of its plastic cards is an interesting development. But its reading of Britain's retail financial market has not always been well judged. The American bank's less than successful rush into money shops in the British high street always looked more attuned to an American-style demand than to the needs of the British public. Could a similar American plunge into promoting private share ownership involve comparable risks?

Certainly the United States is a potentially misleading guide for the unwary. There the banks have recently moved into discount broking – a no frills service for their customers – because they can readily undercut stockbroking firms that have to maintain expensive retail sales forces. But discount broking is for sophisticates who need no advice, and in Britain such people are a relatively small and dwindling band. Between 1945 and 1980 the British private investor has been a consistent seller of shares to insurance companies and pension funds. The habit of private share ownership has gone into abeyance, except for a small minority generally estimated at around 4 per cent of the population. The chief reason is that saving via life assurance and pension schemes has been heavily subsidized by the state, which has granted tax-free returns that are hard to match by investing directly on the Stock Exchange.

The Thatcher government is committed to popular capitalism. Yet it did little in its first term of office to encourage the private shareholder back to the market, and research appeared to indicate that those private investors who bought shares in the early privatization issues such as British Aerospace, Cable & Wireless, Amersham International and Enterprise Oil were inclined to sell out when the price of the shares rose. After re-election in 1984, however, the Tory government applied itself with more enthusiasm to the task and turned the near-£4 billion British Telecom issue into a mass marketing exercise with roadshows around the country, heavy advertising and huge subsidies in the form of commissions for intermediaries such as brokers, solicitors and accountants. The issue attracted enormous interest and 1.7 million individual shareholders. They were promptly rewarded with a huge premium over the issue price as the shares soared in the market.

Whether this very exceptional issue will prove enough to relaunch private share ownership remains to be seen. For a start, the concept of popular capitalism is elusive when translated into basic arithmetic. According to one academic estimate, over 7 million people have no savings; a further 17 million probably have too little to invest the £260 minimum required for a holding in British Telecom; and at least another 9 million have too little to invest with any degree of financial prudence. The minimum size of share portfolio necessary to diversify away from the risk of a share underperforming in the stock market is reckoned to consist of about twenty holdings. Assuming that the smallest sensible shareholding is the £260 stipulated for subscriptions to the original British Telecom share issue, this would point to a potential market of only 3 million people who could safely contemplate share ownership as an investment rather than a gamble.

On the face of it, winning 1.7 million shareholders is not the political breakthrough that the government might have hoped, given that there is probably a fair degree of duplication with the 1.8 million private individuals in Britain who were estimated to hold shares before the British Telecom issue. It was also won at very high cost to the taxpayer, since the issue was substantially underpriced. Yet there is plenty of anecdotal evidence to suggest that many first-time investors rushed into the market and were delighted with the result. The interesting question is whether the potentially misleading impression of the risks and short-term rewards in share ownership they have gained persuades aspiring capitalists to embark on wider stock market activity. When the new, popular capitalists come to experience falling share prices will they take their losses in the same spirit that they take losses in the betting shop? Or will they feel that they are entitled to expect more of the stock market into which the government gave them a heavily subsidized entrée?

In Mark Weinberg's view, the future of private share-ownership in Britain may hang on whether Mrs Thatcher is given a third term. At Barclays, which handles a thousand securities orders a day through its branches, Lord Camoys feels that it is a chicken-and-egg situation: how much should the bank spend on new technology in its branches to encourage private share dealing? John Brew at Grieveson, Grant, which probably runs a bigger private client department than any other stockbroker in the City, is, however, sanguine. He argues that a surprisingly large amount of money is coming out of the housing market back into the stock market; tax-free lump sum benefits provided by occupational pension schemes on retirement are providing another source of funds for investment in stocks and shares. Other brokers, whose minds have been concentrated by the daunting prospect of the Big Bang, are looking to the hitherto neglected private investor as a potential cushion against the coming profits squeeze.

If the changes wrought by the City Revolution do help spread the share-owning habit, it is more likely to be the result of brokers' marketing efforts than the result of the introduction of negotiated commissions. After fixed commissions were abolished on Wall Street in the mid-1970s commissions on orders of up to 1000 shares rose very sharply between 1975 and 1981. Only on bargains involving more than 10,000 shares did commissions come down significantly. The cross-subsidization of small bargains that took place under a fixed-commission system rapidly disappeared as a result of deregulation. The Big Bang is thus a charter for the big battalions; and it is worth noting that some senior officials at the Bank of England regard the government's aspirations on wider share ownership as unrealistic.

Perhaps the crux of the matter lies in the tax system. For it was the tax disincentive to individual share ownership that turned the British private shareholder into a net seller of shares in the postwar period; and it is hard to believe that this great British evacuation from the stock market will be dramatically reversed without significant fiscal change. The Tories admittedly played at the margins of the system by offering better tax treatment for employee share incentive schemes, halving stamp duty and raising the threshold at which capital gains tax became payable. But the Chancellor of the Exchequer failed to make the obvious policy change that would have underwritten his commitment to popular capitalism when the pensions lobby frightened him away from the abolition of tax relief on occupational pension contributions in 1985.

The litmus test of Mrs Thatcher's ideological commitment to wider share ownership will be her willingness either to add to public expenditure by extending the subsidy on privatization stocks to the general run of equity shares, or to offend the pensions lobby. But in the final analysis the government's readiness to subsidize an odd-lot portfolio of privatization stocks probably had more to do with hard-headed political and financial calculation than with Tory dogma. The subsidy helped facilitate the financing of the public sector borrowing requirement while at the same time holding out the prospect of possible votes at the next election as the new shareholders started to worry about Labour threats to renationalize British Telecom.

The one thing that does not appear to have played an important part in the calculation is the fact that the post-revolutionary City, with its giant conglomerates and greatly increased scope for conflicts of interest, will be a much more risky place for the small investor – and indeed for everyone else. All the historical precedents – both in the US and Britain – suggest that deregulation has an awkward habit of pushing up interest rates, blowing down financial conglomerates and bowling out the regulators who are caught on the wrong foot by the rapid pace of change. In the present case the risks are further multiplied by the readiness of governments to turn deregulation into a competitive international game in which they seek to win business from other financial centres on the free-port principle.

The economy's Achilles heel

The problems arise because banks play a crucial role in monetary policy. Their stability is therefore important to the rest of the industrial and commercial system, yet their capital structure makes them vulnerable to any loss of confidence, because they live on borrowed money. Old-fashioned banking textbooks claim that the cardinal sin in banking is to borrow short and lend long. But when the economy is looked at in the aggregate, banks have to borrow short and lend long because there is a mismatch in the system between the savers' desire to retain the right to withdraw their money at short notice and the industrialists' need for stable, medium-term finance. And in practice building societies have always made their living by borrowing short and lending long without being constant victims of mass financial panic. The real point is that financial intermediaries undertake a delicate job and have to do their utmost to maintain the confidence of their depositors. Some will always fall by the wayside. So the question for governments and central banks has always been to decide how far they should leave it to the market to impose discipline on the imprudent and wayward, and how far to pre-empt trouble through close supervision, regulation and last-ditch rescues.

Since the City Revolution represents a return in so many respects to nineteenth-century financial practice it is worth looking at the way discipline was imposed in the City's nineteenth-century heyday. Then the task was left to the markets; and the whole system was vulnerable to bubbles and crashes. The retreat from laissez-faire in the financial system came in the 1860s when numerous speculative companies were floated after an Act of 1861 which authorized limited liability. By 1866 investors' mania for these shaky enterprises had run its course and several bubble companies collapsed. Those London discount houses that had financed the bubble companies were suddenly squeezed on both sides of their balance sheet. Not only were they weighed down by bad debts; they wilted under the pressure of a bank rate that more than trebled to 10 per cent in the twelve months to the end of June 1866, as lenders cut back the flow of credit in response to the cold wind.

The biggest discount house in the market, Overend Gurney, was forced in May that year to ask for £400,000 from the Bank of England. Since Overend had severely antagonized the Bank – to the point in 1860 of organizing a run on the Bank with fellow Quaker-owned banks and brokers – it received a predictably dusty response. Panic broke out in the Square Mile as the business folded and the contagion spread to many of those that had had dealings with the failed discount house. More serious, the country banks precipitated a run on the London banks and finance houses, which eventually extended to the Bank of England itself. This erosion of confidence led to the failure not only of badly managed, insolvent banks but also of financial houses that were basically solvent but unable to realize their assets fast enough to meet the claims of depositors as they were presented. The run on the Bank of England was only stopped when the government suspended the Bank Charter Act which prevented the Bank of England from increasing the note supply.

By the end of December 1866 bank rate was back to 3½ per cent. The Bank of England had won the confidence and deposits of the country banks at the expense of the discount market, so enhancing its position as the bankers' bank. And despite still being a private sector profit-making enterprise, it came to be seen in the wake of the suspension of the Bank Charter Act as a lender of last resort to the whole banking system. The Overend Gurney crisis provides a classic illustration of the high cost to the whole economy of imprudent banking behaviour and of the contagious nature of financial panic. It also explains the rationale for a regulatory structure that has hitherto frowned on conglomeration in the financial sector, because conglomeration creates the risk of cross-infection between one weak subsidiary and another less weak component of a diversified financial group.

How far will the Thatcherite philosophy of self-reliance apply to the City in the aftermath of the Big Bang? Certainly banks, brokers and jobbers will be moving into a much harsher climate. The move to negotiated commissions on Wall Street in 1975 was followed by scores of failures in the brokerage fraternity and numerous mergers as the weak sought to consolidate their position. Few doubt that there will be similar trouble in London. The only question concerns the scale of the attrition. In the gilt-edged market the going is likely to be particularly tough as the Bank of England has removed a whole series of props for the market makers.

The Bank has a legal obligation to minimize the cost to the government of borrowing in the markets, and its perpetual fear has always been that market makers will pull out when the economic climate turns against them; hence its readiness to permit restrictive practices such as an agreed spread (or margin) between the jobbers' buying and selling price on new issues of government stock. It also explains, in part, the Old Lady's determination to keep the discount houses going for much longer than any natural law of economics would have dictated. Yet another outcome was the Bank's practice, until recently, of giving commissions to brokers who sold new government stock to their clients. The working assumption was that the cost of the *pourboire* to City practitioners was tiny in relation to the sums being raised and, in the case of the jobbers, a small price to pay for continuous market making in bad times. The thinking was to some extent shared by the Treasury and the Inland Revenue. Until 1985 they were exceptionally tolerant of tax avoidance in the gilt-edged market whereby insurance companies which paid tax on their gilt-edged income, and pension funds which paid no tax, shunted their gilt-edged holdings back and forth to each other to suit their respective tax positions.

The arrival of the big American securities houses in the gilt-edged market means that the Bank can afford to do away with all the protective subsidies. So activity in gilt-edged will probably come to resemble behaviour in the insurance market where excessive capital surges into the business when times are good and surges out when premiums have been driven down to excessively low levels, causing players to retire hurt. For some British brokers this means confronting completely new kinds of risk in the management of their business. The survivors, according to one leading US investment banker, will be those who grasp the importance of laying off risks with speed and efficiency. Once again the ability to distribute stock will be the key to success.

Officials of the Bank are acutely conscious of the risks that deregulation poses for the stability of the system. In response to the growth of conglomerates they are shifting the emphasis of regulation away from the traditional categories of 'bank', 'discount house', 'broker' and so forth, towards the functions that hybrid financial institutions actually perform in the markets. Particular stress will be laid on whether there is adequate capital to support each individual function undertaken by a given conglomerate in the new system. The Bank, so its officials say, will take all possible steps to prevent conglomerates washing their capital around like the fraudster in the Californian Salad Oil Swindle, who pumped oil from one tank to another just in time to reassure the auditor who was spot checking from tank to tank. And no one is suggesting that the role of lender of last resort should be scrapped. Indeed, the existence of a lender of last resort is an important part of the competitive armoury of an international financial centre in the new free-port game because money always flies, in a financial panic, to the safest assets in the most stable financial centres.

But this raises an enormous problem in a period of deregulation because of a phenomenon that economists call 'moral hazard' – the increased temptation for bankers to act imprudently in the knowledge that a safety net is ready to hand. The conventional wisdom among central bankers is that in the event of a banking crash they should protect depositors, but not the shareholders and management. These last two groups should be obliged, respectively, to lose their money and their jobs *pour encourager les autres*. Yet the bigger the figures involved, the harder it becomes for central bankers to take exemplary action against the perpetrators of financial crises. The point was perfectly illustrated in the Latin American debt crisis: critics of the big US money centre banks argue that their managers took excessive and unbankerly risks in lending to Mexico, Brazil and Argentina because they knew that their banks were too big to be allowed to fail. When Mexico was unable to meet its commitments in 1982 the Federal Reserve and the International Monetary Fund were forced to rescue the American banking system from the consequences of this mass aberration. But there were no strings attached for the aberrant lenders – only for the borrowers. Those who ran the big banks not only survived with jobs intact, but were given reason to believe that, provided they took the elementary precaution of hunting in a pack and playing with very big numbers, the authorities would be incapable of imposing sanctions against them.

It is unlikely that any future financial crisis will occur in precisely the same form. But central bankers have good reason to worry at the response of financial institutions in the 1980s to deregulation. In pre-inflationary days when bankers borrowed and lent at fixed rates of interest, and currency hedging through swaps, options and futures was unheard of, any rise in interest rates or adverse currency movement imposed a natural brake on the expansion of bank lending just as it did at the time of the Overend Gurney collapse in the 1860s. Today this natural constraint has been largely removed by the practice of borrowing and lending at floating or variable interest rates (as, for example, on the average British house mortgage) and of hedging against currency and interest rate risks. As bankers have seen the cost of their borrowings increase and their basic lending business become less profitable, they have, in some cases, responded by seeking out the higher rewards available on higher-risk business. And the risks inherent in such a response are exacerbated by the unattractively named phenomenon of securitization, to which the City Revolution was partly a response.

If the most creditworthy borrowers in the world financial system bypass the banks and raise money directly from the markets, any expansion of banking business will very likely be into poorer-quality lending. And in their search for fee income to compensate for the reduced margins in their lending activities, banks have increasingly been tempted to provide guarantees to their clients that are very similar to the kinds of risk run by insurers. New-style Euronotes, by which banks underwrite the continuous sale by their corporate clients of short-term securities to investors, involve a guarantee that the banks will stump up funds at future times of their clients' own choosing. Few insurers, however, would underwrite a risk where the circumstances in which they have to pay up are unspecified in the contract. And it is a source of growing concern to the Bank of England, the West German Bundesbank and the Japanese Ministry of Finance that these mounting contingent liabilities of the banks could all be called on at the same time in a financial crisis, so threatening the international banking system.

The problems of regulating such business are complicated by competition: any central bank that seeks to impose unilateral controls on the growth of a risky new financial instrument may simply drive business away to another less heavily regulated financial centre. So regulation will tend to move at the snail's pace dictated by the need for international consensus. The resulting lag between financial innovation and regulatory response may well mean that new types of lending and new financial institutions will fall outside the carefully constructed system of checks and balances put together by central bankers under the auspices of the Bank for International Settlements in Basle.

Sovereignty under pressure in the markets

An equally troubling question for the post-revolutionary City is whether the government and the Bank of England will not end up having responsibility without adequate power in a world where familiar rules and relationships no longer hold. For the internationalization of financial markets in the 1980s entails a significant loss of sovereignty for those governments that chose to abolish controls. This means that what remains of the cosy trade-off between the City and Whitehall, by which the City finances public expenditure in exchange for freedom from interference, may ultimately disappear because it becomes an irrelevance; and the government's ability to seek votes by imposing distortions on financial markets may be greatly reduced.

The extent to which the rules have changed can be seen by looking at two key incursions into the British domestic market by foreign financial institutions. The first concerns the deal described earlier in this chapter between the Bank of Scotland and a group of US banks. In a deregulated market, demand for mortgages is rationed not by queues at the building society, but by price; and the price is reflected in interest rates charged by a wider variety of financial institutions that come into the market. What the Bank of Scotland demonstrated was that spare international lending capacity is capable of filling gaps in the British market without regard to the domestic political niceties of home lending. In future borrowers will increasingly be offered the chance to raise money at interest rates which reflect international market conditions rather than ones which are set by British building societies or clearing banks under pressure from government.

The comfortable relationship between the Bank of England and its City flock is also being exposed to new international pressures – witness a second incursion into the British market whereby Citicorp sought to elbow its way into the heartland of British banking in a move that bears close examination. The incident in question arose in 1984 when Citicorp shook Britain's Big Four clearing banks by making an unsolicited request to join the Committee of London Clearing Bankers. Its reason for making this unprecedented approach was that it saw membership of the exclusive (and exclusively British) clearing bankers' club as the key to obtaining access to the British payments system.

The clearing banks gave Citicorp a dusty response, pointing out that it was knocking at the wrong door. They argued that if the Americans wanted access to the payments system, they should apply for membership of another body, the Bankers' Clearing House. The Clearing House's origins went back to the practice of bank clerks exchanging bundles of cheques in a rented room in the Five Bells tavern in Dove Court, Lombard Street, in the eighteenth century and probably even earlier. Undeterred, Citicorp responded with an American-style lobbying campaign. Though few details emerged in public, the authors have established, and confirmed with official sources in Britain, that the US Treasury and the Federal Reserve applied pressure to the British government in support of the American bank's attempt to gain access to the core of the British banking system. As it happens, the Americans were on strong ground. The US economy is one of the most open in the world and the same goes for its financial system. Not only did the Big Four clearing banks have sizeable operations there, but they were not subject to comparable restrictions on access to the admittedly less sophisticated payment systems that operated across the fifty-two states of the union. So the British government found itself potentially under pressure, confronting a powerful argument for reciprocity from an important friend and ally.

At the same time Citicorp itself set in train a vigorous doorstepping campaign in Whitehall. The man in charge was Kent Price, the appropriately energetic American who shares with other Citicorp executives an almost boyish enthusiasm for technology and a disconcerting way of referring to bank branches as 'bricks and mortar distribution points in which people can interact'. Price had come to run Citicorp's London banking operation direct from Hong Kong, where he had successfully muscled in on the banking establishment. He was expected by his peers to give the British a bracing run for their money.

Pointing out to his Whitehall audience that Citicorp reckoned to be the fifth largest bank in Britain, Price argued that an important public utility, the payments system, had become tangled up with a bankers' trade association, the Committee of London Clearing Bankers. His itinerary, in the course of which he set out to explain Citicorp's *modus operandi* in Britain, included 10 Downing Street, where he saw the Prime Minister's personal economic adviser at the time, Sir Alan Walters; the Treasury, where both the Chief Financial Secretary, John Moore, and the Permanent Secretary, Peter Middleton, turned out to give him a hearing; the Department of Trade, at which he met the Secretary of State, Norman Tebbit, and finally the Home Office, where it was the Home Secretary, Leon Brittan, who lent a sympathetic ear to Citicorp's professions of corporate good citizenship. This comprehensive attack coincided with simultaneous lobbying campaigns by Citicorp in the United States (where, according to one Citicorp banker to whom the authors spoke, 8 per cent of the bank's staff are lawyers or lobbyists) and around the world.

In Britain the assault almost certainly amounted to overkill. Mrs Thatcher's distaste for the clearing banks is well known; numerous members of her cabinet felt that the clearers were too profitable by half and too slow in everything except their propensity to raise interest rates. Because the Big Four were uncomfortably aware of this, and had long contemplated reform of the clearing system anyway, they pre-empted hostile government pressure by setting up a committee under Denis Child, deputy group chief executive of National Westminster Bank. Its task was to re-examine the work of the Bankers' Clearing House. The resulting report recommended a complete restructuring of the organization and control of the payments system; and it gracefully paved the way for closer participation by Citicorp and another would-be entrant, Standard Chartered, in the new set-up. In fact the British clearers did not appear unduly worried about the US giant's ambitions in their own domestic market. It is noteworthy that Citicorp's biggest successes in international retail banking had been in countries such as Brazil and Greece where banking systems were relatively underdeveloped.

The American lobbying campaign, launched from Citicorp's offices in Aldwych, halfway between the City and Westminster, was nonetheless revealing about the kind of style and pretensions of the financial conglomerates which were expected to stalk the City in the second half of the 1980s – not least because Citicorp took its case direct to Whitehall. Where others had been content to rely on the good offices of the Bank of England, Citicorp had clearly decided that the Old Lady could only be relied on to look after her own. It was a robust reminder that the new conglomerates were likely to give short shrift to the old club rules by which business in the Square Mile used to be conducted.

Does this mean that the government could run into trouble in the gilt-edged market if the barons of international finance are in a sour mood? Fears on this score are almost certainly exaggerated. In a huge, deregulated international capital market funds will always tend to seek out the best available return. The argument between borrower and investor is thus about the price, not the quantity of funds; and it is likely to be resolved in the same way that it was in the more restricted market of the 1970s when domestic insurance companies, pension funds and banks readily financed a Labour government without being forced by statute to do so.

Far more problematical for the government are the broader implications for the conduct of monetary policy. For with all the traditional financial relationships breaking down and money travelling at high speed across the exchanges it becomes more and more difficult to establish how restrictive (or otherwise) monetary policy happens to be at any given moment. And for the Bank of England the challenge of dealing with more powerful international firms that do not hesitate to invoke governmental support for their corporate objectives comes at a time when its authority and competence have been called seriously into question, following the collapse of the once obscure banking subsidiary of the metal refiners Johnson Matthey.

A failure in banking supervision

Johnson Matthey Bankers' only previous claim to fame was that it was one of five London banks that belonged to the exclusive London gold market. In 1981, when the gold market had sunk into the doldrums, it started to build up a commercial loan portfolio outside its traditional area. Much of the lending, which accelerated rapidly, related to trade finance required by Third World borrowers. Yet the bank's parent failed to support this increase in business into a high-risk area of international banking with a commensurate boost to the subsidiary's capital base. By the summer of 1984 loans to two very questionable Third World borrowers stood at the equivalent of 115 per cent of Johnson Matthey Bankers' £100 million capital; and the ability of these and other clients to repay their debts was beginning to look questionable. An investigation by the bank's own auditors, Arthur Young, conducted at the Bank of England's request not long after the same firm had given the accounts a clean audit report, revealed that the bank was in a potentially serious position.

Word soon started to seep out that something was going wrong. At the end of September that year the Bank of England learned that financial houses in the Far East were ceasing to deal with British banks, some quite unconnected with the gold market, on the basis of rumours of an incipient British banking collapse. On the weekend of 30 September nearly two hundred bankers and their advisers were suddenly called into the deserted City of London to find a solution to the problem.

Johnson Matthey itself lacked the resources to rescue its banking subsidiary, even though it was loosely affiliated to the giant South African mining finance group Anglo American. Initial attempts to persuade the Bank of Nova Scotia, an important bank in the bullion market, to take over Johnson Matthey Bankers foundered because the Canadian bank was not offered adequate guarantees. In the end the Bank of England was forced to nationalize the troubled bank, while extracting £50 million from its parent in exchange for shouldering the burden and persuading twenty-five of London's leading banks to make £250 million available in standby loans. Big US banks such as Morgan Guaranty and Citibank, which had previously financed Johnson Matthey Bankers, played an important part in the rescue. The operation was completed at 8.30 on the following Monday morning, just in time for the bank to open its doors with a reassuring statement for its depositors.

The Bank of England's reasons for hurriedly launching this lifeboat were understandable enough. When America's seventh largest bank holding company, Continental Illinois, suffered a run on its deposits and had to be rescued in June that year, money ebbed away from American to European and Japanese banks. In a very unstable financial climate coloured by the international debt crisis the Bank of England was concerned that money might ebb away from London, starting with the other four banks in the gold market. Among the four was Samuel Montagu, the merchant bank subsidiary of Britain's least robust clearing bank, the Midland. Johnson Matthey Bankers itself had substantial deposits of gold from governments and central banks around the world. The Bank of England feared that London's standing as an international centre could have been threatened by a disorderly collapse in which these important depositors would have been left nursing losses.

Yet the rescue subsequently prompted a barrage of criticism. Some clearing banks felt that they were being required to pay up for the mistakes of a bank about which they knew little and cared even less. Others in the City considered that the Bank's fears for the gold market were exaggerated; if a bank as insignificant as Johnson Matthey Bankers had to be rescued, the problem of moral hazard was likely to become overwhelming. Senior officials in the Treasury scented that the Bank had committed a supervisory blunder; the Chancellor conspicuously distanced himself from any involvement in the affair. A parliamentary row, in which the Social Democrats' leader David Owen started to show an unexpected interest in the workings of the banking system, brewed up to the point where the government was obliged to announce that a joint committee of officials from the Treasury and Bank of England would be set up to review the arrangements for the supervision of the banking system. Much to the surprise of the critics the committee was headed by none other than the Governor of the Bank, Robin Leigh-Pemberton, despite the controversial nature of the Bank's role in the affair.

By the time the committee reported in mid-1985 it was clear that Johnson Matthey Bankers had been appallingly, managed and that supervision had indeed been inadequate. The rapid build-up of high-risk business at Johnson Matthey Bankers was, in the words of one senior banker, the kind of thing that flashes a welter of red lights at even the most junior bank supervisor. In fairness it should be said that the Bank of England did read the signals. Yet it turned out to have shown remarkably little sense of urgency when the ailing Johnson Matthey Bankers failed to send in its returns on time, given that it had already been diagnosed as a problem case; and, despite some misreporting of the bank's position, the regulators could still see that the fast-expanding loan book was unduly heavily concentrated in a way that could jeopardize the bank's solvency if a big client ran into trouble.

In announcing a series of measures aimed at tightening up the Banking Act, the Chancellor of the Exchequer, Nigel Lawson, expressed his 'fullest confidence' in the Governor, Robin Leigh-Pemberton, while simultaneously declaring his conviction that the Bank of England 'to some extent fell down on the job'. It was clear that the degree of latitude that the Bank enjoyed in running affairs in the Square Mile was likely to be further circumscribed in the future. It had lost support not just in Whitehall but also in its own constituency, where senior bankers were becoming increasingly critical of its performance in handling City–Whitehall relations. The politicians, meantime, had questioned the propriety of the Bank's decision to place £100 million of its funds on deposit with its new subsidiary after nationalization without consulting the Treasury; and the Bank's potential losses on the rescue, put at £34 million in mid-1985, were a source of widespread concern. The fiction that the Bank of England was not part of the public sector was thus coming under strain. The best it could do to assuage its critics on the potential loss of public funds was to ensure that its new subsidiary joined Johnson Matthey, the former parent, in suing the hapless auditors, Arthur Young, for damages of up to £248 million.

On the positive side, the Johnson Matthey scandal did at least draw attention to the problems that the Bank of England was likely to face in dealing with conglomerates. A weak owner from outside the banking system was seen to be unable to control or stand behind its banking subsidiary when such backing was important to the stability of the financial system. So steps were taken to ensure a closer relationship between bank auditors and the regulatory authorities; to abolish the legal distinction between banks and more heavily regulated licensed deposit takers in order to impose a uniform standard of supervision; and to seek letters of comfort pledging support for bank subsidiaries from shareholders owning more than 15 per cent in any bank (though whether this would have helped much at Johnson Matthey was open to question).

Yet niggling doubts remained. If the Bank had failed on its own home patch with a bank that carried such obvious indications of trouble to come, could it really be regarded as having a safe pair of hands in the more hazardous game that was likely to follow the Big Bang? What kind of control could it expect to exert in the newer areas into which it was expanding its non-statutory authority, such as the securities markets, Lloyd's of London and the commodity markets? And how far would the new regulators of the Securities and Investments Board, together with the self-regulatory bodies that came under its wing, be able to cope with similar problems, especially when falling prices in a 'bear' market put pressure on firms to take shortcuts and exploit conflicts of interest?

What of the future?

To those who raise these questions the Bank of England might reasonably reply that the most radical reform of City markets since the Great Fire of 1666 could hardly be accomplished without risks and costs; there was no alternative if the Square Mile was to retain its position in international financial markets. The more important question, from the Bank's point of view, concerns London's competitive position now that other international centres are competing aggressively to offer attractive deregulated havens for the footloose financiers of the 1980s and 1990s. Few doubt that the United States and, increasingly, Japan will dominate the international financial markets in the foreseeable future. The whole balance of world economic power has shifted away from the Atlantic towards this new axis. Yet London remains pre-eminent in the time zone that covers Europe, the Middle East and Africa. And in the aftermath of the City Revolution its securities markets will probably come closer than those of the rest of Europe to offering the combination that international financial institutions most prize: the ability to deal cheaply, in large quantities, with minimal disturbance to securities prices, in a stable political framework. So the City of London looks set to hold onto a position as the third leg in the Golden Triangle of international dealing between North America, the Far East and Europe, with other subsidiary centres such as Frankfurt, Zurich, Bahrein, Hong Kong, Singapore, Sydney and Los Angeles playing ancillary roles.

For officials at the Bank of England who have worked hard to preserve London's competitive advantage against a background of relative economic decline this will be an understandable source of gratification. Outside the Square Mile feelings are likely to be more mixed. Leading City figures can often be heard bemoaning the poor quality of Britain's postwar political and industrial leadership. Yet when all is said and done the fact that a City Revolution was needed suggests that leadership in domestic City firms, which have been more heavily protected from international competition than their counterparts in industry, has not been conspicuously impressive. Like the postwar politicians who yearned for a far greater role on the international stage than Britain's new status as a second-rank power actually justified, Britain's financiers aspired to a more grandiose position than was justified by the post-imperial status of sterling in the world financial system. If they succeeded, it was very largely thanks to the enterprise of foreign firms. Circumstances played a key part, too, since the United States chose not to exploit its advantages in international finance until the 1980s and London happened to be a natural beneficiary of the malfunctioning of the world economy in the great inflationary period that began at the time of the Vietnam War in the 1960s.

The City of London was uniquely placed to benefit from the huge imbalances in the global payments system that built up in the 1970s. Both the financial consequences of the oil crisis and the discovery of oil in Britain's own back yard gave the City the chance to deploy skills very similar to those that were used to recycle British capital in the nineteenth century. London-based banks managed to defy the traditional laws of financial gravity: they produced rapidly growing profits in a world of low growth and high inflation. Indeed, the City of London's international activities came close to being an inverse barometer of the health of the world economy.

Since the collapse of the Bretton Woods system of fixed exchange rates in the early 1970s volatility has become endemic in international markets. Corporate finance has turned into the art of minimizing the risks to industry and commerce inherent in this instability; hence, too, the growth of new futures and options markets which provide insurance against currency and interest rate uncertainty. The economic rationale for bodies such as the London International Financial Futures Exchange and its much bigger rivals in Chicago, New York and Philadelphia is that they give companies or traders an opportunity to neutralize risks by locking into a given exchange rate or interest rate in advance of the transactions they make in goods or services. Yet the overall risk in this very unstable system cannot be neutralized: hedging via futures, options, swaps and the rest merely passes the risk from one group of people to another.

In this turbulent economic world financiers in the City of London have become increasingly like insurers. They have, in a sense, been making profits out of the misfortunes of others; notably those in the productive sector of the economy who incur significant costs to reduce the impact of uncertainty on their businesses – a cost which, under the old system of fixed exchange rates, fell on central banks. And there is a risk, in the view of the Nobel prize-winning American economist James Tobin, that excessive resources are being diverted into financial activity in the search for a degree of market perfection that serves no one's interest but that of the market makers. As yet the political will to stabilize the monetary system through international cooperation does not exist. So the financiers may continue to occupy a big place in the preoccupations of governments that are anxious to generate new service jobs in a low-growth world. To return to Jacob Rothschild and Disraeli, revolutions are not to be avoided. But they are a rather depressing sign of the times.

Index

Bank of England – *cont.*
shares, 101–2; and the Stock
Exchange reform proposals,
98–100, 104–5; tries to
prevent foreign takeovers of
British banks, 65
Bank of France, 8
Bank for International Settlements,
228
Bank of London and South America
(BOLSA), 32
Bank of Nova Scotia, 233
Bank of Scotland, 60, 208, 228–9
Bank Charter Act, 224
Bankers' Clearing House, 16, 229,
231
Banking Act (1979), 152
Banque Arabe et Internationale
d'Investissement, 118
Banque Bruxelles Lambert, 118
Banque Commerciale pour l'Europe
du Nord, 28
Banque du Rhône et de La Tamise
SA, 183–4
Barclays Bank, 36, 59, 60, 65, 103,
108, 110, 123–4, 127, 131,
138, 139, 210, 217, 221
Barclays de Zoete Wedd, 100–1,
124, 139
Baring, Sir Francis, 206
Baring Brothers, 7, 8, 10, 74, 75,
103, 113, 129, 133, 134–5
Barnett, Joel (Lord Barnett), 17
BAT Industries, 113, 134, 211
Battye Wimpenny & Dawson, 115
Becker, A. G., 72, 73
Berkshire, John, 65, 69
Berrill, Sir Kenneth, 157
Biffen, John, 91
Bischoff, Win, 71, 75
Bisgood Bishop, 83, 110, 131
Bolton, Sir George, 32
Borrie, Sir Gordon, 96, 156, 158
Bowring, C. T., 21
Brazil, 37, 38, 226, 231
Bretton Woods, 13, 30, 237
Brew, John, 150, 221
Britannia Arrow, 113, 114, 201
British Aerospace, 219–20
British Insurance Association, 149,
152

British Petroleum (BP), 19, 49,
101–2, 206
British Telecom, 19, 49, 70, 86,
130, 140, 141, 220, 222
Brittan, Leon, 230
Broadbent, Adam, 190
Brooks, Raymond, 187–8
Buckmaster & Moore, 117
Bundesbank, 227–8
Buxton, Andrew, 123

Cable & Wireless, 219–20
Callaghan, James, 18, 80
Cameron-Webb, Peter, 162, 184
Camoys, Lord, 100–1, 123, 124,
221
Capel, James, 117, 119, 131
Capel-Cure Myers, 119
Carpenter, Jack, 183
Carter, Jimmy, 29
Cayman Islands, 30, 40
Cazenove, 80, 120
Channel Four, 148
Charlesworth & Co., 111
Charterhouse Group, 111, 132,
133, 135
Charterhouse J. Rothschild, 116,
134
Charterhouse Japhet, 25, 111, 133
Chase Manhattan Bank, 36, 115,
131
Chemical Bank, 60
Chief Registrar of Friendly
Societies, 61
Child, Denis, 231
Chinese Walls, 127–8, 150–3, 210
Citibank, 129, 233
Citicorp, 36, 37, 41, 45, 48, 105–6,
107, 115, 128–30, 136,
211–14, 219, 229–31
Civil Service, 91
Clements, Alan, 148
Clerical Medical & General Life
Assurance Society, 149–50
Clydesdale Bank, 61
Cockfield, Lord, 94
Coleman, R. A., 115
Comery, Ronald, 183
Commercial Union, 169
Committee of London Clearing
Bankers, 16, 229, 230

241